INNOVATIONS IN
Narrative Therapy

A NORTON PROFESSIONAL BOOK

INNOVATIONS IN *Narrative Therapy*

Connecting Practice, Training, and Research

Jim Duvall & Laura Béres

Foreword by David Paré

W. W. Norton & Company
New York • London

Printed in the United States of America
First Edition

For information about special discounts for bulk purchases, please contact W. W. Norton Special Sales at specialsales@wwnorton.com or 800-233-4830

Manufacturing by R.R. Donnelley, Bloomsburg
Production manager: Leeann Graham

Library of Congress Cataloging-in-Publication Data

Duvall, Jim.
Innovations in narrative therapy : connecting practice, training, and research / Jim Duvall, Laura Béres ; foreword by David Paré. — 1st ed.
p. ; cm.
"A Norton Professional Book."
Includes bibliographical references and index.
ISBN 978-0-393-70616-1 (hardcover)
1. Narrative therapy. 2. Psychotherapy. I. Béres, Laura. II. Title.
[DNLM: 1. Narration. 2. Psychotherapy—methods. WM 420]
RC489.S74D88 2011
616.89'165—dc22 2010029692

ISBN: 978-0-393-70616-1

W. W. Norton & Company, Inc., 500 Fifth Avenue, New York, N.Y. 10110
www.wwnorton.com
W. W. Norton & Company Ltd., Castle House, 75/76 Wells Street, London W1T 3QT

1 2 3 4 5 6 7 8 9 0

We dedicate this book to Michael White.
He taught us and inspired us as a mentor
and encouraged us as a friend.
This book would not have been written
without him. He is missed.

Contents

Acknowledgments ix
Foreword by David Paré xiii

INTRODUCTION 1

Part I. Critically Reflecting: From Practice to Theory

CHAPTER 1 The Significance of Story: A Historical, Cultural Backdrop 23
CHAPTER 2 Storied Therapy as a Three-Act Play 37
CHAPTER 3 Circulation of Language 91
CHAPTER 4 Pivotal Moments 122

Part 2. Extending Learning: From Theory to Practice

CHAPTER 5 When All the Time You Have Is Now: Re-Visiting Practices and Narrative Therapy in a Walk-In Clinic 147
CHAPTER 6 Journey From the Underworld: Working With the Effects of Trauma and Abuse 167
CHAPTER 7 Working With the Languages of Addictions: A Story With Pivotal Moments 188
CHAPTER 8 Group Practices With Men Who Have Used Abuse 206

CONCLUSION 228

References 233
Index 245

Acknowledgments

We originally met through the research project from which this book evolved. While we were excited about embarking on a unique project researching narrative practices, it was a daunting undertaking as we were entering uncharted territories. In doing so, we were breaking away from mainstream approaches to research in order to inquire into the therapeutic process, as well as therapeutic outcomes. We needed a significant amount of help and support to meet this challenge. At that point we could hardly imagine our work ever being published as a book.

The ideas expressed in this book echo the voices and reflect the influences of many people who traveled with us on this journey. We particularly wish to thank Karen Young for joining us on this adventure. She graciously agreed to write about her narrative practices in a walk-in clinic for Chapter 5 of this book. It has been a pleasure to reflect on our practices and new ideas with her and we look forward to further research, teaching, and writing projects together in the future.

We would like to acknowledge everyone's influence and offer our genuine thanks for their support, conversations, and contributions, which made it possible to conduct our research and produce this book. Unfortunately, the space available to us will not allow us to include the names of everyone who so generously offered their help and support. We are deeply indebted to every person who has contributed to this project.

First we would like to acknowledge and thank Michael White. He gave generously of his time and knowledge to us. His guidance, mentorship, and leadership provided a primary source of ideas that were foundational to many of the concepts expressed in this book. Michael was encouraging of our original proposal for this book. He read it and then offered us clear feedback about the importance of staying true to our original vision, values, and what we thought was important to write about. He also valued our commitment to critical thinking. He was a superb role model regarding how to center the knowledge of those people consulting therapists. We were inspired by his political and ethical stance and were truly blessed by his friendship over many years.

We would also like to thank David Epston. Even while managing his own grief following Michael's death, David stepped up without hesitation to fill the void and took on much of Michael's previous role with us, offering encouragement for continuing our research and writing this book. He continues to offer us rich consultation to this day. David always has a stockpile of brilliant references and resources to recommend. We particularly want to thank him for pointing us in the direction of Morson's work on Bakhtin. His passion and enthusiasm have been infectious and inspiring, helping us stretch our thinking and move away from taken-for-granted assumptions, to new and less-charted territories, continuing to embrace and develop new ideas.

We are grateful to Jill Freedman, who was always at the end of a telephone if we needed to touch base with her regarding her experience of writing a book, whether it was how to write as coauthors or the process of publishing in general. We have appreciated her patience, generosity, and unfailing interest. Whenever we met at conferences she always asked how the book was coming along and continued to urge us forward.

We would like to thank David Paré for agreeing to read the manuscript and write the Foreword. David's willingness to help unpack, clarify, and question ideas was always welcome. It has been wonderful to have long conversations with David as he is also committed to reflecting upon and researching narrative practices. At one point we spent an entire weekend at his cottage in the Laurentian mountains of Quebec, exchanging ideas around the fireplace, while the snow piled up outside. David's friendship has been a source of constant encouragement, as he also frequently asked about how the book was progressing.

I (LB) particularly thank my husband, David, and son, Liam. They were the ones most affected by this project as I would disappear for days at a time to write with Jim. They supported me by picking up the slack around the home and by showing genuine interest in discussing the ideas and the process of writing over late dinners when I would finally appear from behind the computer. I am grateful to Liam for allowing me to include a short anecdote from his childhood in Chapter 3. I am grateful to David for his enthusiasm for this project and willingness to read drafts of chapters, engage in thought-provoking analysis, and provide such thorough feedback. Jim and I could not have managed without David's faith, and without Caroline's faith, in our ability to write a worthwhile book.

I (JD) would like to thank my life partner and best friend Caroline for her understanding and unfaltering belief in this project. Not only did she also take up the slack in my day-to-day life, she was always ready to listen and offer a "reality test" for our half-baked ideas. Always patient, she frequently helped me bridge yet another technological failure as I would stare in disbelief at my computer. Caroline and our dog, Banjo, constantly reminded me that, "oh yeah, there is more to life than this book project."

We would also like to thank the many staff, volunteers, students, and consultants of the Hincks-Dellcrest Centre, Gail Appel Institute who participated in, believed in, and supported the training and research project. They dedicated endless hours of work and study, through many therapeutic sessions, watching countless hours of videotapes, tracking forms and data, and reflecting on the complexities of the work.

We would like to thank the Master of Social Work students who participated in Laura's graduate elective course in narrative theory and practice and then became part of an ongoing consultation group. They expressed interest in our project and read early drafts of chapters and provided feedback, reassuring us that this was a worthwhile endeavor that would be useful for students. Thanks particularly to Diane, who read these chapters with such care and provided skilled copyediting suggestions. Thanks also to a work-study student, Carolyn, who provided another set of eyes for catching those small spelling and grammar errors and missing references that can otherwise get away from you.

We also thank two of Laura's colleagues at King's University College at the University of Western Ontario: Antonio Calcagno, of the Philosophy Department, who was willing to read earlier drafts and assure us that we had understood Derrida and Deleuze correctly, and Allan Irving, of the School of Social Work, who also read earlier drafts and provided encouragement for what he believed was important work.

We thank the many families who consulted us. They provided us with hours upon hours of high quality "unpaid supervision" as they would humble our efforts with clear and useful feedback regarding what we could do to be more useful with them. Two people participated in writing two chapters in this book. Their feedback and involvement helped us to stay in touch with and strive to improve an ethical practice. We are deeply grateful for the involvement of everyone who consulted us. They have made their way in a myriad of manners into the composite cases provided in this book and also more generally into our approach to working with people. It is a joy and privilege to be allowed to walk with people on their journeys.

We are grateful for the tireless and detailed coordination and copyediting assistance we received from Vani Kannan at W. W. Norton.

Finally, we would like to thank our editor Deborah Malmud at W. W. Norton, for her leadership and guidance. Her influence definitely helped us to produce a better book as she suggested we include further composite case examples and generally encouraged us through this whole process.

Foreword

Reading this book, which crackles with new ideas and creative revisioning of established ones, has been a pivotal moment for me in relation to the authors, Jim Duvall and Laura Béres. As you shall shortly discover, "pivotal moments" are those rewarding junctures in therapeutic conversations when a simple question cracks open a door, shining light on possibilities only thinly imagined; the crack widens as the conversation unfolds, revealing novel and unexpected glimpses of a person, intriguing new versions of their many selves. I thought I more or less had a "read" on Laura and Jim. I've had the pleasure of working and playing with them for several years now—we've been fellow trainers and researchers; we've shared the editing of manuscripts; we've brainstormed research projects and planned conferences together. I've known Laura and Jim in other ways, too. Sliding on one of the Stetsons lying about Jim's place, I've coaxed forth his long-faded Texas drawl, singing and playing old-time music with him late into the night. On those same evenings, I've listened with intrigue to the lilt in Laura's voice—another trace of accent but of the British variety, which she wields with persistent soft-spoken curiosity. Laura's curiosity invites conversations that roam far and wide, from feminist philosophy to Celtic spirituality, punctuated with bursts of her trademark laughter. And so I've had a chance to get acquainted with both their thoughtful and playful selves, but a new door to

Jim and Laura has been thrown wide open for me upon reading this rich and complex rendering of their ideas and practices.

The book resonates strongly with the compassionate and creative work of Michael White, who has inspired so many of us around the world. Laura and Jim each had the privilege of working with and learning from Michael in various ways over the years. It's easy to imagine Michael's delight at a book that pays him generous tribute, while stepping forward in many directions, some signposted but not thoroughly traveled by him. Michael was fond of the metaphor of maps, making it central to the last book he wrote before his untimely passing, *Maps of Narrative Practice*. Some of those maps are evident here–structures and frameworks and sequenced questions, carefully conceived to move conversations to new territories of living. But take a look with a cartographer's discerning eye and you'll see this book also outlines many novel routes, and invites readers to explore them in their own manner and at their preferred pace.

Jim has often said that Michael White did not practice a therapeutic "brand": he practiced "Michael White Therapy." Following on the collective inclination to name things (for better and worse), White's work and the work of his prolific colleague David Epston have come to be called "narrative therapy." This book rightly retains that title because it resonates with a universe of therapeutic approaches sharing the "narrative" moniker, which have circulated the globe. But this book is more than a collection of familiar "narrative maps." It's more like a rendering of what else is possible to know in continuing to work and play with practices that have become well established in a wide variety of therapeutic contexts. The legacy of White and Epston, and of what has come to be called narrative therapy, is evident everywhere, but this book is devoted to "Jim Duvall and Laura Béres Therapy." It is therapy, training, and research that resonates with work that has come before while nudging doorways open to intriguing new possibilities.

The scope of the book defies any attempt to summarize it in a few words. Instead, I'd like to stay with the metaphor of "maps" to shed light on the authors' skillful balancing of two aspects of what for shorthand sake I will call (irony noted) "narrative practice." By "maps," I am referring to particular language, ideas, preconceived questions, and conversational structures, and so on that might be brought into the room by therapists and shared with the persons who consult them. Without maps, therapeutic conversations can inadvertently devolve into unhelpful reiterations of problems, if not the re-perpetration of harm. It takes discipline and intentionality to avoid slipping into well-established traditions of thinking and talking about persons as “disordered.” Therapeutic maps help conversations break free of habitual patterns of deficit-focused talk, honing in on versions of identity that foreground persons’ values and intentions.

That being said, there are certainly challenges associated with working with preconceived therapeutic frames. When therapy is seen as a site where knowledge is jointly constructed by therapists and the persons who consult them, there is always the possibility that preferred developments might emerge at an unexpected moment and in a manner quite unanticipated by any conversational blueprint. There is an art to holding a map loosely, having it ready at hand for consultation while being prepared to fold it away when, at a turn in the conversational path, a new way forward presents itself.

One of this book’s striking features is the balance it manages between this holding and letting go. The authors introduce innovative maps for practice, all the while reminding readers that these are just some among many useful ways forward, and reflecting on how each conversational moment is pregnant with virtually limitless alternate possibilities. The book emphasizes the role of stories and the human disposition for organizing experience in narrative form—a habit traced here to both cultural traditions and cognitive processes. At the same time, we are reminded that nothing is locked down in a world of stories: the frequently playful conversations featured here are free of the crushing determinacy at the center of many psychological traditions. The present moment is always rife with opportunity for revising previous events. That same precious “now,” cradled with reverence in a therapeutic conversation, is also laden with the seeds of countless alternate *futures*, regardless of past events leading up to the exchange of a word, or a glance, or a shared moment of silence.

The authors carefully lay out several possible conversational sequences, including their own ingenious six-step inquiry for developing storyline within a three-act play structure, tailoring conversational exchanges to the direction of the storyteller’s preferred intention, and never presupposing a final destination. They ponder the real effects of the words they choose to describe others, avoiding closed-ended pronouncements or rushes to understanding, and working very hard to stay close to the speakers’ intentions. Assembling their account of practice, training, and research from the ground up, featuring the voices of their many collaborators, they display a commitment to attending to the specific needs and perspectives of the people who consult them, drawing from countless therapy tapes, transcripts, and reconstructed therapeutic conversations generated in a wide variety of contexts. This fits with their preference to be learners, rather than teachers, in therapeutic conversations. Likewise, the research studies they recount are equally targeted to the persons for whom they are intended to be helpful, reminding us of how theories impact participants, and ultimately, the therapeutic outcome.

The result is a book of shape-shifting maps, adaptable to the changing course of therapeutic conversations, and a further crack in the door to practice imbued with an abiding concern for the ethics of meaning-making. May the light shine forth.

David Paré
Ottawa, Ontario
October, 2010

INNOVATIONS IN
Narrative Therapy

Introduction

Research and Critical Reflection as an Evidence Base for Narrative Practices

This book is about narrative practices. We are constantly invigorated and inspired by working with people from a narrative perspective and by teaching narrative ways of working.

White's (2007a) most recent book about conversational maps was one of his most readable and helpful descriptions of how to work with people using narrative therapy skills and approaches. There are in fact a range of useful books for those readers interested in learning some of the theoretical influences that contributed to the development of narrative therapy (Bruner, 1986b, 1990; Derrida, 1976; Foucault, 1980; Vygotsky, 1986) and for those readers preferring some more descriptions of how to begin to learn how to practice narrative therapy (Russell & Carey, 2004; White, 2007a). Our intention for this book is to present some new ideas about narrative practice that developed from our qualitative, exploratory research project. We believe this book will be of interest to experienced narrative therapists and to those who are newer to this way of working because the ideas and practices we will be presenting here have come about from reflecting upon our narrative practices. These ideas can be integrated into the work of experienced narrative therapists, but also stand alone and will be of interest to those who are new to narrative therapy.

Therapists are experiencing increasing demands, by funders primarily, to demonstrate the effectiveness of their therapeutic models. They must also show that they are using evidence-based practices. Critical theorists argue that evidence-based practice stems from a narrow understanding of what constitutes inquiry and research. We recognize the tensions inherent with the wish to be accountable and at the same time remain ethical in our practices while we further expand useful acceptable methods of knowledge formation. This book is a product of a critically reflective research approach that we are continuing to develop. Therefore, this book will also be of interest to those practitioners who wish to reflect upon and write about their work, since we provide descriptions of the research process within this introduction, and the practice chapters also incorporate small case-study research designs that are possible for other practitioners to replicate.

STRUCTURE OF THIS BOOK

Within this introduction we will provide a little of the backstory, by describing the research team, context, and the ideas that influenced the research project. We will particularly discuss the importance of reflective practice and what transforms thinking about our actions into a method of critical reflection (Fook & Gardner, 2007). We will also describe a concept map that developed from our reflection on our field notes and positions some of the new ideas that we will be presenting in the first section of the book.

The first section of the book is composed of four chapters. In the first chapter we provide an overview of the historical and social context regarding the significance of story for therapeutic practice. In the following three chapters we describe three different ideas that came from the research project. These include a new way of working with storyline structure in therapeutic conversations, a discussion about the significance of the circulation of language in therapy, and reflections on pivotal moments of transformation. Composite case examples are included in these chapters.

The second section of this book discusses direct practice. In the first of these chapters we present a description of how narrative practices can be used within walk-in clinic settings; walk-ins continue to be considered a relatively new context within which to provide therapeutic services, and particularly narrative therapy. The next chapter in the second section contains case transcripts that demonstrate narrative skills of working with issues related to past trauma. In the third chapter of the second section we describe narrative ideas as they relate to working with people who are struggling with addictions, using a case-study approach with a woman who attended individual narrative therapy combined with attending Alcoholic Anonymous (AA) groups. The final chapter in this section presents results of a small research project that analyzed the transcripts of a narrative therapy group for men who had used abuse. Composite case examples are also used in the practice chapters in this second section of the book, except in those situations, which are indicated, when people provided direct permission to include their stories.

Provided at the end of each chapter are a summary and a list of questions to encourage and support ongoing critical reflection. One of the challenges inherent in writing is that we run the risk of making a fluid and invigorating practice static and lifeless through the process of trying to pin it down and describe it. We ask you to think of the process of narrative therapy as a film that is playing. We pause the film now and again in order to jot down some ideas and perhaps describe the picture that is in front of us on the screen at that moment, but we then start playing the film again. The process keeps moving and we want to continue reflecting upon it and further describe new ideas.

THE RESEARCH PROJECT

The research project on which this book is based began within a training setting in Toronto, Ontario, Canada, in September 2002. At this point, training faculty Jim Duvall and Eric King at the Hincks-Dellcrest Centre, Gail Appel Institute formed a collaboration with Adrienne Chambon and Faye Mishna, who were faculty members within the Faculty of Social Work at the University of Toronto. Together they developed a method of researching therapy practices as they taught and practiced them in their training program. They hoped that this would begin the process of documenting and examining narrative therapy, which had been criticized for being underresearched. As they began the development of this research team, Laura Béres was also invited to become involved in this project as a research associate. The initial extern training program ran until June 2003, and field notes were generated over these 10 months, as we used an exploratory anthropological field research design, immersing ourselves in the experiences of teaching, learning, and being involved in therapeutic conversations with families who came and received services from the trainee therapists. The following academic year a graduate student was hired in the role of research assistant to continue gathering field notes during the training program from September 2003 to June 2004.

The ongoing research team consisted of Jim Duvall, Eric King, Ellen Katz, Adrienne Chambon, Faye Misha, and Laura Béres. Karen Young and Scot Cooper joined this team at a later stage for discussions about the data gathered during the field work stage.

When we began our field work together, we thought of our research project as being primarily influenced by anthropological field research approaches. Yet, as we now look back on our work together and attempt to develop further methods for examining narrative practices, we have come to realize how important the role of critical reflection was, and continues to be, to this project.

DEVELOPING AN APPROACH TO CRITICALLY REFLECTIVE PRACTICE

I (LB) recently reviewed a range of various conceptions of reflexivity and how they relate to mindfulness (Béres, 2009). I presented D'Cruz, Gillingham, and Melendez's (2007) descriptions of how social work literature since the 1990s has discussed the concept of reflexivity. They pointed out that a certain level of confusion has been created because reflexivity has been used interchangeably with concepts like reflectivity, reflection, and critical reflection. In describing the difference between reflection and critical reflection they drew on Fook (1999) and Healy (2000), pointing out the opportunities of moving away from the dichotomy of theory versus practice, and valuing the generation of theory from practice experience. Here, critical reflection is a practice skill that can be taught to practitioners and students so that they can research their practice.

Fook and Gardner described their model of critical reflection as being influenced by four major traditions: "the reflective approach to practice; reflexivity; postmodernism/deconstruction; [and] critical social theory" (2007, p. 69). These foundations are also all compatible with the philosophical underpinnings and traditions of narrative practices.

First of all, Fook and Gardner drew upon Schön's (1983) model of reflective practice. They suggested that his approach began with "the crisis in confidence in professional knowledge" (Fook & Gardner, 2007, p. 24). Schön articulated the manner in which much professional theory was taught from above, but how practitioners often felt there was a gap between the rules of the theories they were taught and the practice in which they were engaged. He proposed acknowledging this more clearly and supporting practitioners in reflecting upon what they actually were doing in practice, reflecting-*on*-action and reflecting-*in*-action, which could then contribute to developing practice theory. This was more of a "bottom up" process of creating practice theory. Schön suggested that intuition and artistry should be more highly valued again rather than merely relying upon rational scientific methods. He respected the need to take into consideration context and emotion and believed that we should question some of the taken-for-granted assumptions about knowledge and theory.

Reflexivity, as a tradition that has influenced the development of the model of critical reflection Fook and Gardner suggested, is linked to the field of anthropology and the recognition of the impact of the researcher on the field being researched. The type of reflexivity they drew upon is one where the practitioner is encouraged to "look both inwards and outwards to recognize the connections with social and cultural understandings" (2007, p. 28). They take it further:

> Our understanding is a little broader in that we see it as involving the ability to recognize that *all* aspects of ourselves (including physical and bodily aspects) and our contexts influence the way we research (or create knowledge) . . . when we refer to "research" here, our understanding is also broad. We are referring to all the different ways in which we create knowledge—this occurs in more or less formal and systematic ways (depending on the situation), yet is used daily, and often in unarticulated ways, to make sense of immediate surroundings. (p. 28)

The manner in which Fook and Gardner (2007) incorporated postmodernism and deconstruction into critical reflection had to do primarily with their wish to question modernist, linear, and unified thinking. They also were keen to remain alert to the relationship between knowledge and power and to deconstruct the dominant discourses and language that we use that can point to the operation of power in our midst. These ideas remind us also to be attentive to the role of binary thinking in constructing our ideas about difference and the need to be aware of the history of silencing multiple and marginal perspectives.

Finally, Fook and Gardner described the role of critical social theory in shaping critical reflection, focusing on five common themes: "first, the recognition that power is both personal and structural; second, that individuals can participate in their own domination; third, social change is both personal and collective; fourth, knowledge is both empirical and constructed; and last, the importance of communication and dialogue" (2007, p. 35).

Critical reflection, as Fook and Gardner (2007) presented it, is both a theory and a practice. As a practice, it is usually structured over three different days, spread over three weeks, although they suggest this can be adapted to meet various needs. The first day involves preparation of a small group of people and a review of the theories underlying critical reflection. The second day involves each participant in the group presenting an incident from practice upon which they are willing to reflect with the group for the purposes of learning more about their practice. This involves unsettling assumptions and "taken-for-granteds." The third session involves reflections from all of the participants, focusing on what has changed in their thinking and how this will impact their practice. As a theory it can inform our stance in whatever practice we are engaged in and so was also an implicit aspect of our research project.

METHODOLOGY

During the data collection phase of this research project, all of the therapy sessions conducted by trainees or faculty members were videotaped. Written field notes were generated from observing training sessions, therapy sessions, and debriefing sessions. Notes were also taken in meetings we held to review videotapes of therapy sessions, in meetings for group journaling by the trainees, and in research team meetings. The field notes, group journal, and videotapes were all considered the texts, or the collected data, of the study. A content analysis of the texts was then conducted from a phenomenological perspective, identifying and sorting themes, deductively and inductively. This was influenced by a phenomenological approach since we were initially interested in the general essence of the narrative practices as they were experienced in this training and research setting. Through immersion in the texts, the possibility remained for inductive themes to emerge that had not been expected, such as the realization of the importance of circulation of language and pivotal moments. The texts were also examined deductively as we began to identify the manner in which certain narrative therapy ideas, such as centering clients' knowledges and expertise, was taught and supported in this program.

Situating the study of narrative therapy in a practice and training environment made it more possible to reflect on what otherwise could have been taken-for-granted narrative practices. We were in the unique position of being able to observe what the trainees experienced as particular to narrative therapy, as well as include our own participatory observations about what we saw narrative therapy looking like in this particular setting.

THE CONCEPT MAP

Another step of the research project involved the development of a concept map, which emerged from the content analysis of the field texts and tentatively illustrated the manner in which we saw various narrative practices fitting together and influencing one another.

Consistent with an exploratory style of inquiry, our approach was to initially immerse ourselves in the research field notes rather than first reviewing literature, which could have overly influenced our perceptions of the field notes. The result of this immersion was the development of innovative ways of thinking about, and linking together, familiar and new ideas.

In beginning to review field notes, reflecting on phrases and themes, and then beginning to link them together, we noticed that this type of therapy was often referred to as a "therapy of witnessing and acknowledgment" by trainers and trainees alike. This appeared to refer to the witnessing of people's lives, not just the difficulties but also events in their lives that perhaps spoke to other possibilities. It also referred to acknowledging efforts and initiatives and attributing significance to them. These initiatives may have previously gone unnoticed, or unstoried. The acknowledging of these initiatives begins to build themes and alternative storylines in practice. This then led to discussions in the training about what would make a useful conversation. This invited trainees and then the people seeking consultation to reflect upon what was most important to begin talking about and invited them not only to think about the effects of the problem on their lives, but also to think toward preferences early on in the therapeutic conversation. Trainees in the research project at first thought of narrative practices as merely listening to someone's story, but this asked them to think of the "point(s) of the story;" to assist the person who was telling the story to reflect on the reasons for telling the story and begin to think about what was being hoped for in the telling. So, this was the backdrop for the development of the concept map. We recognized that interactions are guided by our desire to witness people's stories, which involve both pain and possibilities, and acknowledging the hopes and values of those people who consult with us.

First Section of the Concept Map: Beginning to Think About the Type of Conversation

In answer to the question "What would make a useful conversation?" trainees began to wonder if a dialogical conversation would be a useful conversation (Figure 1.1). Anderson (1997) described a postmodern approach to therapy as being a dialogical conversation, which contributes to the construction of meaning.

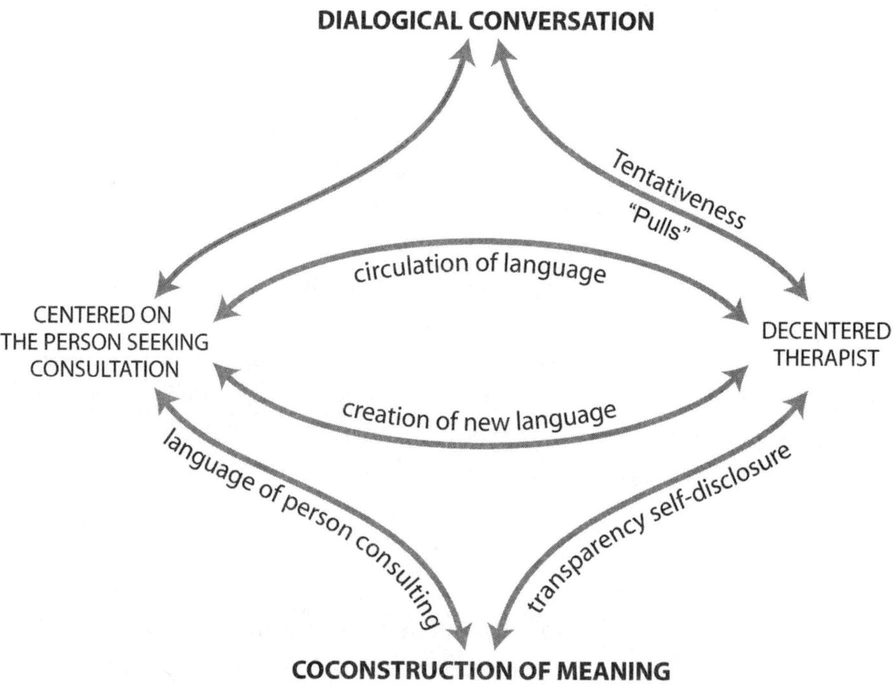

Figure 1.1. A useful conversation.

> Therapy is characterized by conversation/dialogue between (out loud) and within (silent) a client and therapist. I refer to the process of therapy as a dialogical conversation; dialogical conversation is a generative process in which new meanings—different ways of understanding, making sense of, or punctuating one's lived experiences—emerge and are mutually constructed. In turn, the therapy conversation (connected with and informed by conversations outside the therapy room, and vice versa) and the newness that results from it lead to self-agency and problem dissolution. (p. 109)

Guilfoyle (2003), on the other hand, problematized dialogical therapies to a certain extent because they suggest taking up a "not-knowing" stance that implies a giving up of power and expertise. He argued that what happens more usually within dialogical therapies is that power goes underground and is obscured rather than an even playing field being developed. He suggested that it is preferable for power to be discussed within the therapeutic conversation and that the social construction of power be addressed. However, he also acknowledged that in the absence of specific (dialogue enhancement) techniques, therapy is inclined to move toward more monological than dialogical interaction.

What would contribute to the development of a dialogical conversation that would, at the same time, also be critical of dominant discourses of power? These dialogical conversations are not exempt from the overall discourses that strongly influence people's dominant storylines, but represent an intersubjective creation of meaning between therapist and people consulting the therapist. In the training program there was often talk among trainees about the need to move from a position that centered them as experts to a decentered position, which simultaneously centered the people consulting them. It was due to these conversations in the training context that it became clear that this was a significant aspect for these trainees in learning this form of practice as taught in this setting. Through observing the therapeutic interactions and the debriefings of therapy sessions, it appeared as though the combination of decentering the therapist and centering the person requesting assistance contributed to the co-construction of meaning in these therapeutic conversations. In this way the therapeutic conversation becomes a social collaboration, providing more space for the involvement, ideas, and desires of people seeking consultation.

It is important to point out, despite the focus on centering the people seeking the consultation and facilitating dialogical conversations, that the therapist remains responsible for asking particular questions. In this way, the therapist is decentered, yet influential, scaffolding the conversations so that the people seeking consultation can become more in touch with their local knowledges and preferences. Some aspects that contribute to dialogical conversations becoming more narrative in nature involve situating them within a social context. This can come about through reauthoring conversations, the use of outsider witnessing practices, re-membering conversations, and externalizing conversations (White, 1995a, 2007a; White & Epston, 1990). These practices acknowledge the politics of the therapeutic relationship and they assist the person consulting the therapist in developing ongoing supports with others outside the therapeutic process.

It was also clear through observations in the training program that language was significant in relation to the centering of the people seeking consultation and the decentering of the therapist. A primary aspect of the research project began to focus on the circulation of language with regard to the transformation of meaning. Although there remains a slippage in meaning through the expression of language, it does contribute to bringing forth realities. The language that people use is an expression of their lived experience. However, there is often a creation of a new language and, as well, a circulation of existing language. The intentional use of the words of the people seeking consultation privileges their meaning-making activities, but their language often shifts during the conversation as the therapist asks them to unpack what is meant by certain terms and assists them in becoming more "experience near" (White, 1994) in their descriptions. The circulation of language will be described fully in Chapter 3.

We are suggesting that the quality of these conversations between the therapist and people seeking consultation needs to offer a new experience for people as we create a space for dialogical conversations. The therapist's scaffolding of these conversations makes it possible for people to have a new experience resulting in the possibility of movement toward what they could not have achieved in the same way on their own.

"Pulls" were also discussed by trainees and trainers quite often. These had to do with what was evocative and what resonated for the trainee therapists as they participated in therapeutic conversations, suggesting again the need for reflexivity. The ability of therapists to "be present" and reflect in the moment is very important to these dialogical conversations. This makes it possible for them to notice the responses that they are experiencing while listening to people. Often these responses alert therapists to what caught their attention, what images were evoked, what invited curiosity, what was moving, what took them to a similar experience in their own lives. More often these responses represent a sense of transport for the therapist. Although these responses may occur partially as an intellectual experience, they may also be an embodied experience like the "tingle of goose bumps." It is important to reflect on these responses in the moment in order to ensure an ethical and just stance with people, so that we stay focused on what may be useful for them. Some reactions might require a therapist to make a decision in the moment and privately about whether or not it would be useful to discuss those responses. Other pulls might be more in response to powerful interactions occurring in the therapy room and then the people seeking consultation can be asked whether they believe it would be useful to talk more about what has been experienced. This would be done in an invitational manner, rather than suggesting that it needs to be talked about. This, then, ties into decisions about how to be transparent, what to be transparent about, and what to self-disclose. The idea of personal self-disclosure—whether to use it at all and, if so, how much—is quite controversial in the psychotherapy field at large. However, we believe the expression of resonance through self-disclosure can strongly acknowledge people's efforts to face the difficulties in their lives and acknowledge their experience in the therapeutic process.

Second Section of the Concept Map: Moving From Problem to Alternative Storyline

Together, the therapist and people seeking assistance engage in a dialogical conversation, coconstructing meaning from their stories (Figure 1.2). Here it is important to remember that the therapist is not looking for a verifiable "truth," as if there is only one truth to be known, but rather is participating in conversations about the problem storyline and alternative storylines, accepting that they hold multiple truths and multiple meanings. It is true that an adult who has memories of childhood sexual abuse both has been victimized and has survived. It is also true that this person will probably want to move beyond both victimhood and survivorhood. The therapeutic conversation assists people in making meaning out of these memories in such a way that they may move toward preferred views of themselves. (See Duvall and Béres, 2007, for a fuller description of work with survivors of trauma.)

We placed a couple of different types of White's (2005, 2006a, 2007a) scaf-

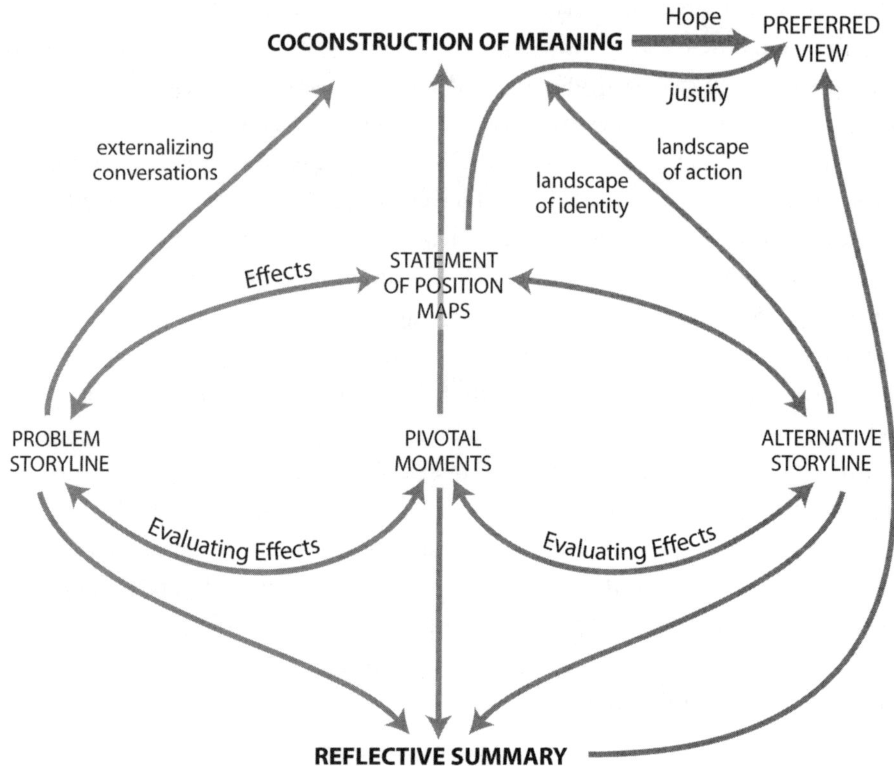

Figure 1.2. Movement to alternative storyline.

folding conversation maps in this section of the concept map to indicate their use in assisting people in moving from problem storylines to alternative storylines through a coconstruction of meaning. This creates an opportunity for people to explore and evaluate the effects of the problem on their lives and to work in the proximity of the therapist to coconstruct preferred storylines. Because the conversation develops and we move from taken-for-granted understanding to new learnings, a gap exists between these two places. That gap is traversed through the scaffolding of the therapeutic conversation, and in this way an incremental and progressive movement occurs from the known and familiar to what is possible to know (White, 2005, 2007a). The questions used to provide this scaffolding invite people into a collaborative conversation. White described these conversational maps and questions as influential, and while they do not choose where a person will go, they point in general directions.

Although, as the previous section of the concept map indicated, there is a desire to maintain a decentered therapeutic stance, this does not mean that the therapist abdicates responsibility over the process of the conversation. It is the responsibility of the therapist to provide the type of conversational scaffolding that makes it possible for the people seeking assistance to cross the above-mentioned gap, which White (2007a), drawing upon Vygotsky (1978, 1986), refers to as the "zone of proximal development." This type of social collaboration opens up space for people to step back and reflect upon those events in their lives that had previously been overlooked, which can now provide chains of associations with preferred stories that would not be possible otherwise.

Statement of position maps also invite people to explore and evaluate the effects of the problem and of possible alternative ways of being. These conversations involve pragmatic building of personal agency. They open up the possibility of thinking in terms of contingencies—"this may happen if I do this, this may happen if I do that"—and reflecting about what can and cannot be known, providing a range of possibilities, which results in problem dissolving rather than problem solving (White, 2005, 2006b).

Through reviewing field notes and videotaped sessions, we began to notice what we have come to think of as "pivotal moments," which will be described fully in Chapter 4. Immediately underneath "Statement of Position Maps" on the concept map is "Pivotal Moments." Pivotal moments appear crucial in the movement that occurs in therapeutic conversations and consist of those aha moments that bring about new understandings. It is important for trainees to become attuned to these pivotal moments, so that they do not become overly anxious about staying focused within a particular conversational map. Rather, it is important that they remain reflective and able to go with the movement that these events can bring about. Morgan and Morgan discussed the link between mindfulness and tranquility and suggest that "tranquility is being pleasantly unruffled by the flow of moment-to-moment experience. It is peace of mind not based on the absence of thoughts and feelings, but on the acceptance of whatever is arising. . . . Therapists require tranquility to act wisely and avoid the mistakes we make when we feel compelled to say or do something in the therapy hour" (2005, p. 78). It is useful to remind trainees that there are times in which it is most important to stay out of the way of change.

Many times people experience a pivotal moment or a shifting of thought as a result of stepping back and reflecting on their situation. This may evoke powerful experiences from their past and link them to what it is they value. As one example of what we have considered a pivotal moment, a grandmother who had custody of her grandson through a child welfare order had brought her grandson for counseling because she was concerned that he may have been sexually abused by his father. They had attended a few sessions, and the grandson usually went into a play therapy room with another therapist while the grandmother, and sometimes also the child protection social worker, spoke with the primary therapist. In one of her later sessions the grandmother spoke angrily and at length about the details that her grandson had given her of the abuse he remembered, asking the child protection social worker how her grandson could have been left in his father's care and abused. She was clearly talking about the problem storyline and the effects, but at a certain point she stood up, said this was very difficult to talk about because of her own history of abuse of which she had never spoken, and then calmly said, "But he'll be okay," which seemed to signify a switch from the past to the future, from an intense and unsettling emotion to a calmness and a moment that we have come to think of as a "pivotal moment." It is useful to unpack these moments and question what was moving about the experience for people. This process of questioning acknowledges people's experience of transport and helps to bring this experience into the present to develop a fuller awareness. This may be a signal that a therapist can move on to statement of position map 2, and/or begin to string together a series of events that will fit within a preferred storyline.

Within this second section of the concept map "landscape of identity" and "landscape of action" have also been included, which are parts of the reauthoring conversation that can assist people in moving toward their preferred views of themselves. The landscape of action has to do with the description of events that could be described as the facts, whereas the landscape of identity or consciousness has to do with people's hopes, values, dreams, and intentions (White, 2007a). These landscapes inhabit both the problem storyline and the alternative storyline in terms of the content covered in these conversations, but do so with a purpose of moving toward their preferences. This occurs through rich story development and through asking about the person's intentions and commitments. These conversations cover past, present, and future as these two landscapes are examined in terms of their effects over time. If a unique outcome, some event that does not fit within the plot of the problem storyline, is discovered, it is then useful to ask about other experiences or initiatives that made that one event possible. On the one hand, finding a unique outcome within a reauthoring conversation might signify that a statement of position map 2 conversation could be started, gaining rich descriptions of a newly noticed skill, moving through the stages of evaluating effects of the skill and then linking this to preferences. On the other hand, it is only when there are a few or more events linked together according to the new preferred plot that the alternative storyline becomes richer and more resistant to any thoughts regarding that event merely being a "fluke." Therefore, therapists might choose to remain in a reauthoring conversation. This again suggests a need to be mindful and in the moment since there are choices to be made about the direction to take in a conversation. This is not a matter of choosing the "right" conversation, but rather being aware of options and flexible enough to move from one to another as it seems useful.

Field notes have suggested that there were not often any explicit discussions about the role of hope or the need to talk about hope with people. After each session, however, the people were given a questionnaire on which they could rank their satisfaction with the session and one of the questions was about how hopeful they felt. In research meetings, hope was also raised as an important aspect of this approach. We believe that the area of hope is much more implicit than explicit within narrative therapy, but needs to be included in the concept map. We also believe that hope is intertwined with the person's dreams, intentions, and preferences as they are articulated within the landscape of identity within the reauthoring conversation and through the final series of questions (the "justification" step) within the statement of position maps.

Externalizing conversations are often thought of as a key aspect of narrative practice. However, these conversations do not represent a "narrative technique," but rather a shift in thinking that acknowledges that problems are situated within discourses and located outside of the individual, separating the problem from the person (Russell & Carey, 2004; White, 2007a; White & Epston, 1990). Trainees can at times get caught up in the notion of there being a "correct" aspect to externalize (Russell & Carey, 2004), but we believe it is more important to think in terms of the philosophical and collaborative stance that assists with moving away from the pathologizing of people and toward the types of respectful interactions that lead to externalizing conversations. These externalizing conversations assist further in the coconstruction of meaning and the movement toward a preferred sense of identity.

Third Section of the Concept Map: The Context

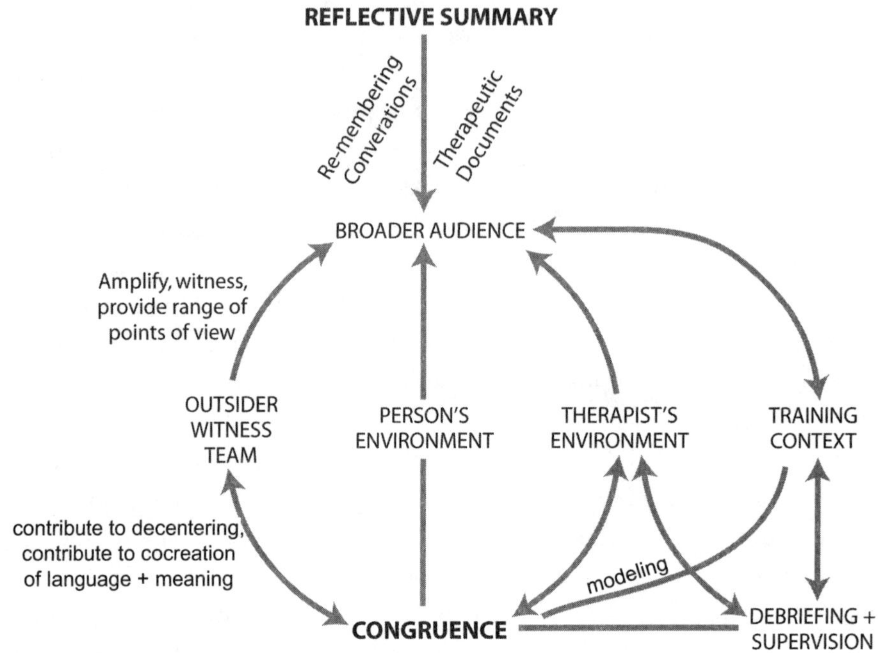

Figure 1.3. The Broader Context.

The broader context in which narrative practices occur, which is discussed in the therapeutic conversations, still needed to be incorporated more directly at this point in the concept map. The "broader audience" of these therapeutic conversations has been added in the third section as the base on which the interactions stand (Figure 1.3). If there was a better way to show how these concepts in the third section are interwoven into all the other concepts, we would use it, but here we rely on using these concepts as the roots to this approach and will use arrows to indicate the manner in which they contribute to such concepts as "decentering of the therapist," "circulation of language," and "cocreation of meaning." Poststructural practices are situated within critical theory and acknowledge the influence of context and discourse in the development of meaning and identity. Therefore, it is also important to remember that it is these ideas within this third section of the map that contextualize the dialogical conversations that occur, ensuring that there is a political and social context for the conversations that take place between the people seeking consultation and the therapist. In fact, these narrative conversations contribute to development of skills and initiatives that can be carried on without the therapist.

The broader audience is made up of the people who touch on the lives of the people who are seeking consultation: the therapist, the outsider witness team and, within this study, the training and research context. What has been impressive in the field notes has been what we have come to consider "congruence" among these various areas, as the trainers and researchers also attempted to decenter themselves and rather privilege what the trainees knew and were experiencing.

Trainees said in group journaling meetings that they had not previously realized how important the outsider witness teams were to narrative therapy, highlighting another unique aspect of narrative practice. They identified the outsider witness teams as not just an extra add-on, but an integral part of narrative therapy that provided important richness. They said that the outsider witness teams could sometimes say things that the therapist was unable to say, that the teams assisted in the decentering of the therapist and could unpack and develop otherwise partial ideas.

We also began to notice that the outsider witness teams can contribute to the creation of a new language and new meaning. One of the trainees commented that if we accept that we are all socially constructed and nothing is done in isolation, then the outsider witness team models this. Many of the trainees, all of whom very much appreciated the contributions of the outsider witness teams, were worried about how they could incorporate the contributions of the outsider witness teams into their practices back at their workplaces, where they would not be able to have access to outsider witness teams. (White, 2006b, has also described how he at times involved outsider witnesses from a list of people who had previously consulted him and who were interested in contributing to the work in this way.)

Re-membering conversations have been added to this final section of the concept map because these re-membering conversations, as another type of scaffolding conversation, are a method of providing an audience to people for what is important to them. They contribute to a multiple storying of people's lives, moving away from a pathologizing individualizing account to a social construction of the problem and, more important, a social construction of their preferences. People are encouraged to evaluate who will be members in their community, based on how the others contribute to the identity the person prefers; people can disqualify some voices and give more authority to other voices. Re-membering conversations are fully described in Chapter 2.

In this third section of the concept map we have also included "therapeutic documents," which do not necessarily broaden the audience but can be another way that demonstrates witnessing and can help bridge people from one session to the next if there is going to be a wait for the next appointment. These therapeutic documents can come in many different styles and shapes (letters as well as poems, as described by Speedy, 2005, and Pentecost & Speedy, 2006), but what is important to keep in mind is that they also can be quite significant as a further summary, or reflective surface, for the people to keep with them when they are going about their day-to-day existence between sessions.

The Narrative Concept Map

When the three sections of the concept map are put together, it is helpful to add further lines and arrows to link the various sections of the map (Figure 1.4). In particular, the third section has been linked back to the second to demonstrate the way in which the outsider witness teams contribute to the coconstruction of meaning and how the whole of the broader audience contributes to conversations about the problem storyline and the alternative storyline. We have also added an arrow from "reflective summary" to "preferred view" to indicate the way in which the reflective summary is best used to support movement toward the preferred view, rather than merely reciting a shopping list of all the various topics covered in a session or a rehashing of the problem.

CONCLUSION

Within this introduction, we have presented the backdrop and context for the research and practice that have informed the development of the new ideas regarding storyline structure, the circulation of language, and pivotal moments, which we will describe in the first section of this book. We have also presented a concept map that came about from the reflective practice and research project. The concept map provides a visual representation of the manner in which the

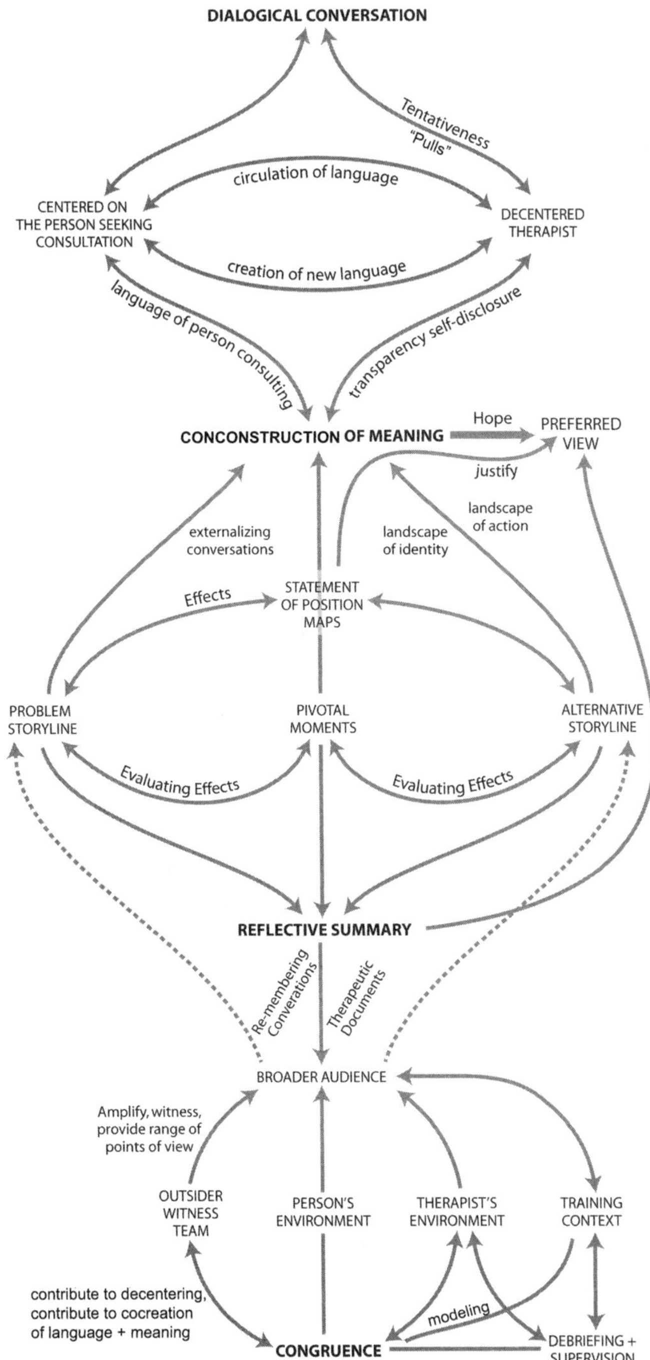

Figure 1.4. The Narrative Concept Map.

various aspects of narrative conversations as well as our new ideas fit together and inform one another. This is not meant to be considered as the *only* way to think about these relations, but rather as *one* way that they can be represented. This concept map may be useful to consider while reading the theory chapters in the first section as well as the practice chapters in the second section, so as to visualize how the various ideas influence and support one another.

Griffiths and Tann (1992) identified five different levels of reflection associated with reflective practice. The fifth level of reflection, which they described as "retheorizing and reformulating," is made up of a cycle of "act–observe–systematically analyse–rigorously evaluate–retheorize–plan–act." We were interested to find out that liberation theology and Paulo Freire's critical pedagogy (2006) have been described as being made up of a cycle of "observe–plan–act–evaluate–replan–celebrate." The addition of the step of celebrating in an otherwise similar cycle of planning, acting, and evaluating seems like a worthwhile adjustment. This reminds us of White's (2007a) discussions of definitional ceremonies, which can mark important learning and pivotal moments of transition. We see the step of writing this book and bringing these ideas to a broader audience as a form of celebration but, as we said initially, this certainly does not mark the end of something, but rather a step in ongoing cycles of thinking, planning, acting, evaluating, retheorizing.

We want to reiterate the importance of critical reflection. We recognize the tension therapists and managers are experiencing in settings where funders are demanding the use of outcome measures and evidence-based practices. We clearly understand the need for accountability to funders and to those people with whom we consult. In the world of pre-test, process, and post-test, we believe that what therapists do in the process is at least as important as the outcomes (post-test). We believe that the process of reaching particular goals is what constitutes the ethics of engagement with people. We also believe that critical reflection offers a model of researching practice, integrating the worlds of theory, practice and research.

PART 1

Critically Reflecting: From Practice to Theory

CHAPTER 1

The Significance of Story: A Historical, Cultural Backdrop

In this first chapter we will illustrate the significance of story from a historical, social, and cultural context, illustrating the relevance of the story metaphor for therapeutic practice. This will provide a context for understanding Chapter 2, in which we will introduce innovative applications of the story metaphor. Although we are excited to introduce "innovative" ideas that expand on existing practices in the area of story, we are also clearly humbled in doing so. In that respect, we strongly acknowledge the foundational contributions of Michael White and David Epston (1990) for their development of the story metaphor. Within this chapter and the subsequent chapter we will revisit those foundational concepts. In addition, we will describe further ideas for extending the development of the story metaphor in therapeutic practice.

THE HISTORY OF OUR JOURNEY

The following will provide a brief history of our theoretical journey, illustrating how our own interest in the story metaphor evolved. The journey contained a number of "forks in the road" surprises, and learnings as we were increasingly drawn toward practicing narrative therapy and interested in the importance of story.

I (JD) was initially trained as a brief strategic therapist and family therapist in the early 1980s and became immersed in the work of the Mental Research Institute and various models of family therapy. In the early 1990s, as we started developing our advanced training program, we began practicing solution-focused brief therapy while working with Insoo Kim Berg and Steve de Shazer. Looking back, we clearly benefited from our involvement with brief strategic therapy, family therapy, and solution-focused brief therapy. Those therapeutic models introduced us to less pathologizing worldviews, shifting our focus from what is wrong in people to what is strong in people (Eron & Lund, 1996).

I (LB) was not overly influenced by any particular family therapy approach. I was influenced by feminist theories as my earliest practice was within a Violence Against Women (VAW) team. During the time I worked with women who had been abused by their partners, I became concerned with the discourses within popular culture that romanticized abuse against women. I was also interested in supporting women's negotiation of those discourses (Béres, 1999, 2001, 2002). This interest led to my doctoral work. At the same time as I was integrating these ideas into my direct practice, I first attended training with Michael White (1995b). The metaphorical pump was already primed and I was completely ready to be inspired by his approach to scaffolding conversations so that he and the people consulting him were able to deconstruct their learning and meaning-making. This was done within a context that examined how people storied their lives and privileged some events over others in the formation of their identity, and also took into account the effects of discourses on the storying process.

It is difficult sometimes to be exact about the starting point of any particular story, and certainly the story of our research and reflective practices begins prior to the 2 years that we gathered field notes from the research project. Prior to that and over time, as our therapeutic and training practice continued to evolve, a number of other influences dramatically changed our philosophical and theoretical orientations and our day-to-day therapeutic practices. Because of these influences, we decided to take time to critically reflect on our work, without the constraints and distractions of working strictly within these therapeutic models. This allowed us to remain committed to the principles of being collaborative, staying respectful, and centering people's knowledge, at the same time remaining open to learning new practices.

During this time, while I (JD, along with collaborators) reflected on the therapeutic process from a phenomenological perspective, I reviewed existing meta-analysis studies. These studies reviewed over 40 years of outcome research in an attempt to identify common factors across therapy models that contributed to positive outcomes in psychotherapy (Bergin & Lambert, 1978; Bohart, 1993; Lambert, 1992; Lambert & Bergin, 1994). Since that time, the authors of this research have continued to contribute to the psychotherapy literature (Bohart & Tallman, 1996, 1999; Miller, Duncan, & Hubble, 1997). One significant common finding emerged from the studies: What people bring to the therapeutic process is what contributes most strongly to preferred outcomes in psychotherapy. This includes their knowledge, skills, abilities, language, cultural beliefs, hopes, dreams, commitments, and preferences. This information was dissimilar from much of the previous literature regarding what contributes to preferred outcomes in psychotherapy. "There, the therapist is the 'hero' who, with potent techniques and procedures, intervenes in clients' lives and fixes their malfunctioning machinery, be they faulty cognitions, weak and ineffectual egos, primitive defense structures, conditioned maladaptive behaviors, defective social skills, or poorly working internal self organizations" (Tallman & Bohart, 1999, p. 91).

Hence, what people bring to the therapeutic process is what contributes the most to preferred outcomes. Within this category (i.e., what people bring to the therapeutic process) the researchers also suggested that there was a subset that was the largest contributor to preferred outcome in psychotherapy and was what they referred to as "extra-therapeutic factors" (Miller et al., 1997). What the researchers referred to as extratherapeutic factors are also commonly understood as the properties of storyline, which are *events* in a sequence, over time, to form a theme, plot, or story (Bruner, 1986b; White and Epston, 1990). What the researchers were particularly referring to were *events* that occur in people's lives that are located outside of the therapeutic process as well as the social influences of others. As we continued to review this outcome literature, it occurred to us that the particularities of what people bring to the therapeutic process, as well as the extratherapeutic factors, could be understood as their story. That is to say, not only do people express their lives as story in the therapeutic process; their lives as lived, both inside and outside of the therapeutic process, are *consti-*

tuted as story. These significant events include such experiences as the birth of a child, separation and divorce, the loss of a loved one, or an epiphany experienced from an everyday event. While excited about this discovery, the challenge with which we were faced became strikingly evident: How do we bring people's stories to the foreground and encourage them to put their stories to work so that they can become performed stories?

Although we came to this discovery through the route of positivist scientific inquiry, which in many ways contradicts poststructural sensibilities, it remained a major turning point in our journey. As we were conducting our own phenomenological process, we suspected that this discovery that extratherapeutic factors (significant events in life) and the properties of story (events in a sequence over time to form a plot) represented the same phenomena. Even though this information was presented in the form of "outcome data," it remained a powerful confirmation for us that when people can more fully express the details of their life stories, it is the single most influential contribution toward preferred outcomes in the therapeutic process. From that point forward we became passionately interested in developing a means of responding to people that encouraged them to fully express their stories. In order to begin our inquiry and put these ideas into practice, it was necessary to have, and reflect upon, many therapeutic conversations with people.

Then, while immersed in many therapeutic conversations, we became aware that it wasn't necessarily constructive to merely elicit and listen to people's stories. The act of cocreating stories with people was not an "anything goes" process. The therapeutic conversation, as the container that holds the story, needed form. The conversation was more productive when there was a guiding framework or "map" to help develop meaning and a sense of purpose in their story.

Because of this new understanding, I (JD) began to study various frameworks for storyline and the therapeutic conversation (Campbell, 1968; Labov & Fanshel, 1977). We were also drawn to the work of Michael White and David Epston (1990) who adopted the story metaphor in their work.

In 1995 we met Michael White. I (JD) had sponsored Michael to present his work in Montreal, Quebec, and Toronto, Ontario. This was an event that propelled our interest in the story metaphor to new levels. Listening to Michael articulate narrative therapy firsthand had the effect of breathing life into narrative practices and significantly grounded our ideas in developing storyline. We found his articulation of narrative practices fresh, inspiring, and confirming of our own work. We continued regular involvement with Michael White through various projects over many years. As it was with others, his influence on our work and our lives was significant. As we had already begun studying storyline frameworks, we were in a unique position to learn from the foundational work of Michael White and David Epston, while continuing to develop our own innovative ideas. We gained a renewed commitment to our practice and were re-energized to plunge into the study of story and storyline development.

UNIVERSAL STORY FORM

It is useful to recognize that the emergence of the story metaphor, as it is applied in the therapeutic process, is situated within a rich historical and cultural backdrop as universal story form. This universal story form spans generations across time and traverses many cultures.

Stories have been a powerful, innermost part of all cultures and communities since the beginning of time. Although the form has many versions, stories typically contain the universal properties of a beginning, a middle, and an ending that brings the story to a close. Story form has endured centuries of storytelling following this collective, time-tested pattern. This simple story form is how the meanings for understanding and living life were adopted and developed by various cultures, communities, and families, and were then passed on through generations. Stories bear and pass on lasting values that form belief systems and discourses, which people use to create their identities and navigate their lives. Although present-day therapists are challenged to respond to the multiplicity, complexities, and shifting discourses of contemporary life, this fundamental story form continues to bring coherence and meaning to them through narrative therapy practices. This time-honored story form provides an unfaltering bridge between the complexities of ever-changing cultural beliefs and therapeutic practices.

Chapter 2 will expand upon the key properties of universal story form as underpinnings for developing various storyline configurations in therapeutic practice. These key properties will include the foundational concepts of Michael White and David Epston (1990), their exploration of the work of Arnold van Gennep, in 1909, and the subsequent work of Joseph Campbell, in 1949, and Victor Turner, in 1969.

French anthropologist, ethnographer, and folklorist Arnold van Gennep (1960) was renowned for his studies of *Les Rites de Passage,* as practiced by a range of diverse cultures. More specifically, he studied the rituals, ceremonies, and celebrations associated with people's "life crisis" (Kimball, 1960). Rites of passage are rituals that people go through in order to progress to the next stage of their lives. Marriage, birth, death, or a time of crisis or transition is marked by rituals, or ceremonies, which may differ from culture to culture but are universal in function.

Evolving from universal story form, the "rites of passage" is a phenomenon that makes it possible for the social values and beliefs that are specific to various cultures to become more visible. The three sequenced phases together form what is known as the rites of passage, and they closely replicate the beginning, middle, and ending configuration of universal story form. The stages of the rites of passage are: the separation (preliminal) stage, the transitional or liminal stage, and the incorporation (aggregation) or postliminal stage. Van Gennep labeled these stages the "schema" of rites of passage, or transition. The word *schema* can be better understood as "pattern" or "framework."

It should be emphasized that van Gennep intended this pattern of sequenced phases to include both "process" and "structure" (or "process" and "outcome"). He was not only interested in the "what" but also in the "how" and "why" (Kimball, 1960). With an overemphasis on demonstrating outcomes in the present-day attempt to research therapeutic models, there is less value placed on how and why those outcomes are achieved. Van Gennep's approach appears more ethical to us as it fills this gap by focusing on the process by which an end result is accomplished. This attention to the qualitative effects of therapy on the people involved constitutes ethical therapeutic practice. In this way, van Gennep's rites of passage is considerably relevant for contemporary therapeutic practice and inquiry.

More specifically, van Gennep drew attention to the characteristic symbolism of rites of passage and the necessity for ritualizing, or punctuating, the transition from one stage, through a threshold, to the next stage, such as a ritualistic passing through a door or archway (hence the term *liminal*, from the Latin *limen*, "threshold"). "He saw regeneration as a law of life and of the universe: the energy which is found in any system gradually becomes spent and must be renewed at intervals. For him this regeneration is accomplished in the social world" (Kimball, 1960, p. viii). Therefore, the liminal, transitional state provides for a regeneration and renewal of knowledge that is made possible through the social collaboration and support of others. Therapeutic practice involving this quality of social collaboration creates a context for knowledge renewal.

Van Gennep connected the rites of passage analogy to an overall story of natural phenomena. Whether routine procedures, or ceremonies that punctuate the seasons, or the changing of the years, in a sense, life itself is an overall story and a rite of passage. The rites of passage has become an integral part of the discourse of sociology and anthropology. Van Gennep's work, although conceived in another time, remains relevant and influential in contemporary thought and popular culture.

Van Gennep powerfully influenced American mythologist Joseph Campbell, and the structuring of his book, *The Hero with a Thousand Faces* (Campbell, 1949). Campbell strongly referenced van Gennep's *Les Rites de Passage* as he developed the journey metaphor into three similar elements: departure, initiation, and return.

Campbell clearly acknowledged the timeless history and universality of cultural stories. He proposed that key stories have continued to exist for thousands of years from around the world, even from disparate cultures, and that they all share a universal story form. He referred to this story form as the *monomyth*. Examples of key stories that share the primary properties of universal story form can be found in the chronicles of Buddha, Moses, and Christ.

Campbell's theories of universal story form continue to have a pervasive influence on contemporary popular culture. He influenced many creative artists who became aware of the promise in Campbell's theories to reveal human experiences in the context of narrative structures. Writers, songwriters, and filmmakers such as George Lucas, Bob Dylan, Jerry Garcia, Jim Morrison, Stanley Kubrick, and Arthur C. Clarke all incorporated his theories of the story metaphor into their work. Contemporary movie examples that are created on his narrative patterns include *Avatar*, the *Star Wars* movies, *The Matrix*, the *Batman* movies, the *Indiana Jones* movies, and *The Lion King*, to name only a few. Examples of books that credit Campbell's influence are Richard Adams's *Watership Down* and J. K. Rowling's *Harry Potter* series.

Van Gennep's work, *Les Rites de Passage*, also influenced the research of cultural anthropologist and ethnographer Victor Turner, particularly his 1969 text, *The Ritual Process: Structure and Anti-structure*. Turner's initial intrigue with rituals and rites of passage was a result of his study of the Ndembu tribe in Central Africa from 1950 to 1954. His involvement with this tribe provided the experiences for his book. The publication of *The Ritual Process* represented a pivotal time in Turner's career as he turned his focus from an exclusive study of the Ndembu tribe and began to focus on complex contemporary societies.

Through his exploration of van Gennep's three-phase structure of rites of passage, Turner subsequently emphasized and expanded the liminal, transitional phase. Turner made the distinction that in the transitional state, which is between the beginning and final phases, people are "betwixt and between," having departed from their previous state but not yet a part of their reincorporated state. They are in a limbo, characterized by humility, ambiguity, test, and a renegotiation of relationships.

It is interesting to note that during the time of Turner's exploration of the liminal state, the social context around him was also in upheaval in the late 1960s. A generation of young people had chosen to embrace marginal lifestyles in protest against the values of mainstream society. Turner's teachings of "betwixt and between" carried strong relevance and resonance for people living in those social times of intense transition:

> It remained Turner's task, based on van Gennep's recognition of the structural similarities of rites of elevation, initiation, healing, incorporation, and transience, to show how this system operated as a way of marking life process in the experience of the people among whom he had lived and worked. (Abrahams, 1997, p. xi).

It is through this contribution to negotiating the complexities of intense life transitions that Turner's exploration of the liminal state became strongly relevant for contemporary therapeutic practice. There has been an overemphasis on assessment, diagnosis, and discharge in present-day practice, neglecting the middle phase of the therapeutic process. This pathologizing approach to present-day therapeutic practices risks totalizing people's identities, with scant hope for alternative possibilities. Turner's work recognized the contextual and transitional nature of people's distress, engaging with them in the exploration of preferred choices and introducing "redressive mechanisms" (Turner, 1977).

The rites of passage pattern introduced a means for understanding and influencing the how, why, and what of story form, providing coherence and vitality. Utilizing processes that exist in many diverse cultures and in the natural world, van Gennep's pattern of the three sequence stages enlivened the storying process. The subsequent work of Joseph Campbell and Victor Turner expanded van Gennep's work through the acknowledgment of life difficulties as transitional, situated within an ever-moving backdrop of context and culture. Key events are ritualized, interpreted, and reinterpreted with others, making possible the renewal and regeneration of knowledge. Regardless of the length of the story through time, the three primary elements of beginning, middle, and end provide the properties to hold a theme, or a plot, and to keep the plot fluid, moving, and on course. This simple pattern of a beginning call to change, followed by a liminal phase containing a quest, finally resulting in a "resolution" or ending, conveys a sense of movement (Campbell, 1949; Turner, 1977; Van Gennep, 1960). This movement is indicated as marking differences through time, a sense of traveling from here to there, tracing identity as transformed through a journey. The application of story form to the therapeutic process offers significant utility as it provides a separation from taken-for-granted, demoralizing ways of experiencing identity and introduces different and "remoralizing" (Frank, 1995) ways of experiencing identity through a multiplicity of possibilities.

As story form provides a journey metaphor, it is important that people are not relegated to the role of passive, observant passengers on their journey. People are invited to become full participants and primary authors as they engage in the revisions of the events located within their life stories. The events within dominant storylines are highly selective, leaving many events outside that are never strung together into coherent storylines. In order to incorporate these neglected events into the revised story, therapists assume an invitational posture, promoting a certain amount of conversational tentativeness, by focusing more on considerations than conclusions, proposing half-baked ideas and speculations, and asking questions more than making statements. This leaves space for people to fill the gaps in their stories by bringing forward the experiences of those neglected events. This encourages people to "step back," reflect, reconsider, and make different meaning of the experiences and events in their lives. People construct meaning from their experiences through a process of rich story development, making possible a restorying of life and identity. This is a fundamental form of human communication.

"What generally happens when we tell a story from our own life is that we increase our working knowledge of ourselves because we discover deeper meaning in our lives through the process of reflecting and putting the events, experiences, and feelings that we have lived into oral expression" (Atkinson, 1998, p. 1).

The act of reflecting on the events and experiences of life is what Bruner (1986b) refers to as the landscape of consciousness. (This, at times, is also referred to as the landscape of identity.) As Michael White (2007a) stated:

> This landscape features the consciousness of the protagonists of the story and is significantly composed of their reflections on the events of the landscape of action—of their attribution of meaning to these events, of their deductions about the intentions and purposes that are shaping of these events, and of their conclusions about the character and identity of the other protagonist in light of these events. Like the development of the plot of the landscape of action, the development of the landscape of consciousness must be reconciled with the *fabula,* the timeless underlying theme of the story. (p. 78)

To further clarify this Michael White (2007a) cited Jerome Bruner as follows:

> In any case the fabula of a story—its timeless underlying theme—seems to be a unity that incorporates at least three constituents. It contains a plight into which characters have fallen as a result of intentions that have gone awry either because of circumstances, of the "character of characters," or most likely of the interaction between the two . . . [In the original]. What gives the story its unity is the manner in which plight, characters, and consciousness interact to yield a structure that has a start, development, and a "sense of ending." (p. 21)

Therefore, when therapists engage in therapeutic conversations with people through the telling and retelling of these richly described subordinate stories, they are more able to reflect on events, bringing rich meaning, understanding, and coherence to their life stories.

The mapping of storylines makes it possible to free identities from problem-saturated stories and journey toward preferred, transformative stories. "Transformative stories are performed stories" (Freedman & Combs, 1996, p. 87). As people begin to perform the preferred storylines they speak and act these previously subordinated stories into existence, more fully engaging with their favored lives.

Storyline frameworks serve as maps that are intended to guide therapeutic conversations while developing meaning, eliciting preferred storylines and reclaiming personal agency. "White reminds us of how Bateson used the metaphor of 'maps,' saying that all of our knowledge of the world is carried in the form of various mental maps of 'external' or 'objective' reality, and that different maps lead to different realities" (Freedman & Combs, 1996, p. 15). A story is a temporal map that traverses the past, the present, and the future. White (2007a) explained:

> Maps like these shape a therapeutic inquiry in which people suddenly find themselves interested in novel understandings of the events of their lives that have been forsaken, fascinated with neglected territories of their identities, and, at times, awed by their own responses to the predicaments of their existence. And I believe that maps like these shape a therapeutic inquiry that contributes to the rich development of therapists' stories about their work and about their life generally, which can be a source of inspiration. (p. 5)

The forms of storylines presented will take into account that all stories are not equal. These storyline frameworks address the range of social contexts in which people's lives are situated. For example, working with a family aspiring to develop a greater sense of intimacy among its members is a different social context than working with an immigrant family that is experiencing the effects of racism and the marginalizing effects of a dominant culture.

Overall, we are proposing storyline forms that incorporate a journey and quest metaphor because these quest metaphors address problems (Frank, 1995) and are strongly pertinent to the therapeutic process. Our development of these storyline forms was powerfully influenced from trial-and-error practice, constantly incorporating feedback from the parents and children who participated in our project. People were routinely invited to offer us feedback regarding their experience of what was useful about the therapeutic conversation and what was appropriate for their particular experience.

Everyone has a story. The parents and children who attended our narrative therapy project customarily began their therapy sessions by telling stories. As stated above, these stories are not merely about people's lives, but actually constitutive of their lives, including their values, language, significant events, hopes, dreams, commitments, preferences, and cultural beliefs. People's individual stories and cultural beliefs are nestled in, and intertwined through, their relationships with others within larger backstories and master narratives. As such, people's identities are the result of social collaboration with others, through shared narratives, taking into account how they view themselves and how others view them (Eron & Lund, 1996; Frank, 1995; Lindemann-Nelson, 2001; White, 2007a).

More often when people initially attend a therapy session, they are caught up in the grips of a dominant negative story and the therapist is not experiencing them at their best. At this time, they are not performing their preferred stories of how they want to experience themselves or how they want others to experience them. This initial expression of their problem story is strongly influenced by the overall cultural discourses in which they live on a day-to-day basis. "Discourses powerfully shape a person's choices about what life events can be storied and how they should be storied. This is as true for therapists as it is for the people who consult them" (Freedman & Combs, 1996, p. 43). It's useful for therapists to acknowledge the effects of dominant stories, but to also be prudent not to accept these stories as total and literal accounts of people's identities. A popular mantra among our faculty when engaging with people early on in the therapeutic process is: "Take people seriously, not literally."

At times people would tell darkened stories, filled with a pervasive sense of hopelessness that their lives would ever amount to anything beyond constant struggle and survival. Other times they expressed stories of disappointment in themselves or someone else. At times they shared stories of fear, as they experienced paralyzing isolation, frozen in time from the aftermath of past trauma and abuse.

People situate themselves as characters within these dominant, oppressive stories, which they come to believe as real and unchangeable. Bruner (1986b) suggested that over time and with repetition, these stories become more rigid and harden, ironically trapping the storytellers within the stories they created themselves. The effects of these oppressive stories strongly influence people's sense of identity, reducing their sense of agency and their ability to see the choices that are available to them. Lindemann-Nelson (2001) stated: "The connection between oppression and identity, I have claimed, lies in the master narratives that are generated by the forces circulating within particular systems of oppression, since these stories construct the identities that are required by those systems" (p. 150). The process of locating identity within master narratives is often the initial step toward moving away from their control and oppression. Identity is interwoven with the voices and exchanges with others in people's social cultural context.

Therefore, although the expression of stories is personal, it is also a social project. Stories are told to and received by someone. They are constructed and sustained among people, requiring a toing and froing. They are produced from a subjective experience of one person and received through a subjective experience of another. They are also shaped by the taken-for-granted metaphors, expectations, and imagery of popular culture. These culturally shaped beliefs and expectations have significant effect on the power and grip of the problem story and the possible introduction of alternative storylines as they travel through the myriad tellers and retellers.

As previously stated, the medium for eliciting people's stories is the therapeutic conversation. Ideas, concepts, and memories arising from this social interchange among the therapists and people who consult with them are mediated through language. Knowledge is renewed and concepts are developed in this mutually influenced dialogical space. This moment-to-moment conversational minutia is the heartbeat of alternative storyline production. Each story is unique and remarkable in its own way.

The parents and children attending our project presented their stories in many different shapes and forms. "Whatever its form, the therapist confronts a narrative—often persuasive and gripping; it is a narrative that may be terminated within a brief period or it may be extended over weeks or months" (Gergen & Kaye, 1992, p. 166). One thing is for sure: The therapist must act in response to the person's telling of their story, taking into account the influence of their backstory.

CONCLUSION

Within this chapter we have introduced the historical and universal significance of story, which through generations across time and diverse cultures continues to thrive in contemporary popular culture. Through the foundational work of Arnold van Gennep and the subsequent development of his ideas by Joseph Campbell and Victor Turner, we have introduced the notion of understanding the distress experienced by people in their lives as both contextual and transitional. For that reason, possibilities for preferred change and personal agency are addressed through the journey metaphor. Therapists play a key role as copassengers on this therapeutic journey.

How therapists respond to people's stories is critically important. People need to tell their stories in ways that make it possible for them to engage in new understandings of their place in the world around them. In the following chapter we will introduce maps for navigating the therapeutic conversation and facilitating the development of people's storylines from the beginning, through the middle phase, and to the end. These maps will make it possible to address the how and why (process) of therapy as well as the what (outcome) of therapy.

Questions for Reflection

1. How can we best attend to both process and outcomes in therapy in order to provide ethically based practices?
2. How can we usefully participate with people on their therapeutic journey, knowing how to be involved and how long to be involved?
3. What skills or attitudes can help us become better at responding to the range of diverse cultural influences that affect people's beliefs and actions in therapy?
4. How have celebrations or rituals marked significant events in your own personal stories?
5. As you reflect back now, do you think that the types of stories you have told about yourself have changed over time? Do you stress some aspects more than others now?

CHAPTER 2

Storied Therapy as a Three-Act Play

As the culture of psychotherapy is immersed in the larger, ever-changing culture of society, a storied therapy is highly pertinent when addressing the effects and the complexities of living in contemporary society. To that end, story is the *raison d'être* of the work we do with people.

In this chapter we will describe how we have expanded the story metaphor into an organizing concept of a three-act play and we will introduce a conversational map that we have fashioned for developing storylines. The three-act play metaphor and the conversational map were both inspired and shaped by a thorough review of the literature, as well as reflective therapeutic practice. In our project, we regularly scrutinized the training and therapeutic experience, contributing to the ongoing adjustment and shaping of practice. Various frameworks were provided for trainees and family members to assist them in reflecting *on* experience and reflecting *in* experience, extending both the theoretical and therapeutic learning. This practice encouraged us to adopt a posture of reflexivity, an awareness of the use of "self" in the creation of knowledge in clinical practice, as described fully in the Introduction. Critical reflection and a posture of reflexivity remain ongoing principles in our practice.

The application of the three-act play and the conversational map will be described, as they apply both to a therapy session and to the overall process of therapy. In order to do so, the chapter will be divided into three primary sections, "act 1," "act 2," and "act 3." In each section we will present detailed aspects of the conversational storyline map, which address the specific aspects of applying the story metaphor to practice.

The theoretical orientation that guides our work is drawn from narrative, poststructural, and social constructionist theory. The story metaphor situated within this theoretical orientation introduces movement, emphasizing the meaning constructed through language and the connectedness of events through time. A story serves as a temporal map, providing space over time to reduce the problematic effects of life transitions on people's identities and their sense of personal agency. People's difficulties are viewed as attempts to adjust to life transitions. The temporal aspect of a storied therapy makes it possible to perceive difference and detect change through time. It also makes it possible to introduce critical thinking and reflective practices, rather than relying on a causal-linear "problem-solving" approach.

We understand our narrative, poststructural theoretical orientation to be a metaphor for therapy and a choice that we have made in our commitment to our work. Freedman and Combs referred to Paul Rosenblatt as follows: "In his discussion, he describes not only what each metaphor highlights, but also what it obscures when used to guide one's thinking and perceptions" (1996, p. 2). Our narrative, storied metaphor is no different from Rosenblatt's description in that it will emphasize certain aspects of therapy and training and de-emphasize others. However, in taking up this philosophy and theoretical orientation we have simultaneously chosen not to take up a traditional causal-linear approach. In this approach there is a risk of totalizing people's identities through the use of labels and categories that are based on an aspect of their experience. These totalizing practices obscure the multiplicity of identity and the influence of people's relevant social context. Our commitment to a poststructuralist, critically reflective approach epitomizes a major discontinuous theoretical diversion away from a traditional approach to psychotherapy. Within the storied, poststructuralist orientation, we understand the conception of self as constructed in the endless reciprocal interchanges with others within a particular social and cultural context. Therefore, we have departed from a conception of self that relies on a "skin-bound container with fixed contents (resources) that we had previously conceptualized" (Freedman & Combs, 1996, p. 17).

Our choice of philosophical and theoretical orientation has significant implications in therapy for both the people seeking consultation and the therapist. For people seeking assistance in therapy, the emphasis on temporal diversity, multiplicity of life, and the influence of a relevant cultural and social context makes space for the reconsideration of identity and the renewal of knowledge. Knowledge is conceptualized as a process rather than a binary tradition of subject and object where one person labels another person. Rather than operating from a framework whereby generalized theory and procedures control the therapeutic process, therapists are able to move beyond and further develop theory through the particularities of the therapeutic practice. In doing so, a storied approach to therapy addresses the complex, ever-changing lived experiences of day-to-day life, perpetually renewing theory and practice.

A storied approach to therapy departs from an information-seeking expedition in an attempt to establish "truth" and focuses instead on a meaning-making exercise. White and Epston explained: "They do not establish universal truth conditions but a connectedness of events across time. The narrative mode leads not to certainties, but to varying perspectives" (1990, p. 78). Parry and Doan (1994) elaborated:

> In other words, it is the *meaningfulness* of the answers given, rather than their factual *truthfulness*, that gives them their credibility. The hearers of the story believed that it was true because it was meaningful, rather than it was meaningful because it was true. (p. 2)

However, this does not promote a relativist stance, where each possible story and identity carries equal weight. It is not a matter of anything goes, but rather that the people we work with will prefer some stories rather than others. We may assist them in stepping outside of mainstream discourses that demonstrate partiality toward certain ways of examining their lives as they step into alternative stories.

We also regard our philosophy and theoretical orientation to be an ethical choice. We believe that we have a moral obligation to collaborate with people, walking beside them as they express their life stories and embark on their therapeutic journey.

STORIED THERAPY AS A THREE-ACT PLAY

Act 1	Act 2	Act 3
The Known and Familiar	**ZONE OF PROXIMAL DEVELOPMENT**	What is Possible to Know
Points of Story Backstory	→ Significant Events Evaluation	Summary *Reflecting surface*
Problem/Crisis	**RICH STORY DEVELOPMENT** Acknowledge initiatives, present moments, arresting moments, aha's, catharsis, sparkling moments, surprises * * * * * * * * * Outsider Witness	Implications for the next steps Re-incorporation of identity conclusions Development of Alternative Story/ receiving context
THIN Identity Conclusions	Temporal Diversity **Migration Of Identity**	**THICK** Identity Conclusions

Figure 2.1. Storied Therapy as a Three-Act Play.

Adapted from van Gennup (1960), Turner (1977), Campbell (1968), and White (1999).

As stated in Chapter 1, stories are organized units of experience, evolving from a universal story form containing a beginning, middle, and ending. We refer to this metaphor of a storied therapy as a three-act play (Ray & Keeney, 1993). The three-act play invokes the rites of passage analogy, adapting it to the therapeutic process (Figure 2.1).

The conversational micromap that we developed is intended to work within the overall pattern of the three-act play. This map includes six points of inquiry, traversing all three phases from beginning to end. The map helps to shape and more fully develop the purpose of the story through each specific phase. Each phase of the three-act play has a discrete purpose that needs to be taken up before moving the story forward to the next phase and developing alternative storylines. These alternative storylines provide a platform for movement away from dominant themes that contribute to a destitute sense of identity, to fertile counterplots that contribute to an inspired and robust sense of identity.

The composition of this conversational map expands beyond the more commonly understood narrative form, which contains properties such as events in a sequence, over time, to form a theme, plot, or story (Bruner, 1990; White, 2007a; White & Epston, 1990). White and Epston clarified the purpose of a storied metaphor as follows: "In striving to make sense of life, persons face the task of arranging their experiences of events in sequences across time in such a way as to arrive at a coherent account of themselves and the world around them" (1990, p. 10).

In addition to the above properties, we are proposing an expanded narrative composition that includes the following stages of inquiry: (1) points of stories (once upon a time, someone was called to do something . . .), (2) backstory (every day . . .), (3) pivotal events (and then, one day . . .), (4) evaluation (because of that . . .), (5) reflecting summary (moral of the story . . .), and (6) receiving context (and finally . . .).

The following outline will illustrate how the problem that brings someone to therapy is situated relative to each distinct phase of the three-act play. In addition, it will show how the six points of inquiry within the conversational map are located in each of the three separate phases to help shape and give purpose to the therapeutic conversation.

Act 1, beginning; separation phase, "perhaps from some status, aspect of identity or role that is determined to be no longer viable for the person concerned" (White & Epston, 1990, p. 7).

1. Points of story: announces what this story is about, that is, what's most important to talk about. Sets the agenda to begin the therapy session.
2. Backstory: develops the relevant social, cultural context. An intelligible frame in which to understand the problem/issue.

Act 2, middle; liminal, transitional, "betwixt and between phase—characterized by some discomfort, confusion, disorganization, and perhaps heightened expectation for the future" (White & Epston, 1990, p. 7).

3. Pivotal events: identifying and reinterpreting the experiences that are located in the significant events in people's lives.
4. Evaluation: locating and judging the effects of problems in people's lives.

Act 3, conclusion; or, "re-incorporation, characterized by the arrival at some new status that specifies new responsibilities and privileges for the person concerned" (White & Epston, 1990, p. 7).

5. Reflecting summary: reflecting on and summarizing movement that occurs in the therapy session or the overall process of therapy.
6. Receiving context: developing a new backstory context to receive changes that have developed and to accommodate the reincorporation of identity.

The three-act play encapsulates the general theme or plot of the story, while each act/phase serves a particular purpose and movement within the overall play. This play, informed by the rites of passage metaphor, provides people with a general map of the experiences that are to be expected in breaking from a problem-saturated life as they ready themselves for the therapeutic journey ahead. People are compelled, rather than convinced, to embark on their journey.

As stated in Chapter 1, van Gennep (1960) pointed out the need to mark the transition from one stage, through a threshold, to the next stage. This remains especially relevant as people move from each act of the three-act play to the next.

Michael White further expanded on the work of van Gennep and Turner's (1977) rites of passage metaphor through his Migration of Identity map (White, 1999). Through this map he continued to call attention to the phases of separation, liminality, and reincorporation as invaluable aids for mapping personal journeys. The migration of identity map begins by inquiring into people's degree of wellness and/or degree of despair, just prior to departing on their therapeutic journey. Their identity conclusions, which are more often thin and negative at this time, are taken into account. The time and date of departure, indicating when people moved from the separation phase and began moving into the middle phase, is logged. During the middle phase of the journey any setbacks or progresses are tracked and graphed, unpacking meaning of the events in a sequence over time through the therapeutic conversation. The final and third phase of the map results in a reincorporation of identity, which incorporates preferred aspects (i.e., skills, knowledges, attributes, beliefs, commitments, preferences, etc.) of people's identities from their past with new realizations and learnings that have been acquired while journeying through the middle phase. The third, reincorporation phase includes reflections on new learnings and perceived difference, implications for identity conclusions, and speculations regarding next steps. Invoking the universal story metaphor, the migration of identity map makes it possible to track difference, movement, and meaning through time.

The three-act play, utilizing the universal story metaphor, offers a lucid means to conceptualize both the entire therapeutic process and a particular session. As Steve de Shazer (1991) stated:

> The conversations that therapist and clients have can be seen as stories, as narratives. Like any story, each case or each session of each case has a beginning, a middle, and an ending, or at least a sense of an ending. Like any story, the conversation is held together by the patterns involved, by the plot. Like many stories, therapy conversations deal with human predicaments, troubles, resolutions, and attempted resolutions. (p. 92)

However, just as we understand our narrative, poststructural orientation to be an overall theoretical metaphor for therapy, the conceptualization of the three-act play and the storyline conversational map are merely organizing metaphors. Metaphors are handy when making sense of phenomenological process. The purpose of the three-act play and the storyline conversational map are to help navigate therapeutic conversations. There are many different types of maps that are useful in navigating therapeutic conversations. Alternatively, for some it may be preferable to use no maps at all when participating in a therapeutic conversation. Therefore, this is *a way*, not *the way*, to organize storyline within a therapeutic conversation. The three-act play and the storyline conversational map do not represent a "truth" claim. These are our ways of conceptualizing storied therapy that are situated within the backdrop of our postmodern philosophical orientation.

ACT 1: SETTING THE STAGE: SEPARATING FROM TAKEN-FOR-GRANTED UNDERSTANDINGS

At this beginning stage, the therapist assumes the position of a welcoming host, engaging with people through a supportive, transparent therapeutic posture while expressing curiosity and interest in their story. This posture is primarily about how to be in relationship with people while facilitating a therapeutic conversation. The focus is on asking questions rather than making statements. Questions, if not done in a cross-examining manner, are invitational and inspired by curiosity. "People can choose how to respond to a question, and when we genuinely listen to and value people's responses, *their* ideas, not ours, stay at the center of therapy" (Freedman & Combs, 1996, p. 277). This posture demonstrates a practice of respect.

When therapeutic conversations work well, they are supportive, with a clear sense of purpose. We engage with people's preferred view of "self." We want them to experience a difference after our conversation with them and a sense of acknowledgment that "finally, someone has heard what I have to say! I was taken seriously." As Freedman and Combs (1996) stated:

> We try to put ourselves in the shoes of the people we work with and understand, from their perspective, in their language, what has led them to seek our assistance. Only then can we recognize alternative stories. Connecting with people's experience from their perspective orients us to the specific realities that shape, and are shaped by, their personal narratives. (p. 44)

Think back to a time when you had a conversation with someone that made a difference for you. How much did your sense of engagement with the conversation have to do with how you were able to resonate with the other person throughout it? Did you feel taken seriously? Did you have the experience that the other person was genuinely listening to you and understanding your perspective? Were you more in touch with how you prefer to experience yourself? You may have experienced increased optimism and a sense of moving more toward your preferred sense of "self." You may have experienced a greater sense of intimacy with yourself and the other person. Afterward, you may have had a sense that even though your circumstances may not have changed, you had a different outlook, you understood things differently, and new meanings were generated as a result of the conversation. Perhaps you experienced more confidence that you could do what you needed to do and felt inspired to do so. Now ask yourself: How was this conversation different from other ones that may have seemed lackluster, uninspired, or even counterproductive?

When beginning a therapy session we assume a conversational, not a traditional, interviewing posture. A conversational posture invites people to express their stories. A poststructural conversational posture helps to deconstruct problem stories while generating new meaning and searching for preferred stories. As a result, therapy sessions are not fact-finding missions, but conversations that encourage the telling and retelling of stories from the past and the coauthoring of possible stories moving into the future.

The poststructural therapeutic conversation is characterized as dialogue among the therapist and people who have come to therapy. It's a mutually shared undertaking, with constant toing and froing between the therapist and people seeking assistance. These conversations are by their very nature moment-to-moment, situated in a backstory of people's lives. While facilitating the therapeutic conversation the therapist conveys a sense of "being in this together."

The therapist begins the session by assuming the position of a welcoming host and beginning with describing the process of the therapy session (e.g., the overall session format, the inclusion of the outsider witnessing team if there is one, note-taking, one-way mirrors, videotaping, duration, etc.) and respectfully asking for permission to use any or all of these activities.

Therapist: So, did you folks come a long way today or do you live closer around here?

Jason: We came a fair ways to get here. We live just outside of town about 40 minutes.

Caroline: We got a little lost coming in this morning. I was worried that we weren't going to make it here on time.

Therapist: Well, I'm glad you made it here okay. Could we take a couple of minutes to check with you about our understanding of what will be going on here today?

Jason: Actually, I would appreciate knowing that. I'm kinda confused about how this whole therapy thing works.

Therapist: I'll do my best to be clear. First, all the rules of confidentiality apply. The plan is that I will be talking with you and get to hear what is important for you to talk about. In addition, there are five people behind the one-way mirror who will be an audience to our conversation. About halfway through our time together we will switch places with the group and listen to them have a conversation about what they heard. They are going to have some ideas, thoughts, and images that they will want to share. At that point in time, we will be an audience to their reflections and listen to what they have heard and what caught their attention in our conversation. After listening to the team's reflections, we will switch around again and I will ask you some questions about what stood out for you or struck a chord for you that you heard in the conversation among the team members. How does that sound to you? Does that sound okay?

Caroline: It sounds interesting and okay.

Therapist: And, the team members would like to take some notes. They will be your words, not theirs. Mostly they will write down particular words or phrases that stand out or catch their attention. Also, I would like you to meet the team behind the mirror if you are comfortable with that.

Caroline: Of course, that's fine.

Therapist: (*Introduces Caroline and Jason to the team.*) And, I'd like to take some notes as well if that's okay. There is so much going on that catches my attention that if I don't write some of it down, it gets lost.

Caroline: That's fine.

Jason: Sure, that's fine.

At this point the therapist becomes a conversational manager, working to democratize the therapy session, inviting family members to introduce themselves, while ensuring that everyone's voice is included.

Therapist: Would the two of you mind just saying a little bit about yourselves at this point and include anything at all that you think would be good for us to know about you?

Jason and Caroline talked about themselves and made themselves more visible to the group. Once this process was completed, they were asked if they had any questions of the therapist. By questioning the therapist, it makes it possible for everyone in the therapeutic conversation to become more visible, reducing the therapist's position as an expert and addressing the inherent and inevitable imbalance of power.

Therapist: By the way, if there's anything you want to know about me, please don't hesitate to ask those questions. I'd be happy to answer any questions that you might have.

Caroline: Do you see families a lot? Is this sort of your specialty? How long have you been doing this kind of work?

Therapist: Yes, I mostly specialize in working with families that may experience a variety of difficulties. I've been working with families for almost 30 years now.

Act 1 is the beginning of the therapeutic conversation and the *separation phase* (to use van Gennep's rites of passage language) of the three-act play. As illustrated above, the therapist's job is to create a supportive environment so that family members can begin to tell their story and slowly distance themselves from taken-for-granted, problem-saturated ways of viewing and doing things (Eron & Lund, 1996). The separation phase is the point at which people begin to move away from the familiar aspects of their lives toward possibilities that are less known. Activities that are particular to the beginning of the therapeutic conversation need to be addressed before moving on to act 2. However, before embarking on the journey phase, and in preparation of the separation phase, effort can be put into anticipating and identifying the challenges and constraints that people are likely to face on their quest. A clearer understanding of these challenges and of the importance of their quest helps people to cultivate a preparedness and willingness to commence the journey. The act of speculating makes it possible for people to imagine alternatives, practicing and improvising new action for the experiences that lie ahead on their therapeutic journey.

Developing Storylines

People may begin the conversation with negative, totalizing identity conclusions about themselves or others. For example, a parent may declare that their 9-year-old son is ADHD (attention deficit/hyperactivity disorder).

Or, people may state that they are depressed. It's useful for the therapist to maintain the view that it's people's jobs to state the problem in this way. That's what they do. People state the problem, crisis, or issue when they come to therapy. The therapist acknowledges the distress that people are experiencing and, through deconstructive listening and questioning, begins to negotiate the definition of the problem in experience-near, nontotalizing terms (White, 2007a). This is particularly important at the beginning of the therapy session because when identity is totalized and gets swept into a category (e.g., ADHD, depression, borderline personality, etc.), it's no longer available for alternative appraisal. Totalizing, global categories invite therapists to relate to abstract concepts rather than relating to the specific people seeking assistance. The practice of totalizing identities through categories and labels creates a distance and disconnect with people, hampering their attempts to discern more productive pathways to alternative storylines. Therefore, the naming, externalization, and deconstruction of the problem helps to establish a different relationship between the problem and the people influenced by it.

As the therapist is presented with totalizing identity statements such as "He is ADHD" or "I'm depressed," people begin to describe the moments and events of the problem-saturated story. The therapist engages with people's telling of the problem story with curiosity and deconstructive listening. In this way, people's stories are acknowledged. At the same time the therapist is listening for what is not being said, yet speaks more to what is important to people.

Careful, deconstructive listening is mingled with deconstructive questions. Deconstructive questions address the totalizing effects of the problem and invite people to reconsider and reevaluate previous negative identity conclusions. As the totalizing effects of the problems are called into question over time, more space is created for alternative storylines to become more visible. The following excerpt from a therapy conversation with a man who has been diagnosed as depressed will provide an example of deconstructive listening and deconstructive questioning.

Therapist: Nathan, given the time that we have together, what's most important for us to talk about today?

Nathan: (*Leans forward in his chair, elbows on his knees, hands clasped and looking down at the floor.*) I'll be honest with you. I never imagined myself going to see someone like you. You know, like a shrink. I'm not really the kind of person that does that.

Therapist: Of course, I can appreciate that you never imagined coming to see someone like me. So, given that this is a new experience for you, how is it that you decided to make this appointment and then came in to talk with me?

Nathan: Well, it wasn't really my idea. I went to see my doctor and he told me that I'm depressed and that I should come see you to work on my depression. (*He raised his head and looked straight at the therapist.*) Can you do that? Can you fix my depression?

Therapist: I'm still a bit confused Nathan. There are a lot of different kinds of depression. Each person's depression is different. It would be helpful for me to know more about your "depression" and your particular circumstances (backstory). Actually, if I could also get to know you away from your depression a bit more, maybe I would be better able to understand what you mean when you say you're depressed. Can you tell me a bit about yourself away from your depression first? And then, I'm curious about how you came to think of yourself as depressed?

Nathan: I wasn't always like this. I had a really good "normal" life. My wife, Rachael, and I had a great marriage and really enjoyed doing things together. I had great friends and an active social life. Everything was going well in my life. Then the company that I worked for downsized and as a result of that I lost my job. I had worked for that company for 23 years and finally made vice president. Then, after all those years, they just dumped me. I found that incomprehensible. I guess I got pretty overwhelmed and miserable after that and just sort of gave up trying. I started having problems in my marriage. After a while, Rachael said she couldn't take being around me the way I was and decided we should separate. She said she needed her space to think about what was going on with us. I had to move out of our home to a little basement apartment. So, in the last 7 months I've lost my job, my wife, and my house. That's why I'm depressed.

Therapist: So, in the past 7 months you have experienced a number of significant losses. You know, Nathan, as I was listening to you describe this series of events, it got me thinking: "Is Nathan 'depressed,' or is what he is experiencing a reasonable response to everything that has happened to him over the past while?" That seems like a big unsettling event to lose your job, and then experience difficulty in your relationship with Rachael, and then moving out of your home into a basement apartment. Given all that has happened, I found myself wondering how you have managed your life as well as you have, in spite of it all. So, reflecting back over all that has happened over the past 7 months, how would you imagine that you could have responded differently?

Nathan: (*Sits up straight in his chair, pauses, and looks down to the floor.*) Maybe with a bit more grace. I got pretty irritable and angry and was hard to be around. I used to be an easy person to be around. I have a lot of good friends, but they have been pretty annoyed with me lately.

Therapist: So, would you say the irritability and anger have gotten in between you and your relationships with other people, like Rachael and your friends?

Nathan: It's like a wedge has been driven between me and Rachael and me and my friends.

Through the conversation so far the therapist has acknowledged Nathan's experience and responses to the powerful events in his life. The therapist then actively accepts and validates Nathan's experience. Then the therapist introduces ambiguity into Nathan's experience by implying that perhaps he is not "depressed" but that his experience could be interpreted as a reasonable response to the powerful and confusing events that have happened in his life. In a sense the conversation moves from diagnosing Nathan as an individual—that is, depressed—to diagnosing the context in which he lives. Finally, the conversation moves from a global, experience-distant category of depression to externalized, specific, experience-near descriptions such as confusion, irritability, and anger.

A posture of curiosity and deconstructive listening incorporates into the therapeutic conversation the practice of double listening. The practice of double listening was developed by Michael White. He described it as follows: "These listening practices are referred to as 'double listening,' which has the potential to open up a wide field of possibilities for exploration" (2003, p. 30). Double listening is important because people's lives are double storied. When we listen to people express their experiences, they are doing so in relation to other experiences that are not being explicitly expressed in the therapeutic conversation but are implied. In this way the therapist is open to hearing whatever people want to say and, in addition, invites them to speak about what they may not have previously spoken about.

Therapist: Earlier you said that you "sort of gave up trying" and became a bit overwhelmed and miserable and then the irritability and anger started getting between you and your important relationships. I'm curious, Nathan.

What is it that you have given up on? Is this something that would be important to talk about?

Nathan: (*Nods his head in agreement.*) I became very overwhelmed with losing my job because it made no sense to me. Actually, I can't remember a time in my life that I felt so confused, overwhelmed, and immobilized. I was a really good employee. It made no logical sense. It felt so out of control. If I could just lose my job after 23 years of being a good employee, then it was like anything could happen. You know, like what's the use in trying then? I think I became so consumed and stuck on the loss of my job that I lost sight of what I had that was important to me. My relationship with Rachael and my relationships with my friends are very important to me. I'm very saddened by what has happened through all of this. Yes, this would be important to talk about. I need to get back on track.

Therapist: So Nathan, would this say that you are the kind of person who values your relationships with other people?

Nathan: Oh yes, that's really the kind of person I am. I'm a people person. I'm not really this person that I've been for the past 7 months.

Therefore, the strength of Nathan's response to these powerful life experiences also speaks to what lies on the other side of his expressions regarding his strongly held values and his preferred sense of identity.

Carey, Walther, and Russell (2009) further expanded on this thinking as they referred to the "absent, but implicit" concept developed by Michael White through his study of the work of Jacques Derrida when they stated:

> If we accept the proposal that people can only give a particular account of their lives through drawing distinctions with what their experience is *not,* then we can tune our ears to hear not only what the problem *is*, but also to hear what is "absent but implicit" in their descriptions—what the problem is *not*. (p. 321)

People can be asked questions that make their strongly held values more visible. What they give value to is shaped by certain knowledges and beliefs about life. These knowledges and beliefs are embedded in stories that are always present, but they lie on the shadowed side of problem stories.

So, the therapist begins the therapeutic conversation by assuming a stance of curiosity, using deconstructive double listening early on in the session. This early phase is where stories are introduced and begin to move the therapeutic conversation forward. As not all stories are equal, the therapist collaborates with people to decide which story is most important for them to express.

Points of Stories: What's Most Important to Talk About? (. . . Once Upon a Time)

Stories are introduced as the therapist inquires about the point of the story. The point of a story serves the same purpose as an abstract when writing a professional article: It is to announce what the story is about. When someone announces the point of the story, the therapist (listener) is signaled to a forward reference that the story is about to begin. The point of the story serves as an invitation to the therapist to participate in and witness the unfolding of the story. It is an entry point into storylines. Therapists pay close attention for the point of the story as they wait for an invitation to move forward and develop the story.

In order to help the story move forward, and gain an understanding of what is most important for people to talk about, therapists restrain their own agenda and hypothesis. They are prudent to avoid "knowing" too soon, intentionally asking questions to which they genuinely do not know the answer. The longer therapists can "not know" and remain curious, the more likely it is that people will provide richly saturated descriptions of the important events and details of their lives. As illustrated in the excerpt of the transcript above with Nathan, a useful question at this beginning stage of the therapy session is posed:

Therapist: Given the limited amount of time that we have with each other, and given everything that's been going on in your life, what's most important for us to talk about right now?

Sarah: Well, out of everything we could talk about, right now my relationship with my son, Grant, is most important to discuss. We're going through a rough patch.

When a therapy session involves multiple family members, different family members may propose various options regarding what's most important to begin talking about. At this point the therapist facilitates a discussion with family members to help them reach consensus regarding a beginning topic to start the therapy session. At this stage, the point of the story, that is, the agreed-upon topic, is framed as a start for the therapeutic conversation. As the conversation proceeds and the story changes and becomes more relevant, family members may prefer to shift the topic. The therapist maintains a curious and tentative stance in order to stay with the family's story as it continues to evolve, move forward, and separate from familiar understandings.

In a sense the therapist and the family members are preparing for a journey, as mentioned earlier, or a quest, as described in the previous chapter. "Quest stories meet suffering [the problem—our addition] head on; they accept illness and seek to *use* it. Illness [the problem—our addition] is the occasion of a journey that becomes a quest. What is quested for may never be wholly clear, but the quest is defined by the ill person's belief that something is to be gained through the experience" (Frank, 1995, p. 115). In a sense the person receives a "calling" to embark on the quest (Campbell, 1968). "The quest narrative affords the ill person a voice as teller of her own story, because only in quest stories does the *teller* have a story to tell" (Frank, 1995, p. 115).

When starting the session people can also be asked to update their story. They can be asked if anything has changed or shifted in one way or another with the problem prior to coming in for the therapy session. Often people have made some effort to decrease the influence of the problem, but their efforts may have gone unnoticed. As well, people may have had realizations or new ways of understanding their situation.

Therapist: What has changed in your view of your situation?

Sarah: You know, I woke up about 3:00 A.M. one morning a couple of weeks ago, sat up in bed, and it just came to me as I looked at my husband laying beside me . . . this is not the man I married (*alerts to the point of the story*)!

Therapist: Would that be important to talk about?

Sarah: Absolutely!

As the therapist establishes the point of the story and what's most important to talk about with people, it's necessary to situate it within their backstory.

Backstory: Creating an Intelligible Frame (. . . Every Day)

Backstory embodies the social context in which people's stories are situated and from which their stories continue to develop. It provides a frame of intelligibility to better understand the overall story and the problem-saturated story. For example, it's relatively futile to ask people how they feel without understanding it within the context of their relevant backstory. This provides a frame of reference. For example, if people say they're "depressed," it remains a word at a global, rhetorical level until it is understood within their relevant backstory, their social context.

When a single-parent, sole-support mother who is living in a tiny apartment over a store with three children, barely scraping by financially because her ex-husband doesn't contribute to the children's child support, says she's "depressed," there is an appreciation for the meaning of the word *depressed* as it is influenced by the *particular* effects of her social context. When a white, middle-aged businessman says he is "depressed" because he has lost money in the stock market, but still holds a position of power and influence, there is a different appreciation for the word *depressed* within the influence and *particular* effects of his social context. People's lives are situated within backstories—social, cultural contexts, influenced by master narratives that shape their beliefs and actions, contributing significance to their stories. These cultural beliefs that exist in people's backstories more often get taken up as truths, contributing to the grip of the problem story. These taken-for-granted beliefs can be called into question and deconstructed to make space for preferred stories.

In order to illuminate people's backstory, the therapist enters into their world. The voices of others who populate the backstory are brought into the therapeutic conversation. The re-membering conversations map provided by Michael White (White, 2007a) provides a useful way to reevaluate and revise relationships with others, thereby purposefully regulating their effects on identity. As White articulated, "Re-membering conversations are shaped by the conception that identity is founded upon an 'association of life,' rather than on a core self" (p. 129). (An example of how this map relates to working with someone managing the effects of addictions is given in Chapter 7.) Therefore, the therapist listens carefully for people to express qualities or characteristics of their preferred sense of self. Those preferred qualities or characteristics are then unpacked and linked to persons with whom they are in association who have contributed significantly to the development of these self-descriptions. These unpacked identity qualities and characteristics provide expanded descriptions that begin to make people's values, beliefs, principles, and commitments more visible. These aren't just information-gathering exercises meant to gather facts through a social history in a thin sense. "Re-membering conversations are not just about passive recollection but about purposive reengagements with the history of one's relationships with significant figures and with the identities of one's present life and projected future" (White, 2007a, p. 129). Involving the influences of others in this way expands the story, livens the backstory, and brings forward persons—past, present, living, or deceased—who have been influential and who support the person's sense of personal agency.

The Socially Constructed Genogram and Re-membering Conversations

Re-membering conversations can be richly developed and illuminate the imagery of people's backstory as it is being described by providing a visual map. A socially constructed genogram (SCG), which is founded upon poststructuralist sensibilities (Milewski-Hertlein, 2001), provides such a map. As poststructuralist thinkers view identity as socially constructed, the mutual influence between self and others becomes highly significant. In addition, beyond the relationship between self and other, the interpretation of text, broader cultural discourses, and master narratives influence the personal sense of reality.

Unlike the traditional genogram (McGoldrick & Gerson, 1985), which describes family and relationships in a positivist view, the socially constructed genogram provides an alternative map for understanding the multiplicity of identity, family, relationships, and culture. The socially constructed genogram accounts for the view that meaning and understanding are generated socially, within conversations with others (Anderson, 1997; Anderson & Goolishian, 1988). However, this intersubjective dialogue referred to by Anderson and Goolishan (1988) does not exempt people from the influences of the wider cultural discourses. The SCG also takes into consideration the power and political influences of the broader cultural discourses.

As identity is viewed as occupying territory, the socially constructed genogram conveys the spatial aspect of identity in relation to others. As people are able to visually locate their relationships with others in a desired proximity of closeness or distance, they are able to avoid assumptions about relationships based on discourses regarding the entitlements of the biological family. This makes it more possible for them to explore the quality of those relationships.

The SCG makes it possible to unpack and explore the particular meaning that is embedded in the key experiences between people through re-membering conversations. White (2007a) spoke to this when he stated:

> Re-membering conversations provide an opportunity for people to revise the memberships of their association of life: to upgrade some memberships and to downgrade others; to grant authority to some voices in regard to matters of one's personal identity, and to disqualify other voices with regard to this. (p. 129)

When someone talks about their family, or particular family members, we can question the meaning of those words and understandings. There is an acknowledgment that these words describing family are culturally defined, and the meanings and experiences of family change significantly in various cultures. Milewski-Hertlein wrote: "The deviation from the nuclear family is not just a Western tradition. In China, children can be raised apart from their fathers with their mothers in a group of women" (2001, p. 25).

The re-membering conversations and maps developed by Michael White, together with the socially constructed genogram, both sustained through a poststructural sensibility, serve to enliven the backstory. The socially constructed genogram calls attention to the significance of backstory when understanding identity.

Creating the Socially Constructed Genogram

The socially constructed genogram is created through a collaborative effort between therapists and the people who consult them. It is not a static device meant to diagnose and establish normative conclusions about people's relationships with others, but a fluid map for aiding in the interpretation and renegotiation of relationships. This reinterpretation creates the opportunity to critically reflect and restory relationships toward more preferred understandings. As one's life is continually changing, the socially constructed genogram reflects those changes through time.

When creating the SCG with someone, there are options available. One option is to simply print a number of diagrams of approximately five concentric circles. Then they are ready for use in each therapy session with people who consult us. Another way is to simply draw the circles in the moment on a blank piece of paper. Then the therapists can explain the concept of the genogram to the people consulting them. In doing so, they can invite people into the deconstruction of traditional understandings of family and relationships. People are invited to express their relationships on the SCG as they actually experience them and then they are encouraged to explore the meaning of those relationships. People are encouraged to expand the traditional understanding of relationships to people (living or dead), pets, archetypal heroes, friends who are like family, and so on. People are invited to place themselves in the center circle of the SCG. Then they are asked to place others in respective circles based on their closeness or distance, or importance or lack of importance, or preference or lack of preference regarding their rating of their relationship with them. Their relationship to the other person (e.g., father) is indicated by writing it onto the SCG.

The following are excerpts from a conversation with a 15-year-old boy who was dealing with the effects of living in the aftermath of his parents' separation and divorce.

First Session with Luke

Therapist: It appears there are a number of people in your life who have different relationships with you. Do you think it might be useful to have a look at these relationships with these people and clarify your associations with each of them?

Luke: I guess it would. Sometimes it gets pretty confusing.

Therapist: (*Introduces the SCG.*) Sometimes it can be useful and interesting to map out relationships visually on this piece of paper with all of these circles. Would it be okay with you to locate the people in your life in relation to you on this piece of paper?

Luke: Sure, why not?

Therapist: (*Places the SCG on the table in front of Luke.*) Okay, first, can you place yourself in the center circle by writing your name there?

Luke: (*Writes his name in the center circle.*)

Therapist: Now Luke, I would like you to take a minute and reflect on the relationships in your life. As you think about these relationships, imagine where you would place them on this map. The relationships that you would like to have closest to you, or who you consider to be most significant and closest to you now, would be at the inner circles and the people who you would prefer to keep at more of a distance or who are distant to you now would be at the outer circles. This can include people who may not be alive anymore. Or, it can include people you don't even know, or people you look up to, or someone you may admire from afar, a rock star, a superhero, an actor, or even an imaginary person. It could even be a pet or a stuffed animal. You can start anywhere you like.

Luke: Okay, I get it. (*He starts to put names within the inner circle. He starts by writing the word* Grandpa.) My grandpa died about 7 years ago, but when he was alive we were close.

Therapist: (*As Luke places each name on the SCG, we discuss the nature and quality of the relationship.*) So, what was it about your relationship with your grandpa that made it possible for the two of you to be close?

Luke: Well, we did things together. He made time for me and always took the time to explain things carefully in a way that I could understand. He would often say, "Do you follow what I'm saying to you, Luke?" He would do that in a calm and patient manner until he was satisfied that I understood what he was trying to explain to me or teach to me.

Therapist: So, what have you learned from your grandpa that you carry with you today?

Luke: He taught me a lot of things. I have a lot of respect and admiration for him. I think what I learned the most from him is how to be calm. He also taught me how to slow down and pay attention to details. Sometimes he would say to me, "Luke, it's in the details." I guess I would say that he taught me a lot about how to be calm and patient.

Therapist: If he were here now, what do you suppose he would say that you have contributed to his life?

Luke: I think he would say that I was his companion. Grandpa and I were buds. I gave purpose to his life.

Luke continued to place his dog, Smokey, his best friend, Jordon, and his mother in the inner circle and then placed other friends and relatives at various positions on the remaining circles. As he placed each person in their respective circle on the SCG, we discussed the nature and quality of the relationship and the reason for that person's particular status in Luke's life. By combining the socially constructed genogram with the re-membering conversation map, each relationship would get unpacked, marking the contributions made to the person from Luke and the contribution to Luke's life by that person.

The SCG can also provide a useful visual map to re-vision future, preferred states. After constructing a SCG to illustrate the present state of people's backstory, they can be asked if they would like to construct a map that would represent how they would like their life to look in the future. This future-oriented SCG would show what it would look like if all of their relationships were revised to represent an association with the significant others in their life that they would prefer. The therapeutic conversation can include discussions about what would need to be different for this change in relationships to occur.

Therapist: Luke, now that you have placed various people on your map in a way that reflects your association with them, are there any of those relationships that you may want to change in the future? You know, if you could change things to suit your life the way you would ideally like it to be.

Luke: Well, truth be told, in a perfect world I really would like to have a closer relationship with my dad. (*Luke had positioned his father at one of the outer circles on the SCG.*)

Therapist: Is it okay to start another map to represent your relationships with people in the future? On this map you can place people relative to where you would want them to be in the future.

Luke: (*Places his father close to the second circle from the center.*) Since he's remarried it has been harder to spend time with my dad. I'm guessing that we will never be really close, but I would like it if we could be closer than we are. I think he wants to be closer and spend more time together. It's just more complicated now.

Therapist: Would it be useful to talk about the relationship that you have with your father and the relationship that you would like to have with him?

Luke began talking about his longing to spend more time with his father and to develop a closer association with him. The SCG assisted a re-membering conversation and opened up possibilities for future conversations that could include his father.

Recruiting Significant Others to Attend Therapy Sessions

It can be quite useful to recruit the participation of significant others in therapy sessions. In this way we bring the people that populate the person's backstory into the therapy room with us. Again, using similar points of inquiry from Michael White's (2007a) re-membering conversations, people can be recruited into commenting on what they have appreciated about the person's intentions and efforts to move forward toward their preferred life. People can be consulted who have already made similar journeys, who can share their stories, showing what they did that provided them with the skills, knowledges, and inspiration to get through their personal quest. Although their stories are not completely germane, they do provide resonance and ideas for challenges that lie ahead. The social support and maps of others can offer reassurance to people while they are experiencing the distress inherent in the transitional phase. During these times of uncertainty it can be validating to know that others have already been through these trying times, endured, and moved on to other things. It can be reassuring to hear people talk about what got them through challenging journeys in their lives and how they experience themselves differently as a result of it. When sharing the stories about these challenging journeys, people may describe the details of their struggles in such a way that demonstrates the determination that is developed through these experiences. The details of these conversations help people prepare for their journey in pragmatic ways as they hear about past events that contain rich details of the trials and errors involved. These conversations inspire resourcefulness and inventiveness as people relate these experiences to their own beginning journey.

Second Session with Luke and Friend Jordon

Therapist: Welcome, Jordon. Thanks for joining Luke and me in this conversation today. Luke said that he considers you to be a valued friend and that you have been on a similar journey as Luke.

Jordon: Yep, Luke's my best friend. I've got his back. I would do anything for him. By "similar journey," if you mean my parents splitting up. Been there, done that.

Therapist: Jordon, what have you appreciated about Luke's efforts as he's gone through his parents' separation? Is there anything that you have noticed that stands out for you?

Jordon: You bet there is. Luke's the iceman. He always manages to stay calm, even when things are tough. When my parents split up I got pretty angry for a while. It wasn't a pretty picture. A couple of times I really lost it and had to learn new ways of dealing with the whole mess. I had trouble. But Luke's been a class act. I've learned how to chill by watching him go through his parents' split-up.

Therapist: Having been through it, is there anything you could tell Luke that you think might be useful to him on his journey that you learned from your own experience?

Jordon: Luke and I, we've talked about this before. (*Speaks to Luke directly.*) What I found is things get better over time. Life's just different now. Sometimes it feels weird. But it actually did get better.

Luke: Sometimes I get really down when I see what my parents are going through and sometimes what they are doing to each other. So how did you hang in when things were really tough like that?

Jordon: My lifesaver was I had good friends. Sometimes just being with my friends and even with their parents got me through when my own mom and dad weren't doing well. I also got more involved in playing sports. It helped me to stay busy and focused.

Jordon and Luke continued to compare stories related to their similar journeys. Jordon's recalling of the stories from his experience offered Luke hope that he could have a closer relationship with his father over time.

Constraints and Master Narratives

It's also important to identify constraints that exist in a person's backstory. What is it that holds them back or gets in the way of doing what they need to do? A person's ability to perform their story and confidently experience personal agency is contingent on how they are situated in the backdrop of their life. As illustrated above, "the extent to which our moral agency is free or constrained is determined by our own—and others'—conception of who we are" (Lindemann-Nelson, 2001, p. xi). How we act and make sense of our identities is strongly linked to how we perceive others viewing us. "This includes his construction of the other person's motivations and intentions and his view of the other's view of him" (Eron and Lund, 1996, p. 43). This may include family and friends who are located within the immediate social context, or it may refer to others who are out there in the broader discourses of culture and society. People's identities and sense of moral worth can become vulnerable or impoverished when a more powerful social group views them as less important and prevents them from inhabiting identities that are worthy of full moral respect. In this case, a person may be experiencing the degrading influence of a master narrative (Lindemann-Nelson, 2001). People experiencing this sort of oppression might require help to resist the influence of the master narrative through affiliation, advocacy, and the development of an organized counterstory.

The transition from act 1 to act 2 indicates the end of the first phase of the rites of passage, within the journey metaphor (Turner, 1977; van Gennep, 1960). This marks the beginning of the journey. This transition begins with a separation from familiar ways of experiencing life, to a liminal, ambiguous journey phase characterized by a quest that addresses the problem story and, at the same time, strives for personal agency. "For me, taking a journey into the unknown with a map in hand always fills me with anticipation" (White, 2007a, p. 7). "The meaning of the journey emerges recursively: the journey is taken in order to find out what sort of journey one has been taking . . . it nevertheless represents a form of reflexive monitoring" (Frank, 1995, p. 117).

The entrance to act 2 serves as a threshold, much like a doorway, entering the quest phase of the therapeutic conversation. The rites of separation (van Gennep, 1960) mark the time from which people have expressed the point of the story, situated the story within the overall backstory, and are moving toward it, but have not yet crossed through the threshold into the liminal phase of the therapeutic conversation. This is a very important beginning step in the therapeutic conversation, where the therapist needs to be careful to move slowly and not jump to conclusions about what needs to be discussed. Joseph Campbell referred to this first phase of the journey as the "departure . . . beginning with . . . the call to adventure" (1968, p. 41). This is a time that the person experiences distress of some sort that requires a separation from their previous sense of identity that may no longer be as pertinent. "It marks what has been termed 'the awakening of the self'" (p. 42). Campbell described this phase further as follows:

> But whether small or great, and no matter what the stage or grade of life, the call rings up the curtain, always, on a mystery of transfiguration—a rite, or moment, of spiritual passage, which, when complete, amounts to a dying and a birth. The familiar life horizon has been outgrown; the old concepts, ideals and emotional patterns no longer fit; the time for the passing of the threshold is at hand. (pp. 42–43)

Campbell's view is that once the person accepts the call (the problem or the issue), then the first threshold is crossed. "Eventually, the call cannot be refused" (Frank, 1995, p. 117). Even though significant effort and intention may have gone into plotting this course so far, in preparation for the liminal phase of act 2, it is prudent to remain open to the possibility that people may pause at the threshold and return to the familiarity of what they know. This response may indicate a need for further preparation, and can be seen as using necessary judgment, rather than being experienced as failure. Significant journeys are rarely linear experiences, simply moving in one direction, ramping up continuously while life improves measurably with each day that passes. More often a significant journey requires planning, reconsideration, and readjustment of plans as we move toward a preferred future.

Once people have accepted the call and are ready to depart from the familiarity of their life and move through the threshold from act 1 to act 2, the therapist graciously invites them to pass through the threshold, moving their story forward to the journey phase of the therapeutic process.

The following passage is from a therapeutic conversation with a woman who has recently divorced and is experiencing the effects of worthlessness and isolation. This passage will illustrate movement from the separation phase and accepting the call to move through the threshold to act 2.

Juanita: I've been thinking a lot about how isolated I've been since my divorce from Carlos and how the blues had me slowly retreating into living my life away from people who matter to me. It's like being trapped on a desert island all by myself. I just feel isolated, worthless, and more and more fearful of doing what I need to do to reclaim my life. Some days I don't even leave the house.

Therapist: So over time, since you and Carlos divorced, you have begun to experience a sense of isolation and worthlessness that feels like being trapped on a desert island.

Jaunita: Well, yes. And, like I said in the last session, I can't continue to live like this. The more I live like this, the worse it gets.

Therapist: You no longer want to live like this. You want to move toward something different?

Jaunita: Yes, I've made a decision. As scary as it is when I think about it, I just have to take some risks and do things to get my life back. I want to move

> from being stranded on this island and move back to the mainland. You know, when I think about it, even the bit of work that I have done with you and the team so far has helped. I think I have already moved from an island to a peninsula. I even phoned an old friend last week and arranged to get together with her. Believe me, that's different than what I would usually be doing.

In order to bridge this transition, therapists offer people a reflecting summary of the therapeutic conversation in act 1 prior to moving to act 2. Although we believe that it is important to provide reflecting summaries at regular intervals during the therapeutic conversation, this particular summary serves to punctuate the threshold to act 2. In a sense, this reflecting summary is the threshold, the portal to act 2.

As implied, this summary is a form of reflective practice. At this point, the therapist facilitates a process for people to look back over the session thus far, reflecting on what stands out in the conversation, noticing any difference. "When people move from being in a conversation to reflecting on it, they become audiences to themselves. This puts them in a better position to perform meaning on their own emerging narratives" (Freedman and Combs, 1996, p. 192). The reflecting summary begins with what Michael White refers to as an "editorial" (2007a, p. 46). The therapist may say: "I'm now better able to understand what's important to you and therefore, what's important for us to talk about in the time we have together today." By addressing what is important to talk about, the therapist addresses the "call," the rationale, the purpose of embarking on the therapeutic journey. This is discussed in descriptive, experience-near terms, using people's precise language. "At this time care is also taken to ensure that people have the opportunity to articulate all the complexities of their position on the effects of the problem" (White, 2007a, p. 46). Reflecting on experience in this way introduces people to the possibility of learning, since the process of reflection "allows its examination and improvement" (Fook & Gardner, 2007, p. 24). People are invited to state clearly what they are separating from that no longer serves them and what is important to them that they are called to move toward.

The reflecting summary is a process that "is based in ethical postures that value openness, transparency, multiple viewpoints, and the decentering of the therapist" (Freedman & Combs, 1996, p. 284). Inviting family members to reflect on the therapeutic conversation "is a *political* act, the purpose of which is to share power among all the participants in therapy" (p. 191).

However, simply reflecting on the conversation without a scaffolded and eliciting process would lack focus and purpose. This focus introduces a way of "knowing" that is relevant with people's local knowledge and sense of purpose. Therefore, it is an *inductive* (informed by the person), rather than a *deductive* (informed by the theory) process (Fook & Gardner, 2007). Rather than depending on professional knowledge, this process elicits people's local knowledge. It invites people to clarify gaps between the imposition of master narratives and the values that they are drawn to in their lives. They are asked identity questions that encourage "expressions of subjectivity" (White, 2007a, p. 99). The therapist scaffolds carefully crafted questions that help people mine the conversation in a way that produces learning and realizations that may not have been recognized or even valued in a deductive approach. Local experience becomes the focal point for understanding people's preferences (e.g., "What do you think stands out that's the most significant thing we have talked about thus far?") The following excerpt illustrates a reflecting summary that facilitates movement through the threshold to the journey phase.

Therapist: Jaunita, when we began our conversation in the last session, you also talked about a profound sense of loneliness, isolation, and self-loathing. Today you are saying that you have made a decision that you are no longer content to continue living like this and that you want to move off of this island of isolation to the mainland and get your life back. You also said that you have already moved to a peninsula. So, is that movement toward getting your life back?

Jaunita: Yes, I suppose it is. Even that much movement wasn't easy, though.

Therapist: Of course not.

Jaunita: There's lots of things I need to talk about. Yes, I really need to start taking some risks and move forward. I want to stop feeling so dragged down.

Therapist: So, when we started last session you stated that you were experiencing isolation and self-loathing. You also stated that through our conversation and your involvement with the outsider witnessing team that you have experienced some sense of movement. You also said that you have taken the initiative to phone an old friend and have arranged to get together with her and that was different. And you have said that you have decided that you want to get your life back. Jaunita, have I understood you correctly? Is this what you understand? Are you saying that you are ready to move forward and would like to proceed with our conversation?

Jaunita: Yes, that's what I understand and yes, I have definitely decided to move forward. I don't want my life to go on like this. I want my life back!

Jaunita has clearly stated her desire to move forward and has accepted the "call." This is an intentional state. She is ready to proceed to the journey phase and act 2 of the therapeutic conversation.

Reflecting on their backstory invites people to reconsider the relationships of others and consider adjustments to the proximity and subsequent influence of those relationships. This reflecting summary encourages people to question taken-for-granted assumptions, simultaneously making space for new understandings. What becomes important is an appreciation for the multiplicity of identity, the complexity of experience, and a value placed on local knowledge in an ever-changing context. This process helps to sharpen people's focus and clarify their purpose for the challenges that lie ahead in act 2.

ACT 2: EMBARKING ON THE JOURNEY

> This fateful region of both treasure and danger may be variously represented: as a distant land, a forest, a kingdom underground, beneath the waves, or above the sky, a secret island, lofty mountaintop, or profound dream state; but it is always a place of strangely fluid and polymorphous beings, unimaginable torments, superhuman deeds and impossible delights. (Campbell, 1968, p. 48)

The point of the story was elicited in act 1, moving the story forward through the therapeutic conversation, while the person disembarks from familiar territory and, "perhaps from some status, aspect of identity, or role that is determined to be no longer viable for the person concerned" (White & Epston, 1990, p. 7). The backstory has been illuminated, making influential discourses visible, as well as significant others who populate the person's life. This illuminated backstory provides a social context in which to understand the influence of the problem and relationships of others. The threshold linking act 1 to act 2 of the three-act play has been traversed. Now, in act 2, it's time to embark on the journey, the quest, and the raison d'être of the therapeutic process.

This liminal, journey phase of the therapeutic conversation enters into the territory of possibilities that are not yet known, where things mean not quite what they meant before. Michael White (2007a) further depicted the journey phase as follows:

> When we sit down together I know that we are embarking on a journey to a destination that cannot be precisely specified, and via routes that cannot be predetermined . . . and I know that the adventure to be had on these journeys is not about the confirmation of what is already known, but about expeditions into what is possible for people to know about their lives. (White, 2007a, p. 4)

As a means to facilitate movement, in order to traverse the liminal phase, Michael White (2007a) introduced the idea of the zone of proximal development (ZPD) into narrative therapy. The ZPD is a concept developed by Russian educational psychologist and social constructionist Lev Vygotsky (1986). It refers to the difference between what people can achieve individually and what they can achieve with assistance from someone else. The ZPD, according to Vygotsky, is "the domain of transitions that are accessible" (Gredler & Shields, 2008, p. 85). "A ZPD does not refer to a specific task, or a single transition, but a broader domain or phase that includes many learning transitions and movements within in it" (p. 86). Vygotsky was clear that his focus on the ZPD was to offer psychologists and educators an alternative choice from "an old delusion that implies development must complete its cycles for instruction to move forward" (p. 86).

It is critical that the therapist and the person seeking consultation maintain a working relationship in which incremental movement can be accomplished through this transitional stage. Rich dialogue is a key feature of the ZPD. An enriched therapeutic conversation provides fertile ground for concept development and knowledge renewal. The conversation between the person and the therapist becomes the medium in which the therapist incrementally scaffolds learning through a succession of small transitions across the ZPD. The person is able to obtain learnings that may be just out of reach, perhaps a step beyond what they previously understood.

It is the therapist's responsibility to facilitate a scaffolding process that supports movement. This scaffolding process operates from a belief that qualitative transformation occurs through a sequence of small changes that accumulate gradually. As people receive feedback regarding their efforts, analyze the events in their lives, and evaluate their experiences in a collaborative therapeutic environment, their potential for critical reflection expands. Tinsley and Lebak (2009) emphasized the need for a collaborative environment of trust and shared understanding to produce incremental knowledge development. They stretched their thinking and engaged their imagination. As people's understanding increases, their confidence to take necessary action increases accordingly.

As the person acquires new knowledges and skills, the therapist decreases assistance until it is finally tapered off. Much the way a building site crew removes the scaffolding after completing the construction of a building, the therapist removes influence from the therapeutic process. This range of therapist's involvement assumes that therapy itself is a rite of passage, intended to prepare a person for managing the complexities of life. In posttherapy life, when a person addresses an issue, although the therapist is not present, the person makes independent use of the earlier collaboration with the therapist.

While scaffolding the therapeutic conversation, the therapist invites people to describe the details of their story. Maintaining curiosity and deconstructive listening, the therapist's questions bring forth new worlds of experience for consideration. Deconstructive questions open up space for possibilities that will reach beyond usual concerns and familiar ways of experiencing everyday life. Creativity, choice, and realizations emerge from the experience of responding to these deconstructive questions and delving into the inevitable gaps that exist in problem-saturated stories. These new realizations can be strung together into chains of associations, which begin to form alternative storlyines. These emerging alternative stroylines provide foundations for people to influence future events and develop a renewed sense of personal agency.

The following transcript of an adolescent boy will illustrate how alternative storylines emerge in therapeutic conversations.

Therapist: Sam, I was just wondering if you could tell me a bit more about this bothersome habit that has developed with you.

Sam: Well, sometimes I bother other people a lot. You know, like pester them.

Therapist: What do you mean when you say bother or pester others? Could you describe what you are doing at those times? Maybe you could give me an example.

Sam: Well, I can get pretty annoying. I get too intense sometimes. I ask a lot of questions when I don't understand something, especially when I disagree with someone. I really pester my big sister, Linda.

Therapist: Okay, so you ask a lot of questions. Does this mean that you are a very inquisitive person? (*Deconstructive questioning.*)

Sam: Oh yeah, I definitely am.

Therapist: Have you always been inquisitive like this?

Sam: As far back as I can remember.

Already the conversation between the therapist and Sam begins to shift toward a double-storied account and an acknowledgment of a different aspect of Sam's identity, which could be understood as inquisitiveness. Sam verifies that he has been inquisitive "as far back as I can remember."

Daily life is the locale of problem-saturated stories, which are largely dominant over other realities people could experience, were they not eclipsed, forced from view, and relegated to the shadows. The routines and repetitious events inherent in daily life often distract people from noticing discrepancies within their stories. As Morson pointed out when reflecting on the work of Mikhail Bakhtin: "People act out patterns or do what the laws have prescribed; their actions instantiate, but never exceed, rules or pregiven laws. What people do not do is genuinely choose, even though they might imagine otherwise" (1994, p. 21). Like fish in water that cannot see the water, people become unwittingly trapped in invisible and pervasive dominant discourses, subjugated to the gripping effects of master narratives.

In spite of that, the discrepancies to the problem-saturated story are always present. Like panning for gold, the discrepancies can be found as traces embedded in people's values and commitments, glimmering through as expressions of how they would like life to be otherwise. These traces, often scattered throughout the therapeutic conversation, are clues to alternative storylines. They may appear as discrepancies between the version of story told and details of actions taken, incongruous elements, or implicit statements. These traces and clues can be identified, questioned, and brought forward. Therapists are responsible for noticing these traces, clues, and inconsistencies, holding them up through reflective summaries, contradicting the dominant narrative, while proposing alternative understandings. These discrepancies and traces are always found in the experiences located within the events that constitute the overall theme of people's lives, but may not have been noticed previously. These experiences and events are located in the "landscape of action" and are the "stuff" of the journey phase.

Therapist: So, being inquisitive is something that's pretty strong for you.

Sam: Well yeah, when it's working for me. Like lately I've been more interested in my schoolwork and I got a B+ on a test. It's the first time in a long time that I studied hard for a test and it actually paid off. It felt great! But mostly, when I'm inquisitive it just comes out as pestering people and I'm just wanting to get my way. Like when Linda told me last week that I couldn't stay out until 3:00 A.M. at a rock concert, I just kept pestering her and asking her, "Why not? My friends get to stay out till then!" (*Although there is an emerging storyline of Sam becoming more interested in school, there remains a risk that the dominant storyline of his pestering habit will overshadow it.*)

Therapist: Are other people in your family inquisitive?

Sam: Mostly it's just me.

Therapist: So, although there have been some new developments with being inquisitive about your schoolwork, are you worried about this bothersome habit of pestering people?

Sam: Yes, I actually am concerned about how it affects Linda. She's a good big sister. I feel bad when I get her upset with me. She probably doesn't know that I feel bad. And I'm also concerned for me because it's really not a good way to do things. I'm just starting to realize that. Linda said that I'm acting immature when I pester her like that and that I need to grow up and act my age. I think she's right. It just got to be a really strong habit. I mean I don't want to grow up doing this.

Therapist: Why is that, Sam? If you grew up doing this, what effects would that have?

Sam: Well, you know. Like when I'm a 36-year-old adult and my boss tells me to do something, I'll need to work with him. He's not going to like it if I'm really annoying and pestering him. I really want to get rid of this.

Therapist: How long have you been concerned about the pestering affecting the rest of your life? (*Traces of a double story that speak to what Sam values and what he wants for himself.*)

Sam: Well, I've been thinking about it more lately. It just gets everyone around me all tense, especially Linda. She gets frustrated. She even tries to avoid me sometimes. We used to do stuff together. Sometimes she would take me with her when she would go shopping or when she would go visit her boyfriend. He's a really cool guy and would play video games with me. But lately she doesn't ask me to go with her. Maybe she thinks I'm too much of a pain to be with. She's probably fed up with me. I'm starting to feel kinda guilty about how I've been with her.

Therapist: What do you think this says about what's developing in you (*double story*)?

Sam: Well, I think I'm starting to think more clearly. I think I'm understanding more that Linda is being a good big sister and that she is being responsible when she tells me I can't do something, like stay out till 3:00 in the morning at a rock concert. I'm sort of able to take things in now and think about it. I used to just think Linda and my parents were just being controlling and mean, but now I'm starting to think they're not really that way. When I really think about it, Linda is a great big sister. When I'm not pestering her, she's actually pretty fair and a lot of fun.

Therapist: Well, what is it about Linda that you consider to be fair and a lot of fun?

Sam: Well, when she says no, she says it for a reason. She's being responsible and protective. I can see that now. She's always watched out for me when we were growing up because she's a bit older than me. I think I just got it in my head that she was controlling and mean and got into this really bad habit of pestering and annoying her when I didn't get my own way. When I stop and think about it, she's actually a great big sister and fun to be with.

Therapist: What does that say about Linda and what's important to her and what she stands for? You said that she watched out for you when you were growing up and that she's fun to be with. What sort of sister is she?

Sam: Well, I think she's a really great big sister and she is a really solid person. You know, like she didn't have to watch out for me growing up. She could have just done her own thing, but she always took me along with her. She never seemed to mind having me around. She's actually a really cool person. Everybody likes her. She has lots of friends and they all think she's a lot of fun.

Therapist: (*Reflecting summary.*) Sam, so far you've told me about this habit of pestering people, particularly your sister, that you would really like to get free of. You mentioned that this habit has developed over time, and that you're starting to realize that it's not a good way of doing things. You said that you don't want to grow up like this and have this pestering habit affecting the rest of your life. You also talked about being an inquisitive person and that you've been that way as far back as you can remember. And you said that you've been more inquisitive in school lately and even studied hard and got a B+ on a test. It seems like things are changing a bit and you are having realizations and ideas about how you want to be when you grow up. Sam, am I understanding this correctly?

Sam: Well, when you put it like that, actually, I'm sort of understanding it differently as we're talking about it.

The previous example with Sam illustrates how the discrepancies to the problem-saturated story are found as traces embedded in the therapeutic conversation. Sam expresses how he would like his life to be otherwise. It's the therapist's responsibility to notice and address the traces, discrepancies, and clues to alternative storylines. These traces and clues to the emergent alternative stroylines are brought forward in a reflecting summary. Following the reflecting summary Sam continued to talk more about how he wants his life to be different.

Pivotal Events (. . . and Then One Day)

Commonly understood properties that constitute a story, or a narrative, in order to ascribe meaning to experiences in life are articulated as events that are strung out in a sequence over time to form a theme, plot, or story. However, just as all stories are not equal, nor are all events equal. Each event contains its own uniqueness of human action, within a particular context of time, which is not simply a generalized production of previous events over time. Morson articulated this notion well when he clarified Bakhtin's understanding: "It is essentially related to the irreducible particularities of the unrepeatable moment in which the act occurred" (1994, p. 22). These qualities, as well as the thing toward which the unique and precise action is oriented, are what gives the event what Bakhtin referred to as eventness (Morson, 1994):

> Eventness—a key concept for Bakhtin—is indispensable for real creativity and choice. Bakhtin emphasised that the loss of choice entered into an ethical prob-

> lem, "for ethics depend on the sense that what I do at this moment truly matters." Without it, the event becomes a mere shadow of itself, and the present moment loses all the qualities that give it special weight. (p. 21)

This eventness, these irreducible and unrepeatable particularities within events, is what makes each person's story remarkable, different from another person's, and worth telling. For there to be eventness, there is an awareness of multiplicity. This awareness of multiplicity provides numerous options to allow experiences to occur that develop alternative storylines while preventing experiences that constitute problem storylines. These significant, marker life events can all be pressed into service (Morson, 1994):

> In such a world, time ramifies and its possibilities multiply; each realized possibility opens new choices while precluding others that could have been made. The eventful event must also be unrepeatable, that is its meaning and weight are inextricably linked to the moment in which it is performed. Choice is *momentous.* It involves *presentness.* (p. 22)

Although events arranged in a sequence over time may contain similar experiences, the events are not entirely the same. To focus only on similarities and sameness is not likely to produce new options. Eventful events are separated by unique particularities. These particularities constitute eventful events that can produce movement and new options. These events contain elements of mystery, astonishment, and personal choice. They cannot be replicated and their outcomes cannot be predicted.

Indeed, significant events that possess an inherent eventness can serve as base camps that one can return to time and time again, repeatedly exploring the rich experiences they contain, reinterpreting them to better serve present-day life. A great deal of lived experience falls outside of what can be storied at any one time and, instead, exists as details that have been relegated to the shadows. As people are more strongly resonate with these pivotal events, they can become more engaged and involved in unpacking them when exploring alternative storylines.

Consequently, certain events are much more powerful and influential than others, significantly shaping beliefs and understandings about life and identity. Therefore, not all events are necessarily eventful. Significant events are pivotal, at times containing irrevocable decisions, changing the direction of life's course. These events are typically more affectively loaded, more *meaning-full*, and, because of that, more proximal to recount and explore.

To better understand important events in life, they must be made available for reexamination, reinterpretation, and reconsideration. That requires that we step back, reflect, and evaluate the effects of the experiences located in the pivotal events of our lives. Pivotal events will be discussed fully in Chapter 4.

Evaluating Effects (. . . and Because of That)

Meaningful shifts in our identities require us to evaluate the effects of problems and experiences of life. In this phase of the journey people are invited to reflect on the effects of the problem on their life, through revisiting and reinterpreting those experiences located in various events.

This evaluative aspect of the therapeutic journey engages in an exploration of the relativity and multiplicity of meanings. Through the scaffolding of the therapeutic conversation, the therapist strives to generate meaning through dialogue. Gergen and Kaye (1992) explained:

> This involves a reconception of the relativity of meaning, an acceptance of indeterminacy, the generative exploration of the multiplicity of meanings, and the understanding that there is no necessity either to adhere to an invariant story or to search for a definitive story. (p. 181)

This reflective, generative conversation becomes key to the reauthoring process.

The relational proximity and moment-to-moment collaboration of the therapist with the people seeking consultation becomes increasingly significant at this stage of the journey. By engaging in reflective practices, people continue to distance themselves from the constraints of the problem, moving incrementally toward an increased ability to manage their life.

The act of reflection enables people to evaluate their relationship with problematic events from different points of view. This multiplicity of views has delimiting effects on what were limiting beliefs. It emphasizes the notion that beliefs are not invariant truths and that they can change. "For those who adopt it, this stance offers the prospect of a creative participation in the unending and unfolding meaning of life" (Gergen & Kaye, 1992, p. 183).

Reflective Exercise
As an example, take a moment to experience this simple exercise. Draw an S on a blank sheet of paper. Consider this S your life map. At the bottom of the S write the word *BORN*. At the top of the S write the word *NOW*. Next, you will be asked to do something that's impossible to do, but do it anyway. Starting at the bottom of the S. list the four most significant events in your life in chronological order. Above each event write one sentence, or a word or two, describing what you learned from the experience.

Now reflect on the events. Were the events all equal, or were some events more powerful, having more significant influence? Were they all positive events, were they all negative events, or were they a combination of both? Which did you learn the most from: the positive, the negative, or somewhere in between?

Now, try one more thing. Out of the four events, pick the event with which you are most emotionally connected. How does this event influence your beliefs and the way in which you experience the world? Consider the following questions:

- Are these beliefs, resulting from the influence of this event, still relevant in your present life?
- If you were to revisit and reconsider the experiences in this event, would you find other experiences that may have been diminished or relegated to the shadows of your original response?
- Would you prefer to retain your original interpretations, assumptions, and beliefs, or do your think you could revisit this event, reinterpret it, and change them to better suit your life as you live it now?
- Would the event and the meaning interpreted from it seem different if you were
  - 20 years younger or older?
  - from another culture?
  - another gender?
- As you remembered the event, did previously forgotten experiences reappear in your memory? If so, did these experiences offer alternative meaning that may contribute to different identity conclusions?

The process of reflecting on experiences produces a progressive distancing from the problem. It also makes possible a *relativizing* of experience (Gergen &

Kaye, 1992), positioning people in relationship with problems. These transformative dialogues invite people to consider how they might act differently if they operated from different assumptions. What abilities, commitments, and preferences were related to previously hidden experiences that become more visible that they might call upon?

Therapist: (*Reflective questioning.*) Sam, let me ask you another question. Suppose you were that 36-year-old adult man that you were talking about earlier and you were looking back on your life now as a 15-year-old. What advice would your 36-year-old self give to your 15-year-old self about how to get your life free from "pestering" and "annoying"? What advice do you think you would give yourself about your relationship with Linda?

Sam: Wow, good question. It's kind of a hard question, though. (*Gazes off to the side and thinks about his answer.*) Hmmm, I think my 36-year-old self would tell me to learn to be patient and focus. Sort of like the Karate Kid when his teacher taught him to be patient and think. When things got tough they went fishing. Then they weren't so reactive and annoying like I've been. I also think my 36-year-old self would tell me to treat my sister better. She's right. I have been acting immature. I don't want people to think I'm immature. I don't like the way things are between us right now. I want to do things together with Linda and have fun the way we used to do.

All this to say, do people take for granted their beliefs and understanding of the world around them, as though they are true, and therefore unchangeable? Or can they step back and reflect on the experiences and events of their life, reevaluate them, reinterpret them, and reconsider them to more accurately fit their present life as it is being lived? As Fook and Gardner put it: "In this sense, the reflective approach tends to focus on the whole experience and many dimensions involved: cognitive elements; feeling elements; meanings and interpretations from different perspectives" (2007, p. 25). Rather than emphasizing dominant aspects of events, a reflective approach examines the multiplicity of experience located within significant events.

Cultures, beliefs, stories, and identities are formed from the interpretation of experiences within events. The understandings that we have, or the meanings that we ascribe to events, are constrained by the cultural context surrounding them. As well, the more significant the event, the more likely that it will strongly shape our beliefs about our identities and the world around us, increasing the possibility that we may take these beliefs to be real or true. However, these past events can be revisited and reinterpreted to better serve present life.

As we work with people to reflect on their experiences, it becomes increasingly important that we are mindful of our use of self and our influence in the minutia of the therapeutic conversation. Fook and Gardner stated: "We are often responsible for interpreting, selecting, prioritizing, sometimes seeing and not seeing, and using knowledge in particular ways that are to do with a myriad of things about ourselves and our social and historical situations" (2007, p. 28). As we participate in reflection, transparency becomes a highly valued operating principle, in an effort to make known to people the history and context of our ideas. We not only reflect *in* action, but *on* action, making our own ideas visible to people.

As we studied the parallel effects of both therapy and training, reflective practices were integrated into each therapy session of our training and research project. Student therapists were constantly encouraged to reflect on their practices, emphasizing transparency and ongoing skill development.

This reflexivity has twofold benefits for the therapists and people who consult them. It provides a reflective, practice-based process whereby therapists can extend their knowledge and skills, thereby extending the limits of their theoretical orientation (Bird, 2006). For families seeking assistance, their knowledge and preferences are recognized and privileged, making it possible for them to extend their learnings and move toward preferred action.

The following statement of position maps (maps 1 and 2) (White, 2007a) provide an example of Michael White's micromaps that are available for scaffolding the therapeutic conversation, encouraging movement through reflection and reevaluation of the relationship with problems, as well as skills, knowledge, commitments, hopes, and attributes.

Statement of Position Map 1: Mapping the Effects of the Problem

1. *Naming the problem.* In the process of naming the problem it becomes externalized and objectified in relation to the person(s). The externalizing process is considered to be a counterpractice, as typically it is the person who is objectified and pathologized in the practice of therapy. A comprehensive examination of the problem is undertaken, effecting further distancing from it.

2. *Exploring and naming the domains and influence of the problem.* In this cat-

egory, an inquiry is undertaken to explore where the problem lives (e.g., school, home, work, community). By determining specifically where the problem is located, the pervasive influence of the problem is deconstructed and the relative influence and effects of the problem are determined. Simultaneously, the relative influence of the person over the problem is determined and made visible.

3. *Evaluating the effects and influence of the problem.* At this stage of the process the effects of the problem on the people are evaluated. People are asked to take a position on the effects of the problem on their life (i.e., Is it a good thing, a not so good thing, or an in-between thing? Would they like to continue with the problem in their life the way that it exists, eliminate the problem from their life totally, or change their relationship with the problem?).

4. *Justifying the evaluation of the effects and influence of the problem.* People are asked to justify their position regarding the effects of the problem on their life. If the effects of the problem are experienced as negative, then why is that? What do people's position on the problem say about their values and what is important to them? They can be asked to speculate regarding what difference it might make for them being more in touch with these values.

Statement of Position Map 2: Mapping the Effects of the Skill or Initiative

1. *Negotiating and naming a skill, unique outcome, or initiative to standing up to the problem.* There are always gaps in problem stories that contain unique outcomes, skills, and times that people took initiative to influence the problem. More often these exceptions to problem stories become visible as the therapist is exploring statement of position map 1 with people. When this happens, the therapist can shift the conversation to map 2, continuing to unpack the skill, attribute, or initiative.

2. *Mapping the effects and potential effects of the skill, unique outcome, or realization.* In this category, an inquiry is undertaken to explore where the domains of the skill, unique outcome, or realization are located (e.g., school, home, work, community). People can be asked how the development of the skill, unique outcome, or realization has affected the influence of the problem. Is there as much space for the problem in the person's life?

3. *Evaluating the effects and potential effects of the unique outcome, skill, or realization.* The real and potential effects of the skill, unique outcome, or realization on the people's life are evaluated. People are asked to take a position on the effects of the skill, unique outcome, or realization on their life (i.e., Is it a good

thing, a not so good thing, or an in-between thing? Would they like to continue with the skill or attribute in their life?).

4. *Justifying the evaluation of the effects and influence of the skill or attribute.* People are asked to justify their position regarding the effects of the skill or attribute on their life. If the effects of the skill or attribute are experienced as positive, then why is that? What do people's position on the skill or attribute say about their values and what is important to them? They can be asked to speculate regarding what difference it might make for them being more in touch with these values.

Literature and training risk oversimplifying the therapeutic process. Any seasoned therapist knows that the therapeutic process is messy and complex and does not represent the orderly, linear fashion in which the scaffolding maps are presented above. As these maps are used the therapist and people seeking consultation zigzag back and forth among them. As the therapeutic conversation progresses, the emphasis becomes more and more oriented toward map 2 and the development of people's skills and attributes. The different levels of inquiry encourage reflection and incremental, steady movement through this transitional phase.

Reflection invokes rich story development, which evokes katharsis (see Chapter 4 for an explanation of why it's *katharsis* with a *k*) through realizations, aha moments, and epiphanies. As these realizations occur people are transported to new worlds of possibilities. These realizations and preferences can be strung together to form chains of association, forming preferred stories that stand juxtaposed to the problem story.

The transitional phase of act 2 is not a search for certainty and truth based on the gathering of information, but instead it strives for the generation of rich meaning, developing a sense of purpose that is resonant with people's sense of preferred identity. As a preferred story is developed, people become prepared to cross the second threshold into act 3, the final *reincorporation phase* of the three-act play.

As stated previously, reflecting summaries are an aspect of reflective practices. Throughout the session the therapist offers summaries at regular and frequent intervals for people, reflecting back key words and phrases, summarizing the conversation as they continue through it. This inductive posture invites people to "step back," pause, and reflect on the conversation, taking up a position on what was said. Reflective summaries help people express themselves, speak out, and make discernments about their lives. Their discernments often contradict dominant themes, illuminating gaps between the influence of the problem story and their own strongly-held values and preferences.

However, the reflecting summary that we are referring to at this point is a key aspect of the storyline as it approaches the threshold to act 3. Like the entrance to act 2, this process summarizes the therapeutic conversation to this point, including act 1 and act 2. Following the rich story development and scaffolding conversation of the liminal phase, this second primary reflecting summary invites people to reflect back over the entire session, revisiting realizations and consolidating their fresh position before crossing the threshold to act 3.

The reflecting summary makes it possible for people to move the therapist back on track, if necessary. In providing the summary the therapist in a sense says, "This is my understanding of what you came in with today, what we discussed, and the realizations and consideration that you experienced as a result of that conversation. However, that's my view. What is your understanding?" People can now offer *their* reflections of the therapeutic conversation, reducing any potential gaps in understanding before moving into future speculation and the receiving context.

The following excerpt will illustrate a reflecting summary with a woman who had experienced trauma and abuse.

Therapist: Dianne, at the beginning of our session today you strongly expressed your desire to get free of the overwhelming feelings of sadness, despair, and self-loathing that you have been experiencing for many years. You said that there were many times that you found it hard to even get out of bed and face the day. You also described how you no longer gained the same satisfaction from normal everyday activities that you used to enjoy. You said that you had given up playing guitar and hardly ever saw your friends anymore. You made a point of clearly stating that you do not want to continue living like this and that you want to rejoin your life. As we talked you said that it was time to face these feelings of despair and you decided to stop trying to overcome them, but instead, just let these feelings be. Dianne, then you continued to talk about how you would really like to feel better about yourself and that you would like to be true to yourself and take back control of your life. You recounted one event in which "suddenly things were different." You said that after that event your past and your invasive memories no longer had strong control over you and that from that time forward you started taking control of your life. When I asked you what you would like to bring forward with you from your previous life, prior to the abuse, you said your strong sense of "determination and creativity." You continued to describe ways that you had learned to take back control of your life. For example, you learned to regulate your visits with your parents and no longer visit them when your father is drinking. You learned that walking helps you feel better. Then you learned that going for a walk with your friend Patti helps as well. Then you realized that even going for a walk by yourself helps and gives you time to reflect. Then, as we were talking, you realized that you had already started taking control of your life more than you had previously thought that you had. Then you described an aha moment when you realized that that you could "just let it be" and stop trying to make the fears and bad feelings go away. Instead, you have learned to focus your interest and attention on other things. You said that maybe you would get your guitar out of the attic and play it this weekend.

Dianne, these are my words and my memory of our conversation. There was so much we talked about that I'm sure I've left some things out. Is this your understanding of what we talked about? Have I got this right? Is there anything that you would change or add to what I just said? (*The summary allows people to correct the therapist and regulate their mutual understanding.*)

Dianne: (*Smiles*) Well, you were close, but there was more. I also said that I started taking control of my life by dividing some household responsibilities with my husband, John. The most important one is that he has agreed to take responsibility for our finances. I realized that a huge problem was that over time I've taken on too much responsibility. I've become overresponsible. It's too much! I'm constantly trying to do everything to take care of others, which creates more anxiety for me.

Therapist: All right, that's helpful to know. So, in addition to what I said, it seems like you have experienced two major realizations or aha moments. Those are that you have realized that rather than trying to make the memories and bad feelings go away, you could just let it be and instead focus your interest and attention on other things. The other realization or new learning you've had is that you have been overresponsible in trying to take care of others. You've learned that you can share some of those responsibilities. So you have already started sharing responsibility with John and he is now responsible for your household finances.

Dianne: Yeah, that's it. Now you've got it. The responsibility for the household finances was a huge burden for me to assume by myself. As I said, it was really contributing to my anxiety. Already that has made a difference in how I feel.

Dianne has expressed a desire to bring her sense of determination and her creativity forward from her past and to press these two qualities into service in her present and in her future. In addition, she has noted a number of realizations and new learnings that can also be put to work in her current project of rejoining her life, moving toward her preferred identity, and reclaiming a sense of personal agency.

People are invited to reconsider their identity conclusions as a result of being refamiliarized with their strongly held values through the therapeutic conversation. Part of the process of reincorporation involves bringing forward preferred aspects of identity that reside in people's past. More often, these preferred aspects of identity have been overshadowed by the problem story and, therefore, have been unavailable for consideration. It's the therapist's responsibility to provide scaffolding in the therapeutic conversation that helps people revisit these preferred aspects of their identity that are located in the past. People are asked to revisit those aspects of identity and reconsider their potential effects if they were to be brought into their current life. As they revisit and reconsider these aspects of identity, they become reconnected with them and are more able to incorporate these aspects by utilizing new learning and developments that were generated through the therapeutic conversation. The integration of preferred aspects of identity brought forward from people's past with new learning and perspectives generated from the therapeutic conversation constitutes the beginning of the reincorporation of identity.

ACT 3: THE REINCORPORATION OF IDENTITY

Act 3 of the three-act play moves toward a reincorporation of identity (van Gennep, 1960; White, 1999) and a speculation regarding future steps that people may take as they move forward in their preferred lives. Reincorporation of identity is experienced when people find that they've arrived at another place in life, where they experience a fit that provides them with a sense of once again being in touch with themselves and with preferred ways of living.

This third phase of the three-act play brings the therapeutic conversation into the present. At this stage people are encouraged to simultaneously look back and look forward. They reflect back over the summary gathered moving into the threshold of act 3, reviewing their new understandings and preferred aspects of identity that had been previously relegated to the past. They look forward, speculating about the effects of their new understandings, reincorporated with previous preferred aspects of their identities on possible futures, making connections among their individual and social worlds.

Therapist: Dianne, as you look back now, can you think about those qualities that you have decided to bring back into your life from your past? You recalled a sense of strong determination and your creativity. As you integrate those skills and values that were aspects of your former self with the new realizations that you just spoke of, like being able to let it be and focus on other things, and being able to share responsibility with others, in addition to all the other learnings you have mentioned, how do you imagine this making a difference for you? You know, if you were to look even 3 or 4 months into the future, how do you imagine this making a difference in how you are experiencing yourself?

Dianne: (*Gazes up and to the right, imagining.*) Well . . . (*pause*) I think I will be more true to myself. I think as I look out the window, I will start to see some of the beauty and not just the darkness. I also think I will have a closer relationship with my husband and my daughter. I will have some of the intimacy with my husband that we used to have. I think I will actually enjoy spending time together with them. I will be doing things and enjoy doing things with them, instead of just going through the motions. I think if I can just "let it be," I will be more at peace with myself and like myself more. The self-loathing has been very consuming. Yes, as I think about it, I think I will start liking myself more. This will make a big difference. I think I will start to experience the normal ups and downs of life like everyone else and it will no longer be the extreme highs and lows like it has been for years. (*She looks at therapist, pauses, and smiles.*) . . . I never knew I had this in me. Maybe there's hope. That was a good question.

Receiving Context

At this closing stage of the three-act play and the therapy session, the therapist moves to help people maintain their distance from the old story. There is an emphasis on the development of a future and receiving context that serves the purpose of holding the new preferred story.

Revisiting the re-membering conversation and backstory from the beginning of the session, the therapist collaborates with family members to recruit a wider audience to populate the new preferred story.

New stories can be vulnerable to harassment by the old story. Tricky habits can sneak in from the shadows, bringing with them self-doubt, temptation, and relentless influence to return to taken-for-granted ways of seeing and doing things. Isolation increases the vulnerability of new stories. A receiving context that is inhabited by others who validate and support the efforts of people to perform their new story makes them far less vulnerable to the influence of the old problem story.

Having experienced new understandings and realizations from their journey through the transitional middle phase of act 2, now in the reincorporation phase people are able to experience a renewed sense of life as an open process, "the sense that what I do at this moment truly matters" (Morson, 1994, p. 21). This revelation brings with it personal choice and creativity, contributing to a sense of hope when developing a future, receiving context.

It's important to gather the themes of the new story. In doing so people can view their receiving context as a project and be asked to name that project. The naming helps to create a new overarching frame in which meaning can be indeterminate and continually redeveloped through time.

Therapist: Well, I'd like to ask you another question. You just said, "Maybe there's hope." So, that gets me wondering, as you continue to gaze into the future, what needs to happen to make space for that hope to develop and take root? Who will populate your new life that will contribute toward the development of hope? Who do you value the most that you would like to invite into closer relationship with you? Who will be in your inner circle? Conversely, which relationships would you like to keep at a distance? What will you be doing that you are not doing now that will contribute to you "liking yourself more"? Could you build me a picture?

Dianne: That's a big question. It's going to take some thinking to answer it well!

Therapist: I know. Can you answer it anyway? Take all the time you need.

Dianne: You know, I'm really excited about getting close to John again. The abuse and trauma have had real effects on him as well. It created a weird kind of distance in our relationship that went on for quite a while. We haven't been intimate for a few years. Yet that whole time he was supportive of me. He used to say to me, "You'll get through this. I'll be here when you're ready." He's my best friend. He deserves to have his wife back. John is definitely in the inner circle.

Therapist: So, the abuse created a distance between you and John to the degree that you haven't been intimate for years. Yet, he remained supportive to you the whole time. Dianne, what do you suppose that says about John's ideas about being a partner to you and about being your "best friend"?

Dianne: It says that our relationship is important to him and that I matter to him. It also says he's not self-centered. He was able to absorb the pain and frustration and have empathy for me and have some understanding for what I was going through. He didn't let my fears and self-loathing destroy our relationship.

Therapist: You said that you're "really excited" about regaining your closeness to John. If the fears and self-loathing created distance between the two of you, then what do you suppose would help to regain the closeness in your relationship? Any ideas about what would be an antidote to fear and self-loathing?

Dianne: (*Pauses, looks down at the floor.*) Well . . . I'm thinking courage. The courage to be close and intimate after all this time and distance. Let's face it. It's probably going to be a bit awkward at first. Since he has been so patient and understanding, maybe I should take the lead. You know, as I'm thinking, maybe I'll ask John out on a date. Even if we went to dinner and then went to a movie or went to listen to some music, that would be a good start. I think that could be fun. Fun must be an antidote to fear!

Dianne continued to express her ideas about regaining closeness in her relationship with John and described a number of ways that she would go about doing so. The more she talked about it, the more her attention focused on revitalizing her relationship with John and away from fear and self-loathing.

Therapist: Who else will you be inviting into your inner circle?

Dianne: Well, obviously my daughter, Jessica. She will be happy to have her mother back. I mean, I've done things with her. I take her to music lessons and go to school functions and all of that. But now I won't just be going through the motions. Just like my relationship with John, I'm excited about really connecting with Jessica. I want to spend time with her and do things with her.

Therapist: How old is Jessica again?

Dianne: She's nine. These are important years and I don't want to miss them.

Dianne continued to discuss her ideas about what it means to her to be a mother and how she learned through her own past abuse how important it is for Jessica to experience a strong and stable connection with her that she can count on.

Therapist: Are there any other people that you would like to invite into closer relationship with you as you create your new life?

Dianne: Yes. I have already started to rekindle my relationships with friends. Patti is a good example of someone who I would like to keep a closer relationship with. Just our walks have made such a difference already. While we are walking we're talking about all kinds of things. Last week she invited me to join a creative writing club that she belongs to. It's a group of five women who get together once a month and talk about their writing and learn about creative writing. I think I would really like that. I'm ready for my creative part to come alive again. I also think it would be good to get to know the other women around the common interest of creative writing.

The conversation thickened considerably as Dianne described all of the possible benefits of rekindling her relationships with friends and what these ideas of friendship meant to her. She also talked about the benefits of bringing her creative side "back to life" through the creative writing club. She also spoke of her intentions to take guitar lessons.

Therapist: Dianne, we've talked about a number of relationships that you value and want to keep closer to you. It's been exciting listening to you talk about all of the many possibilities as you initiate these changes. I'm wondering though, what relationships would you prefer to keep at more of a distance?

Dianne: (*Leans forward, looks down at the floor.*) My relationship with my father needs to stay at a distance. He's my mother's husband and I will accept that. But, I can't reconcile all of the terrible abusive things he did to me. It took me a long time to figure out that I need to take control of my relationship with him. He tries to be charming. But I learned that he still cannot be trusted. If I give in just a little bit, he takes advantage of that and starts to make advances toward me. I've come to terms with this. It just is what it is now. I would like to have a closer relationship with my mother. But, it's complicated. I have a hard time forgiving her because I know she knew my father abused me and didn't protect me from him. She lives in a state of denial. For now, I need her to stay at a distance with my father. She's making her own choices. Maybe this is something that can be revisited over time. I've wasted too much energy and too many years trying to figure her out. Right now I need to move on with my life. Other important people need me and love me. It's time for me to focus my attention on those relationships.

Therapist: Dianne, you have really described a detailed picture of what your life will be like as you move into the future and rejoin your life. This seems like quite a project filled with lots of new possibilities. Would you say this is like a project that you have started working on?

Dianne: Yes, I suppose it is like a project.

Therapist: Well, projects are often easier to think about and become involved with when they have a name. What do you think? Would you like to give this project a name? For example, The *blank* Project. Perhaps you could pick a name that has particular meaning for you.

Dianne: Well, one name comes to mind. How about "The Let It Be Project." I think that has been my most powerful realization lately. I need to stop fighting it and struggling with it and just let it be.

Dianne has described her receiving context in powerful ways that inspire hope and possibility for living her preferred life. She has populated her life with closer, valued relationships. She has also described possible actions that she will take to invigorate and sustain those relationships in order to create her new life. These ideas and actions are the details of personal agency.

CONCLUSION

We have introduced two innovative concepts in this chapter: (a) storied therapy as a three-act play and (b) the conversational map, which includes six distinct points of inquiry. These concepts work together, expanding on two pioneering and foundational concepts regarding the application of story to the therapeutic process.

The first concept, storied therapy as a three-act play, expands the rites of passage analogy (Campbell, 1968; Turner, 1977; van Gennep, 1960), which was also a further expansion of universal story form that has been handed down through many cultures and many generations. The rites of passage analogy became a foundational concept to the therapeutic process when it was applied through the pioneering work of Michael White and David Epston (1990). Michael White (1999) continued to develop the rites of passage analogy through his migration of identity map and, although it initially had enormous influence on the creation of narrative therapy, that influence has faded over time. With the introduction of the three-act play our intention is to reintroduce, revitalize, and enliven the rites of passage analogy and universal story form. The three-act-play metaphor is innovative in that it has further developed these foundational concepts, bringing more clarity, purpose, and cultural relevance to the overall therapeutic process. Through the distinct framework of the three-act play, the purpose of each phase is more clearly defined and punctuated, clearly marking each stage of the rites of passage.

The three-act play creates space for people to improvise new ways of viewing and doing things, engaging with creativity and choice, and exploring preferred meaning. In doing so, it offers an approach that acknowledges the multiplicity and fluidity of life and identity. All of these activities contribute to a sense of personal agency.

Much the same as in poetry or music, the overall form creates an arrangement, a configuration in which endless acts of movement and creativity are made possible. Without form, the poetry, music, or therapeutic process lacks coherence and purpose. The three-act play provides space for discreet movements within the time-tested patterns of universal story form and the rites of passage analogy.

The second innovative concept that we have introduced is the conversational map, which is integral to all three phases of the three-act play. The conversational map is innovative in applying the expanded framework for story to the therapeutic process in the following ways:

1. *Points of stories:* We make a distinction that all stories are not equal and we need to engage with people around the stories that hold the most value for them. This helps people focus on what is most important for them to talk about and what they want to have different in their life, their "calling" (Campbell, 1968). They assist people to separate from the problematic aspect of their life during the first phase of the three-act play.
2. *Backstory:* The backstory provides an intelligible frame for people's stories that needs to be addressed and placed in a social context before moving to act 2 of the therapeutic process.
3. *Pivotal events:* This represents one of the most significant aspects of the conversational map. Just as all stories are not equal, nor are all events equal. We have illuminated the value of locating events that have particular significance in people's lives, revisiting them and reinterpreting the experiences within them.
4. *Evaluation:* This point of inquiry in the journey phase places a particular emphasis on inviting people to "step back" and reflect on the events of their lives, engaging creativity and choice. A renewed sense of personal agency is established when people regain a sense that "what I do at this moment truly matters" (Morson, 1994, p. 21).
5. *Reflecting summary:* This aspect of the framework invites people to summarize their story at the closure of a therapy session, highlighting points of resonance and holding the therapist accountable for their understanding of the story at that point in time.
6. *Receiving context:* Although this is a concept that was explored by White and Epston (1990), it was not discreetly integrated into a storied framework. Providing a future orientation, the receiving context assists in repopulating people's future backstory, building audience in order to sustain their newly developed preferred story.

The integrated frameworks of the three-act play and the conversational map together offer a lucid and robust means for conceptualizing the therapeutic process, whether therapists are conducting a single session or are working through the entire process of therapy. The frameworks are useful to beginning therapists, offering them maps in which to develop their unique learning and practices.

Experienced therapists can experiment within these time-tested storyline frameworks, creating opportunities to extend their theoretical and practice wisdom.

A richly developed story depends on therapists' constant and close attention to the circulation of language and special, pivotal moments. The following two chapters will thoroughly address the application of these concepts to a storied therapeutic conversation.

Questions for Reflection

1. When beginning a therapy session (act 1), what unique skills, particular to your own practice wisdom, do you draw on when inviting people to develop the meaning and purpose to their story?
2. How do you use critical reflection when eliciting people's backstory and addressing the cultural discourses and master narratives in which their lives are situated (e.g., race, ethnicity, gender, spirituality, sexual affiliation)?
3. Are you transparent in situating yourself within a cultural backdrop as a therapist?
4. How can you maintain a posture of reflexivity (an awareness of the use of "self") in your practice, so that you can transparently and routinely reflect on your work with people in order to constantly inform your theoretical learning and continuously develop your therapeutic skills?
5. What particular decentering principles or skills do you use in order to manage ambiguity and remain tentative when inviting people into rich story development during the middle (journey) phase of the therapy session (act 2)?
6. How can you best use your reflexive posture in response to people's moments of realization and epiphanies in order to acknowledge and support transport (act 2)?
7. How do you invite people to reflect on a therapy session in order to notice movement and difference (act 3)?
8. How do you conceptualize a therapy session and/or the overall therapeutic process?

CHAPTER 3

Circulation of Language

In this chapter we will describe how our experiences within our field research inspired us to begin to reflect much more critically about the use of language within therapeutic conversations. We have found that the works of philosophers Deleuze (1994), Deleuze and Parnet (2002), Derrida (1974, 1978, 1991), and Foucault (1965, 1973, 1980, 1997) have contributed greatly to our understanding of the complexity and fluidity of the social construction of meaning through the words we use. We will describe some of their ideas that we have found the most interesting and relevant for considering therapeutic conversations. Since people use language to tell us their stories, our reflections regarding the use of language will also touch upon aspects regarding story and the issue of "voice" of the teller of the story. This raises issues of an ethical nature because we need to be committed to being careful about how we use language to talk and write about people and their stories in professional settings and within written recordings.

During the field research phase described in the Introduction, as we reviewed videotapes of sessions as a research team, we began to notice and have conversations about the specific use of language in these sessions conducted by both trainees and trainers. The trainees were encouraged to be careful with the use of their language and to be sure to encourage the people consulting them to reflect on what would be the most suitable words for them to use to name the problem to be externalized or the name of any alternative skill that was being developed and supported through telling their story (these are the first steps within externalizing conversations, which have been described in Chapter 2). What we began to realize, though, was that the therapist, whether a trainee or trainer, would at times offer tentative suggestions as to the words that could be used to describe ideas.

White (1995a, 2007a) suggested the need to be careful and precise in the use of language, ensuring that we intentionally use the words and phrases of those people with whom we are consulting, rather than interpreting what they say. It is important, however, to be thoughtful and purposeful about which words, and what types of language and ideas, to pay attention to. One of the trainees realized that, although he had been attempting to center the language of the little girl with whom he was meeting, privileging her ideas and thoughts, he had inadvertently reinforced the problem by spending a great deal of time discussing her use of the word *darkness* as it related to her worries. An example of using language in such a way that it opened up possibilities, on the other hand, was when a trainee therapist was meeting with parents of a young boy, Jamie, who was very slow in the mornings preparing for school. The parents talked about how he sometimes just seemed to not be able to focus on what needed to be done. They asked him how it was that he was able "to focus and give his attention to playing with Lego blocks, but he was unable to focus and get ready for school." He said that he went into his "Lego zone." The trainee therapist wrote a therapeutic document/letter (therapeutic documents are described in the Introduction) to the family and asked about this Lego zone and wondered about whether there were other zones he ever accessed. (It should be noted that these therapeutic documents are significant for supporting the circulation and development of language outside of the therapeutic setting.) When the family returned for a follow-up session, they reported that they had begun using this word and concept "zone" in their conversations together. They reported in their follow-up session that this had led to many productive conversations as Jamie talked about further zones he was able to create and what he would be able to do to create a "getting-ready-for-school zone."

Mum: It was really nice to get your letter and of course we read it to Jamie. Well, he actually asked us to read it to him almost every night. And then we could, like, remind him about his zones if he was slow in the morning. We'd say, "Remember you said you were going to make this new getting-ready-for-school zone?!"

Therapist: And how's that coming along, Jamie?

Jamie: Fine. I have all kinds of zones so I can make them whenever I want.

We have had the opportunity to observe numerous live and videotaped counseling sessions of Michael White's conversations with people, as he presented these in workshops and conferences. We also were able to observe the manner in which he took notes in these sessions, and it was clear that he not only suggested the necessity to be careful and intentional in the use of people's language, but in fact he was also very careful in acting as a scribe for those people consulting him. He would take precise notes, slowing the conversation down and saying, "Do you mind if I just write that down? That sounds very important." This had the result of privileging and centering the language and knowledge of those people consulting him. Clearly the decisions he made about which words and phrases to privilege were not neutral, but came from a position that was committed to assisting people make thought-out decisions about their life course, based on their own values and dreams, rather than merely responding to societal pressures. His was a political position (White, 1995a).

As we examined videotaped sessions within the research project, however, we began to realize that it was also possible to carefully introduce new and different words and language into the conversation as long as it was done tentatively and respectfully in a spirit of discovering meanings together rather than imposing an understanding or interpretation. It did not appear necessary to *only* use the other person's language in order to center their preferences and hopes for their life. (When we do introduce a new word into a therapeutic conversation, we usually acknowledge that this is our word and ask if it resonates for the other people or if they would prefer to suggest a different word.)

An example of a therapist tentatively introducing a new word into a conversation was presented to us as we watched a videotaped session of one of the trainers in conversation with a young boy who was experiencing difficulties with what his mum described as "low self-esteem and temper tantrums." The mother and father were both present in the session also, and initially, Tommy, 9 years of age, was wandering about the room as the therapist began to ask what they should talk about in that session.

Therapist: So you have some concerns and we may not have to pick only one to talk about in the hour we have together, but if we did have to pick one, which would it be?
Mom: Low self-esteem.
Dad: Low self-esteem and a tendency to threaten suicide.
Mom: (*to Tommy*): Sit down, buddy.
Therapist: Your mom and dad said they'd like to talk about self-esteem. Does that sound like something you could talk about some? Maybe?
Tommy: Okay.

Through the first step of the externalizing conversation the therapist attempted to encourage Tommy to describe the feelings and their characteristics before moving on to having him describe the effects of these feelings in his life (the first two steps of scaffolding an externalizing conversation). Obviously the type of language used for these steps is adjusted for people, depending on their age and their level of concept development. Many children enjoy the playfulness of describing their problems in this externalized manner (White, 2007a) and also enjoy drawing pictures of the problems or using puppets and play-therapy equipment (Ball, Piercy, & Bischoff, 1993; Freeman, Epston, & Lobovits, 1997). This particular young boy, however, was quieter than some and appeared to be having some difficulty in finding the words to describe the feelings. Therefore, the therapist asked the mom and dad to describe more fully what they meant by self-esteem. Following a discussion about the effects that they had all been observing, the therapist introduced the tentative notion of certain ideas seeming to be *sticky*, thereby introducing this word and concept into the conversation.

Therapist: What do you mean when you say self-esteem?
Mom: He says nobody likes him. It's like everybody hates him. He says he has no friends and has the tendency to say people hate him. Then he says, "Now you're angry with me," and I say "No, I love you." I always say those words, but he seems to think the opposite. He makes me cry when he puts himself down.

Therapist: When you respond like that, are you trying to reassure him, telling him he's loved?

Mom: Yeah, trying to make him feel better.

Therapist: It hurts you, makes you sad. What would you like for him instead?

Mom: I just want him to have confidence. I ask, "Do they say they don't like you?" And he says, "No, you can just tell."

Therapist: So, it's like he guesses?

Mom: Yeah, and I tell him it's not true.

Therapist: Paul, can you add anything to what Cindy's been saying? His, um, trouble? Would you call it self-esteem, trouble with self-esteem, or with worrying people don't like him, or an idea people don't like him?

Dad: It's both. He calls himself stupid. But he's doing fine at school. I tell him not everyone is good at everything.

Therapist: So, is your response to tell him the things he's good at? Does it help?

Dad: He calms down.

Therapist: Um, Tommy, your mom and dad are describing some times when it seems like you get this idea that people aren't liking you.

Tommy: Uh huh.

Therapist: Yeah, is that an okay way to talk about it or is there another way you'd like to talk about this, um, problem? At first we talked about it as a self-esteem problem and now we're talking about it as an idea people don't like you. Is there another name for it?

Tommy: The reason I keep saying that I'm stupid and people don't like me is because every time I ask people at school if I can play with them they say no, like there's something they don't like about me. It's hard when my friends don't want to play with me.

Therapist: You have friends. . . .

Tommy: They make fun of me and say they don't like me. They call me things.

Therapist: Sounds hard. What would you call that, what they're doing?

Tommy: Making fun.

Therapist: Doesn't sound like fun, does it? Seems a bit mean.

Tommy: That's why I say I'm stupid.

Therapist: So, when they say that, you get the idea it's got to do something with you, yourself?

Tommy: Yeah.

Therapist: Yeah, okay. Is that kind of a sticky idea? Does that kind of stick around with you?

Tommy: Yeah. Because I tried making other friends but none of them are my friends.

Therapist: So, I guess, on account of those people, friends, saying those things to you, making fun and being mean, this sticky idea gets going that other kids might not like you.

Tommy: Uh huh.

Therapist: When that idea is kind of sticking to you . . . what happens?

Tommy: That makes me think and say to myself that I'm dumb and stupid and maybe I should just kill myself. It's all that sort of stuff, when people aren't nice.

Therapist: So, really huge ideas get going and say hard stuff to you and to your mom and dad.

Tommy: I get really frustrated and it feels like I've had enough.

Therapist: Yeah, when you get frustrated, that's when these drastic ideas come and you think about hurting yourself. Did I get that right?

Tommy: Yeah. I've just had enough of people making fun of me. I'm fed up. I might as well do it. Then people would be happy 'cause I wouldn't be around anymore.

Therapist: Is that one of the things the sticky idea says to you, that they'd be better off without you?

Tommy: Uh huh.

This word seemed to make sense to him and his parents even though they hadn't originally come up with it themselves. If they hadn't begun to use the word, if they hadn't made it their own by beginning to talk about sticky ideas and the very real and powerful effects of these sticky ideas in Tommy's life, then they could have looked for and tried out other words. As it was, he was able to begin to imagine how he could counteract the stickiness of the ideas in order to protect himself from them sticking to him. At about the midpoint of the session the therapist asked the family if there had been any times when the sticky ideas hadn't stuck around as much.

Mom: Last week was a perfect week. He had a little temper tantrum this morning, so it must have been the sticky stuff.

Therapist: So the sticky stuff got in there this morning, but the whole week you said was pretty good—perfect, you said.

Following a discussion in which the parents described their observations of what had gone well the week before and shared some guesses as to why they thought things had gone well, Tommy then shared some of his guesses about why it had been a better week. In particular, he said it had really helped that he and his older brother had decided to be friends again.

Tommy: I don't have to worry. I might as well throw it away. I've got my brother as a friend now.
Therapist: I might as well throw it away?
Tommy: Yeah. We used to fight constantly.
Therapist: So, you've done stuff to change that. How many times did you have to say to yourself that you didn't have to worry and you might as well throw it away?
Tommy: A lot. Every day.
Therapist: How did it work, saying that?
Tommy: It really worked well. And now I listen really well.
Therapist: Was that about throwing it away?
Tommy: Yeah, all of it.
Therapist: Quite a lot happened over the last week. The sticky idea got loose a bit.
Tommy: I just tore it off (*demonstrating, by pulling imaginary things from his clothes*).
Therapist: You tore it off!
Tommy: Yeah, like I made my life a whole new life.
Therapist: You did? Getting these sticky ideas off you can make a big difference, can it? I'm getting excited.
Tommy: (*Interrupting and speaking with more excitement*) It's like I was a magnet and it all stuck to me, but now I'm a person so it all fell off (*again indicating this with his arms*).
Therapist: Like you demagnetized? That's amazing (*Tommy, smiling*).

From time to time in the conversation as the young boy occasionally had some difficulty describing his experiences, the therapist was able to also include the parents through horizontal scaffolding of the conversation. (Horizontal scaffolding is used to develop an idea at a particular step of the therapeutic conversation prior to moving up to the next step in the conversation.) In this way, the parents appeared to become excited about externalizing the worries with this type of language. In picking up this language of "sticky ideas" and "sticky stuff," the parents moved away from the potentially pathologizing accounts of their son that totalized him as someone with "low self-esteem" and "temper tantrums" and rather supported further concept development and a freeing up and movement of his identity. Initially, we worried in our research team meetings that the practice of introducing a new word like this could be considered overly directive by the therapist and not centered enough on the other's language. We began to realize, though, that this had been a useful and hope-inducing conversation for the young boy and his parents; the word had been introduced tentatively and there was room for the family to adjust and use the word as they wished.

Another example had to do with the time an outsider witness (outsider witness teams are also described in the Introduction) tentatively suggested a word, commenting that she had noticed the mother's strength. When the mother returned to the therapy room, she said she had been drawn to the word *strength*, but she thought of it as more a matter of perseverance. A trainer, via an earpiece, suggested that the trainee therapist could ask if there was a history of perseverance in the mother's family. This led to a long story about how much perseverance there had been throughout her family as they immigrated to Canada. The one word/idea/concept (strength) triggered another and opened up space to explore what was meant and what was useful to explore together (perseverance).[1]

Michael White (1995b, 2005, 2006b, 2007b, 2007c) often referenced the contribution of the philosophers Foucault, Derrida, and Deleuze to the development of narrative therapy. In one of our last conversations with Michael prior to his death in 2008, he indicated that he was planning to study Derrida and Deleuze further because he recognized their particular contribution to thinking

1. Adrienne Chambon, one of the research team members, was particularly interested in how these examples we discussed seemed to have something to do with the circulation of language. We are indebted to her for bringing this to our attention and triggering our interest in understanding this further.

through his concept of "the absent but implicit." In my (LB) last training session with him in December 2007, White (2007c) described the steps of a conversation about the "absent, but implicit" as often starting with people bringing a complaint to a session. Whenever a conversation started this way, he would suggest it would be useful to name the experience about which the people were complaining, like the first step of an externalizing conversation. Thinking of every emotion or thought as an action or reaction, he would ask if the people's reaction (even if only a feeling) suggested that they were standing up against that experience of which they were complaining, or whether it meant they were going along with it. For instance, people may complain that a particular friend is always late when they make plans to meet. This may be experienced as disrespect or diminishment and the people may feel angry about it. The people may realize that by feeling anger and complaining about this behavior of always being late, they are in fact taking a stand against disrespect and diminishment. It is then possible to ask people to tell a story of how they came to recognize and stand up against this kind of behavior and how they began to realize that this was something important to do in their life. The point often is that if people complain about disrespect, this is because they have previously experienced (at least once) respect. They know what disrespect is because they know respect. In the initial complaint, however, respect was absent from the conversation, although it was implied. (An even more straightforward and simple example could be of a child tasting a new food and saying it is sour. The child only knows it is sour because she has previously tasted sweet and knows the difference.)

White said that he wished that he had stressed the importance of "the absent but implicit" in therapeutic conversations even more, and he planned to write much more about the importance of Derrida and Deleuze to these ideas. Maggie Carey, Sarah Walther, and Shona Russell continued with this project about how these philosophical ideas can assist us in expanding our understanding and skills of facilitating conversations about the "absent but implicit" (Carey, Walther, & Russell, 2009). Holmgren and Holmgren (2009) and Winslade (2009) have also been highlighting the importance of Derrida and Deleuze, as well as Foucault, for narrative practices. Interestingly, and yet perhaps unsurprisingly, Derrida and Deleuze can also assist us in further understanding the complexities of language and the challenge to work ethically within the limitations of language.

THE VULNERABILITY AND TENTATIVENESS OF LANGUAGE

Words within language, whether spoken or written, whether inside or outside of a therapeutic conversation, only ever partially represent that which is being described (Dooley & Kavanagh, 2007). They do not speak to a stand-alone object that is separate from our observations of it. They do not represent a truth to be discovered totally outside of us as the observers of an object or creators of an idea. There is always something lacking within the word, something missing, or something different implied and contrasted within the word (as in the "absent but implicit" conversation about disrespect and respect). Derrida moved away from the position that philosophers before him maintained of using the image of a circle that could encapsulate, catch, or set up a border around a truth (Dooley & Kavanagh, 2007). Derrida suggested that language is vulnerable. We like the word *vulnerable* since it can, itself, suggest a range of reactions. Vulnerability might be considered a weakness by some, or something beautiful by others. It could suggest something fragile, with an openness and flexibility, rather than something more rigid and constraining.

Derrida also wrote of cinders, and words being like cinders (Derrida, 1991; Dooley & Kavanagh, 2007). He wrote of cinders as coming from something, from that which had been consumed by fire. They are different from the fire, yet still contain warmth and can be rebuilt into a fire. Yet they are also vulnerable because they will crumble into ashes. The cinders are not able to actually indicate what was in the fire. In the same way, a word can exist in relation to something but cannot capture everything about it. The example given in Dooley and Kavanagh was about a cat. A cat is a thing outside of the person who might speak about the cat, but the word *cat* does not capture everything there is to say about a cat. It could trigger different images of cats in different people's minds. It could trigger different kinds of reactions in people who like cats than in people who dislike or who are afraid of cats. However, even separate from these triggered images, Derrida would suggest that the word also contains difference (*différance*) and that people hearing the word also need to consider what a cat is not—a cat is different from a dog, for instance. Concepts, and the words used for those concepts, do not stand alone, but are only understandable because of differences . . . what a word lacks. When Derrida talks of "*différance*" he is describing how a word (a "signifier," as he also referred to it in *Of Grammatology*

[1974]) is not only different from the thing it describes (the "signified") but also is describing what that thing is by saying what it is not. It is as if when we say or write a word, that word is like an image within a mirror. However, we are also comparing the idea of that word with other ideas. It does not stand alone but rather within a field of comparisons, perhaps as if we are standing in a room of mirrors.

It is therefore important to be careful within therapeutic conversations to be on guard against jumping to conclusions based on what we initially assume is meant by certain words. Rather we need to always be committed to asking more about what is meant by the people in front of us saying those words, and committed to being perhaps more playful (at times) and creative in using a variety of words in a variety of ways. This would provide the opportunity for those people to more fully describe what they mean and assisting them in finding ways to think through their experiences and put them into a storyline structure through language. Bird described this as "languaging into existence" (2008, p. 7). Since the storyline is made up of the landscape of identity as well as the landscape of action, it can be helpful to ask the people consulting us what certain actions or events in their storylines suggest in terms of what is important to them, or what it is they give value to. This helps us move away from limiting the possible meanings of the words and stories, encourages double listening, and opens up space for richer descriptions.

For example, in the following transcript the therapist is asking John, who has come to consult her, if he could speak more about his reactions to his mother's comments to him after hearing that their priest from 25 years ago had been charged with having sexually abused children in their parish.

John: So when I visited my mother that day she said to me that she couldn't believe he had been charged with abusing those kids and she said, "Oh my God, you were that age then too. Oh my God, don't tell me he abused you too. Oh my God, it would kill me if he touched you."

Therapist: How did you react to that? What went through your mind when she said that?

John: Well, I figured I couldn't tell her. I figured it would kill her. I still haven't told her, because she's sick and it really could kill her.

Therapist: How would you name or describe that reaction you had to your mom's comment? You were saying earlier that you are having trouble with anger and depression. Um, are they in reaction to your mom's comments or are they more in response to the priest and the Church?

John: I know other good priests so I wouldn't say I'm angry at the Church, well, maybe I'm angry at the Church for how they have handled it, but I'm not so angry with my mother. Well, but it was really, really hard to not be able to tell her, for her to pretty much tell me not to tell her.

Therapist: Um, so how did that affect you then, when she said, "Don't tell me he abused you too"? If it wasn't so much anger, but it was hard, what was that like? Could you describe it a little more so I could perhaps understand?

John: It was more like silencing, it was like shutting me up.

Therapist: Could you say more about what it was like—the silencing and shutting up? Do you think visually? Would an image come to mind? Or would you describe it more in terms of a physical sensation in your body?

John: It was like a tightening in my chest, a shutting up and shutting down at the same time.

Therapist: What does it speak to, do you think, that despite feeling silenced, and what seems like some frustration about that, that you've decided not to tell her anything yet?

John: You know what? I may have been a bit angry. I might have preferred a different response, but the fact is that I love her and I'm concerned about her health and well-being and what it means is that I care about her and that's what's most important to me right now. I might tell her in the future if things change, but I don't have to yet. I'm so relieved you aren't telling me I have to tell her. I was kind of worried you might.

The therapist reported, regarding this conversation, how differently this first conversation had gone than she had expected. She had expected that John would have expressed anger at the Church, and her previous training would have had her assuming she understood the anger and encouraging John to break his silence rather than protecting his mother in this way.

Rather than relying on an assumption that John would be angry at the Church and at his mother, as well as jumping to conclusions about what that anger was like and what it meant, the therapist slowed down the conversation. This made space and time to circle around these ideas and engage in a conversation in which John was able to describe what these words meant for him in this situation. She provided him with the chance to explain what was important to him and was therefore underlying his decision not to tell his mother about his own experiences of abuse.

As we have indicated, Derrida was not interested in capturing a meaning or truth by containing it within a circle. A spiral might be more in keeping with these notions. We continue circling or spiraling around a word, but keep the circle open as we develop fuller understandings and descriptions. It would be similar to Michael White's (2007a) notion of zigzagging between the landscape of identity and the landscape of action within the reauthoring conversation map, described in the Introduction and in Chapter 1 about storyline, where there is a commitment to looking for details and thickening the meaning of a story. Although Derrida realized the tentative and vulnerable nature of words and language and that they are always so very incomplete, they are also full of possibilities. For instance, we think of the number of times Michael White was consulted by families of children with a diagnosis of ADHD and the playful and creative manner in which Michael was able to move beyond the words used in a diagnostic label like that. At times he might ask, "Oh, what color is your ADHD?" through his commitment to externalize and name the problem and later move on to talk about the effects of "Mr. Mischief" in the child's life. Michael did not need to battle the diagnosis but rather, recognizing how incomplete the words were, he was able to begin to use the possibilities instead.

How can we further work with this awareness of the incomplete and vulnerable nature of language as a possibility rather than a limitation? Are there any metaphors that could assist us in remembering the need to maintain an open mind to multiple possible meanings instead of responding to pressures within work settings to quickly assess and diagnose with labels?

THE METAPHOR OF "GRASS" AS OPPOSED TO "TREE"

Deleuze and Parnet (2002) wrote about how the image of a rhizome has been useful for them in understanding the way that they thought and wrote together. A rhizome is a type of plant and root system like grass, or strawberries (Holmgren & Holmgren, 2009), that spreads underground and pops up here and there. Each little strawberry plant looks separate and distinct in the garden, but they are all linked together underneath the surface. There is no knowing where the next strawberry plant will appear. This is quite different from the manner in which a tree grows. As the translators of Deleuze and Parnet's book said:

> [This] is therefore not an "interview" or a "conversation"—although it has elements of both. It grows in many directions, without an overall ordering principle. To use Deleuze's terms it is the book as . . . "rhizome." There is no hierarchy of root, trunk and branch, but a multiplicity of interconnected shoots coming off in all directions. It is both an explanation and an exemplification of Deleuzian pluralism. (p. xi)

They included their concerns regarding the linear and oftentimes hierarchical structure of interviews and this reminds us as we begin therapeutic interviews or conversations to be sensitive to the effects of such a structure. Taking into account Deleuze and Parnet's (2002) thoughts on the image of the rhizome can assist us in this, so that we can move away from merely a back-and-forth exchange, rather acknowledging the complexity of language and thought and the creation of ideas and the movement of identities.

The following brief transcript offers an example of working with Sally, a successful professional woman, who was referred to counseling due to depression. She presented as highly intellectual and experienced with previous therapy. She was well-versed in therapeutic language and diagnosis. Although from a narrative perspective we would attempt to externalize and move beyond these types of labels, some people begin the process very attached to these descriptors and it is unhelpful to argue or try to persuade them to give them up at this point. It is, however, still very important to move beyond a surface understanding of what is meant by the word *depression*, and rather ask for fuller descriptions.

Therapist: You mentioned how helpful it was to receive the diagnosis of depression and anxiety. Could you tell me a bit about the ways it has been helpful? Um, you know, I think depression and anxiety can be experienced quite differently from one person to another so it helps me be a bit more clear if I can understand how it has affected you and also how the diagnosis has affected you.

Sally: It's just given me a way of understanding myself and why I can't concentrate sometimes and why at other times, although my head is racing, I can't seem to catch the right word. It's also good to feel like part of a group of others who are the same as me. They've prescribed some medication that works sometimes, but this angst keeps coming back and that's what I really want to talk about with you.

Therapist: Angst? What brings that about? What's it like?

Sally: It's my personal demon that keeps coming back. Things can be going okay and then it rears its ugly head and gets me thinking about the meaning of existence again. Is there a God? Why, if there is a God, is life so irrational so often? I want things fair and rational and in an ordered universe. I fight arbitrariness. I'm terrified of nonexistence. Depression is like a demon. It's tricky.

Therapist: You've talked about your profession being very orderly too. Does that give you another way to fight arbitrariness too? Perhaps you could, in fact, say more about what it is you mean by arbitrariness and what it is about it that bothers you so much?

Sally: I enjoy playing intellectual games, but sometimes I would rather be blissfully unaware. The greatest arbitrariness is death—the unknown and unknowable death. So, I have railed against arbitrariness in my work. I'm committed to that, but I'm left floundering in my own singular reality.

Clearly, these descriptions that Sally has provided are unique to her and are not always part of a diagnosis of depression. If the therapist and she had begun debating whether it is useful or not to diagnose, then they would not have been able to move on to rich descriptions of how she is attempting to make meaning of her life.

Deleuze and Parnet (2002) went on later to admit that although they problematize the way in which dualisms are set up in language, they recognized they were setting up a dualism in opposing the rhizome to the tree as a way of describing and considering the interconnectedness of thought and creativity. What they appeared to like about the grass metaphor also is how grass can grow between the cracks of paving stones and they suggested the importance of "lines of flight"; lines that will come out of the middle of spaces, lines that will crack open other ways of being and thinking, opening up spaces for creativity, movement, and growth. This provides a nice metaphor for how people who consult us may also be able to grow and flourish through the cracks and margins of mainstream pressures and expectations. In fact, in Chapter 7, in describing working with the language of addictions, Becky tells her story of having felt pressured for many years to label herself as an alcoholic, but how she has found it liberating within narrative conversations to realize she does not need to be trapped by that label, but can grow through and past it.

Although we had been thinking of what we observed as the circulation of language within therapeutic conversations, this metaphor of a rhizome perhaps is more clearly descriptive. Each word or concept used within a therapeutic conversation, whether spoken by the therapist or the people who have come to consult the therapist, is not a stand-alone word (like a tree) that has sprung forth solely from the speaker. Rather, if we attempted to follow that word or idea back, it would more likely show a crisscrossing and weblike tangle of strands leading back to multiple sites. Each word tentatively suggested by the therapist also would have multiple influences and paths. The therapeutic conversation does not unfold in a direct and linear manner, but rather creates itself from the intermingling of many voices, many ideas. It is useful to remember this in a therapeutic conversation, maintaining the space for the exploration of all these ideas rather than overly focusing on assessing and pinning down certain words as capturing certain truths about the people consulting us. These ideas about moving away from linear cause-and-effect relationships between things and the words used to describe them resonates with ideas we will discuss in the next chapter. There we will discuss moving away from linear images of time in order to open up further possibilities for people. Real life and the therapeutic process are far messier and more complex than the linear images we have often relied upon to attempt to describe our experiences.

THE ETHICS OF RECOGNIZING OTHERNESS

Wyschogrod (1989), discussing the impact of Levinas on Derrida, said that Levinas described violence in two different ways. Levinas talked not only of how violence is done to the individual when the individual self is lost or subsumed into totalization, but even more important for him, perhaps, was how violence is perpetrated when the self draws the other into "sameness."

White (1995a, 2007a) was concerned about moving away from totalizing and pathologizing accounts of people. He meant that when we focused on just one aspect of someone's life or one characteristic, there was a danger of totalizing that person based on that one characteristic or aspect. (If we think back to his work with children who had received a diagnosis of ADHD, he would be concerned that the label would totalize the children and they would only be thought of within those terms, rather than as individuals responding to the effects of high levels of energy and troubles concentrating.)

However, what Wyschogrod (1989) meant here about Levinas's worries about the self being lost in totalization is the violence that is perpetrated on an individual when he or she is understood to be just the same as everyone else and there is no room kept for difference. An example of this would be if I (LB) had imagined Becky as limited in her possibilities based on general knowledge and experiences with others who had struggled with addictions. There will be some similarities, but we must ensure that we maintain the space and time necessary for looking for and recognizing the differences also. Wyschogrod went on to suggest that Levinas was concerned by the violence that can be done by the group that does not recognize differences in individuals, but also by the violence done by individuals (perhaps therapists) assuming that the other individuals are the same as the therapists themselves. This is something that we raise with our students often. We believe that it is important to move beyond empathy (Duvall & Béres, 2007) because there is a danger in assuming that we understand someone else's experience because we can empathize, based on some similar experience perhaps, or maybe merely based on our attempts to put ourselves in the other's shoes. There is risk in this because the other person is different, is "other," and may not react in the same way we would have done.

Wyschogrod then went on to also suggest, "Representation conceals, while pretending to reveal, the seething turbulence of being" (1989, p. 191). This is very important. We may all think that as we discuss ideas and concerns in therapy, our words are representing what we mean, but they may be concealing just as much as they are revealing, due to how limiting and vulnerable they are. There is the risk of jumping to conclusions based on our initial surface understandings of the words being spoken by the people consulting us as represented in the above transcripts:

> For Derrida . . . each element acquires meaning only through a play of differences, the intersignificative relations to one another of elements which themselves lack self-present meaning. Each element is so interwoven with every other that it is constituted only by the traces within it of the other bits in the chain or system. There are no independent meanings but only traces of traces. (p. 192)

This would suggest that all meanings within language circulate, spiral, zigzag, and weave back and forth between various discourses. How can we escape from the dangers of limiting our understanding of one another and the ideas that are being discussed? How can we be mindful about language in such a way as to support and even encourage the movement from one territory to another, as discussed in relation to the rites of passage and migration of identity metaphors in Chapters 1 and 2?

LINES OF FLIGHT AND MIGRATION

May (2005), discussing Deleuze, said:

> How we think about our world and how we live it are entwined. Our ontology [our philosophy of being—definition added] and our practical engagements are woven together. This is true not only for the philosophers. It is true for everyone. A world that consists of particular things with strict borders that interact with other particular things (with their strict borders) according to particular natural laws will call us to certain kinds of living. For instance, if particular things are what they are and nothing else, then we will not waste our time imagining what else they might be or might become. (p. 72)

It is as if May and Deleuze are speaking directly to therapists. Why would we bother talking with people about their problems or listen to people's stories if these problems and the problem stories are the only way things could be? May (2005) wrote:

> If we abandon this way of thinking of our world, then alternate ways of living may appear to us. If things don't have strict borders of identity and if the relations among them are not reducible to natural laws, then we can no longer be sure of what a body is capable. Perhaps there is more going on in our world than is presented to us. (p. 72)

Deleuze and Parnet described three different types of lines, one of which May appears to be referring to as a border. They said that the first type of line is the one that is used to create various segments and set up dualisms. Their examples included male–female, white–black, childhood–adulthood, home–work. They also suggested that there is a more fluid or molecular type of line that segments but is less linear, is less constraining, and allows for more movement back and forth across categories. Finally, they suggested that there is a line of flight, which cuts across categories and involves movement and creation. They used a geographical metaphor to describe travel and movement, and in so doing, raised the examples of nomads, migrants, and the sedentary. Although the sedentary clearly stay in one place, they suggested that the nomads, despite their constant wanderings, also stay within certain geographic areas. The migrants are the ones who leave one territory for another. In discussing this line, however, they also said that "what matters on a path, what matters on a line, is always the middle, not the beginning or the end. We are always in the middle of a path, in the middle of something" (2002, p. 28). This is like the liminal phase in the rites of passage and migration of identity metaphors. How much of some conversations are actually only sedentary or nomadic? Do we sometimes merely wander like nomads, but stay within a previously known territory? How much more liberating for people if therapeutic conversations can contribute, through the careful use of languaging of ideas, to a true line of flight from one territory of being to another, moving from the preseparation phase, through the liminal phase, and on to the reincorporation phase (van Gennep, 1960).

As an example of attempting to move away from black-and-white, either-or thinking, the following segment of transcript comes from a 10th session, with a young man who initiated counseling because he said he had been struggling with what he had initially indicated he thought was a sex addiction.

Philip: I had a bad week a couple of weeks ago. I can go a week or two and start thinking that everything's okay and I've beaten it and then all of a sudden I'm getting out of my car at the massage parlor again. I convince myself it's okay 'cause they're in the business. I get so sick with myself, because I wasn't brought up to be like this.

Therapist: There are so many discourses about love and sex and intimacy. What has contributed to your understanding?

Philip: I was raised in quite a religious home and I was raised believing that sex is a natural and good thing, but should be shared in marriage, not like I've been doing it. But my beliefs and behaviors seem so far apart. I still believe this but it's difficult to believe it when it isn't the norm to believe this. I'm either a saint or a sinner. And, when I'm living like a saint I know I'm living a lie. When I pay for sex I pretend it's my first time. I pretend to be innocent.

Therapist: Can you unpack the pretending to be innocent, pretending it's your first time?

Philip: It's the excitement. Ten percent of the time I think it's okay to go and if it's just about getting rid of the desire it isn't too bad.

Therapist: So, 10% of the time you say you think it's okay. Does that mean it's something other than black or white at that time?

Philip: Yeah, this old friend from school told me he thought it was really good I was trying to change stuff about myself. I can be the equivalent of a functioning alcoholic. There can be joy-filled *ways* to enjoy sex. Not just one way.

Therapist: How is it different for you then, when you move away from that saint or sinner, black-or-white thinking?

Philip: Well, it's like I said, more ways open up. I can choose how to be. I've been all muddled about sex and intimacy and scared of intimacy, so I avoid sex with intimacy and figure I'll be okay, but I want people to know me. I don't want to be so secretive. I want to be more sensitive to the fact that people aren't defined by what they do.

This conversation was explicit in attempting to unravel the discourses and the influences on words and ideas that shape our identities and our possible identities. Philip had been stuck in a to-and-fro back and forth between attempting to be what he understood was a saint and then, if he couldn't hold himself to those particular standards, found himself behaving in a manner that he would then describe as sinning. It was important that the therapist not take up a position of making a judgment about Philip's behaviors but rather continue to be committed to assisting him in reflecting upon the effects of having set up this dualism and then opening up other possibilities for the movement of his identity into preferred territories. This is also an example of time ramifying for Philip, as options and choices open up. The idea of time ramifying will be discussed in the next chapter in regard to pivotal moments.

INTENTIONAL AND CREATIVE STAMMERING WITHIN LANGUAGE

Despite the fact that Deleuze and Parnet (2002) problematized the notion of dualisms, they also acknowledged how very difficult it is to move away from dualisms within language. They admitted that it is not possible to rid ourselves of dualisms totally, and so they suggested the creation of "stammering" to open up a space between dualisms that will push against mainstream uses of language. They went on to say:

> It is probable that a multiplicity is not defined by the number of its terms. We can always add a 3rd to 2, a 4th to 3, etc., we do not escape dualism in this way since the elements of any set whatever can be related to a succession of choices which are themselves binary. It is not the elements or the sets which define the multiplicity. What define it is the AND [capitals in original], as something which has its place between the elements or between the sets. AND, AND, AND—stammering. And even if there are only two terms, there is an AND between the two, which is neither the one nor the other nor the one which becomes the other, but which constitutes the multiplicity. This is why it is always possible to undo dualism from the inside by tracing the line of flight which passes between the two terms . . ., the narrow stream which belongs neither to the one nor to the other, but draws both into a . . . becoming. (pp. 34–35)

Deleuze and Parnet (2002) used this image of a narrow stream wearing away a path at another point in their writing. In following a different line of flight or a different path, we can make changes, go against the grain. Rajchman described Deleuze's use of the French word "*fuites*" as meaning "leaks" as well as "lines of flight" (2000, p. 12). The notion of these lines of flight also being like leaks fits well with the notion of a stream of water slowly wearing away a path or our understanding of boundaries, margins, and the seepage that can occur *through* as well as *across* boundaries. Fisher and Augusta-Scott (2003) were the first to highlight for me (LB) the problems inherent with the effects of dualisms in therapeutic interventions, particularly in relation to working with abuse in intimate relationships. In earlier approaches to working with men who had used abuse, there was a pressure to assess whether a man was abusive or not abusive, which relied on the dualism of abusive–not abusive. However, this did not fit well with the experiences of the female partners of men who had used abuse. They rarely saw their partners as completely abusive and, in fact, if a professional counselor were to assess the men as "abusers," then they ran the risk of totalizing them and leaving no room for them to be anything other than abusive. It is crucial that we contribute to multiplicities and the spaces between dualisms since they provide far more choices for those people who consult us.

These spaces between the dualisms open up the possibility for a line of flight from previously constraining labels that open up more than just two choices. The above transcript of Philip opening up a space for himself to have further choices than either saint or sinner was an example of moving beyond dualisms, while also discussing the multiple sites and discourses that contribute to our thinking of the extremes on this continuum.

Deleuze and Parnet (2002) appeared to be suggesting that the greatest creativity and movement occurs in the in-between, which allows us to escape from the constraints forced by dualisms and the lines that set up segments or sets. If the words and language we use in therapeutic conversations cannot escape the use of dualisms, difference (Derrida's *différance*), and contrasts, if there is slippage and we can never be sure that the word used is being understood the same way by each person in the conversation, then it is crucial to keep in mind the vulnerable nature of language, as Derrida points out. However, it may also be useful to take up some of Deleuze and Parnet's suggestions about how to use language in a different and more creative style. This style is a manner that will acknowledge these difficulties and limitations of language and can be more playful or creative in constructing a space for movement of understanding and identity. Deleuze and Parnet said:

> A style is managing to stammer in one's own language. It is difficult, because there has to be a need for such stammering. Not being a stammerer in one's speech, but being a stammerer of language itself. Being like a foreigner in one's own language, constructing a line of flight . . . we must be bilingual even in a single language, we must have a minor language inside our own language. . . . Proust says: "Great literature is written in a sort of foreign language. To each sentence we attach a meaning, or at any rate a mental image, which is often a mistranslation. But in great literature all our mistranslations result in beauty." (pp. 4–5)

Misunderstandings perhaps can move us on to further questions, further reflections, possibilities. and beauty within therapeutic conversations also. We do not need to be so worried about getting it right.

These ideas about stammering reminded me (LB) of when my son was very young, perhaps 4 years old. He had developed language skills at a very early age, speaking in full sentences prior to the age of 2, but at the age of 4 he developed a stammer, which he outgrew within a year. I have a clear memory of him during this time, trying to describe an event that he had experienced, when he suddenly stopped in frustration and said, "Oh, I don't have the word for it." His vocabulary had not quite caught up with his ability to think and experience and I wonder if this also contributed to his stammer at the time. Stammering is probably more representative of our thought process and the way in which our thoughts jump about, but there is often a narrative smoothing that occurs as we take our jumble of ideas and attempt to describe them in the spoken or written word. We've begun to realize the importance of keeping open a space for the exploration of thoughts, ideas, and feelings rather than too quickly moving to the smoothing out of these stammerings, hiccups, and bumps along the way.

Frank, in discussing the various types of storyline structure that people take up when describing their experiences with illness, described one as the "chaos narrative" (1995, p. 97). He pointed out how difficult and unsettling it can be to listen to someone who is describing their experiences this way because they use a "staccato pacing of words," using a list of events that don't always seem to follow a smooth narrative pattern. He quoted Nancy as using "and" often: "And if I'm trying to get dinner ready and I'm already feeling bad. . . . And then she's in front of the microwave and then she's in front of the silverware drawer. And—and if I send her out . . . And then . . ." (p. 99). Frank went on to say that the "chaos narrative is always beyond speech, and thus is always *lacking* [his emphasis] in speech" (p. 101), which is again consistent with Derrida's notion of lacking and difference in language. We are not suggesting that we should be encouraging people to develop chaos narratives because, as Frank points out, these are so very unsettling for the person who experiences herself within chaos and for the listener. However, it is possible for someone to move beyond the experience of chaos and then look back and discuss their experiences within a narrative order. Frank described Gilda Radner as having been able to summon up all her strength to write about the interruption that cancer created in her life, which she experienced as chaos at the time but was able to put into a coherent story through her commitment to writing about it. We wonder if there is a way to bring about stammering without bringing about chaos. If people come to counseling, they often do want to interrupt patterns in their life and develop new ways of being, and this can feel unsettling and disruptive at times. As we also think back to some of the videotaped sessions of Michael White that we have seen over the years, we wonder if his style, which at times appeared bumbling (although he was a brilliantly skilled therapist), was a commitment on his part to not too quickly engage in narrative smoothing that would have shut down further opportunities for reflection and unpacking of ideas. As he consulted in countries other than his native Australia, he would often use his accent and his unfamiliarity with the others' accents as a reason/excuse to say that he did not understand a word, that he had misheard, sometimes playfully, a word, and the conversation would be pushed on into new territories as he and the others looked for ways of understanding one another.

We have often said to students that in learning how to work in therapeutic conversations, it is very useful to reflect on "taken-for-granteds" and unpack what a person means by certain words. It is too easy, when both people in a conversation speak the same language (with the same accent), to jump to conclusions and assume that they understand one another. Clearly, they think, we both know what "sadness" means. We have pointed out that those people who are learning this work in a second language have an advantage in some ways because they are more likely to ask for clarification of meaning more often, and not assume they have understood fully. So, we were interested to read of Deleuze and Parnet's (2002) suggestion that even if we only speak one language, it may open up more possibilities within conversations if we approach speech and writing as if we are speaking in a second language, stammering and having to reflect further on each word, category, and concept. Bird also indicated that "the revisioning of the prescriptive conventions of the English language is often more difficult for the English speaker. In this instance the taken-for-granted usage of language needs to be brought into focus before it can be reconstituted into the relational" (2008, p. 4). She developed her own ideas and methods for practice—influenced by family therapists, feminists, and narrative therapy, through Michael White and David Epston—creating and using what she called "relational language-making" instead of using conventional language structures. In a recent graduate course I (LB) taught in narrative therapy, one of the students in the class was originally from Poland and English was not her first language. She added greatly to our in-class and online discussions, as well as practice interviews, as she looked up definitions of words we used and gently pushed us to be clearer about how we were using words, versus how they were defined and how they might be used in everyday conversations. These were excellent reminders for us all and necessary for us to keep in mind in all therapeutic conversations.

Chambon also wrote beautifully about the unsettling work of inquiry and the "destabilizing and productive language in Foucault's writings" (1999, p. 71). Her own use of language is evocative and I (LB) have often thought of this following description that she provided regarding Foucault's stance that transformative knowledge is disturbing: "It disturbs commonly acceptable ways of doing and disturbs the person implementing it. It ruffles the smoothness of our habits, rattles our certainties, disorganizes and reorganizes our understanding, shakes our complacency, unhinges us from secure moorings" (p. 53). This shifting and unsettling, unhinging and ruffling can all be part of a therapeutic conversation as people move from what has become familiar into the unknown and on into new possible territories. Regarding Foucault, Chambon noted that he often made use of poetic language in his writing, moving us away from the comfort of rational analysis. He mixed various stylistic genres and she said that his "playfulness with style is to be taken as a serious act, which means attending to language differently. He makes us aware that language shapes the reality we see" (p. 77). Chambon reminds us to be careful of academic and professional language that presents itself as fully objective, neutral, or transparent. There are effects on people based on the language we use, so it behooves us to use language carefully and ethically. We believe this is especially true in written reports that we may be required to produce about people within our work settings. Most organizations and professional licensing associations demand that we maintain written notes of our meetings with people, including the results of assessment tools perhaps, and the setting of goals. We are required to maintain progress reports and finally a list of outcomes in a closure summary. We strongly believe that these demands are not neutral but come from certain ways of thinking about the world and the people who request services. Although the codes of ethics of our licensing associations may demand that we maintain reports, we believe that it is just as important to consider our ethical relationships with the people of whom we are writing. Frank's (1995) ideas are significant for those of us working in the counseling and therapeutic worlds. Any profession needs to be aware of the impact of the power of language and knowledge (Foucault, 1980) and the effects of talking about and writing about people and their stories in such a way that privileges the professionals' accounts over the people who have come to consult them. Frank linked the notion of ethics into a sense of postmodern responsibility that harkens back to Levinas's thoughts on the "other" and charges us to move beyond rigid ideas about professional ethics, which limit our full ethical engagement with others.

We need to think through the long-lasting and real effects of how we describe people and their situations and make it clear that we are never able to make objective truth claims, but that we are stating observations and opinions.

PRIVILEGING THE VOICES, MEANING, AND STORIES OF THOSE IN THERAPEUTIC CONVERSATIONS

Deleuze and Parnet (2002) also pointed out their concerns regarding a form of violence they saw occurring within psychoanalysis. They wrote:

> If you go to be psychoanalysed, you believe that you will be able to talk. . . . But you don't have the least chance of talking. Psychoanalysis is entirely designed to prevent people from talking and to remove from them all conditions of true enunciation. We have formed a small working group for the following task: to read reports of psychoanalysts, especially of children; to stick exclusively to these reports and make two columns, on the left what the child said, according to the account itself, and on the right what the psychoanalyst heard and retained. . . . It's horrifying. . . . It's an amazing forcing, like a boxing match between categories which are too unequal. (p. 81)

What appears to have horrified Deleuze and Parnet the most is the number of times within the accounts it says that Melanie Kline "interpreted, *interpreted*, INTERPRETED" (their emphasis in the original). They went on to say: "It is said that there is no longer any of this today: significance has replaced interpretation, the signifier has replaced the signified, the analyst's silence has replaced the commentaries . . . we see no important changes" (2002, p. 81). These are necessary reminders to those of us involved in therapeutic conversations now, to be on guard against any temptation to slip into these types of conversations of which Deleuze and Parnet are horrified, or to re-create these types of interpretations in written assessments.

Sample of a Written Assessment

In working in counseling settings of all types, therapists are expected to maintain written assessments, ongoing progress reports, and, finally, closing summaries. We provide here a brief sample from an assessment document to demonstrate how important we believe it is to be precise in our writing about reporting what has been told to us. This is in order to ensure we do not slip into the types of writing where it can appear as though we are interpreting and making our own judgments. When we do enter our opinion, it is important to make it clear that it is our opinion and not a matter of absolute truth as reported by the professional. We believe being committed to this style of writing is based upon a relationship of ethics with those people consulting us, and also stands us all in better stead if reports are ever subpoenaed by court. (Of course, people are told in their first meetings that although all notes are kept confidential, there is always a chance that records could be subpoenaed.)

Initial Assessment Summary

Initial contact:

Joanne Smith telephoned to request an appointment for herself and Robert Johns. She indicated that they had been married for twenty years, but she was in the process of separating from him. She said that she was looking for some assistance in discussing the separation process with him and negotiating how to support their 16- and 18-year-old children through the process.

Background information:

Joanne reported in her first joint session with Robert that they have been married for twenty years and have two teenage children. She also indicated that she has been thinking about separating for almost two years and is quite frustrated by the fact that she does not believe Robert is taking her concerns seriously. Robert suggested he was taking her seriously but still hoped to convince her not to leave him and their children, Ricky, 18, and Melissa, 16.

They both agree that they are financially secure. It would appear, based on their descriptions, that although they will both experience a drop in their income as they separate, they will both continue to be able to live financially comfortably. Joanne reported in the session with Robert that she has found him overly controlling of her and of the children and although she would not describe any of his behaviors as abusive, she wants more of her own freedom now. She also indicated that she is worried about how controlling Robert can be of their children, stating that she felt Ricky was old enough to be allowed to make his own decisions about what to study at university, for example.

Initial assessment:

Robert reacted to Joanna's description of him being controlling by giving examples of how he had been absent from the family home for much of the time that he was working full-time and how he had attempted to fill that gap by trying to be helpful, connecting Ricky and Melissa to jobs and volunteer opportunities as young teens, as one example. They were able to have a conversation in session about the possibility that he may not have intended to be controlling, but how these behaviors could still be perceived as having been controlling. They both appeared to be very committed to what would be best for their children.

Based upon their descriptions of their relationship and how they interacted with each other in their session together, I also had the impression that Robert has not given up hope in his relationship. I am concerned that in his attempts to try to convince her to change her mind, he may present as controlling again. I checked privately with Joanna about any safety concerns and she says she has no concerns at this time.

We believe it is appropriate to include our opinions, but it is important to be clear that they are only our opinions and not a privileged interpretation. In order to be clear, we can indicate what those opinions are based upon and make sure also that we follow up in progress reports describing how our opinions have altered as aspects of the others' lives change.

Frank (1995) also described his concerns about how doctors have interacted with people, silencing their stories within modern times, but he noted changes occurring within postmodern times as people are taking back their voices and doctors are beginning to privilege people's stories to a greater extent. He went on:

> The story of illness that trumps all others in the modern period is the medical [or professional—our addition] narrative. The story told by the physician becomes the one against which others are ultimately judged true or false, useful or not.... What is relevant here is ... that a core social expectation of being sick is surrendering oneself to the care of a physician. I understand this obligation of seeking medical care as a *narrative surrender* [his emphasis] and mark it as the central moment in a modernist illness experience ... she agrees to tell her story in medical terms. "How are you?" now requires that personal feelings be contextualized with-

> in a secondhand medical report. The physician becomes the spokesperson for the disease, and the ill person's stories come to depend heavily on repetition of what the physician has said. (pp. 5–6)

That someone needs to surrender narratively to the professional does not sound consistent with Levinas's notions of ethics. Moving from the premodern world to the modern world and then to the postmodern world, Frank (1995) suggested, involves changes in the issue of voice. Frank argued that what is distinct in postmodern times is the manner in which people are feeling a need to find a voice again that appears to be their own voice.

> *Postmodern times are when the capacity for telling one's own story is reclaimed* [his emphasis]. . . . Voices tell stories. Stories are premodern. . . . In the modern period the medical story has pride of place. . . . The postmodern divide is crossed when people's own stories are no longer told as secondary but have their own primary importance. (p. 7)

CONCLUSION

In this chapter we have presented a description of how our interest in the circulation of language grew from our research and observations of many hours of therapeutic conversations. What has become clear to us is that it is crucial to realize, on the one hand, how incomplete language is for describing people's experiences and stories and, on the other hand, how complicated and full of multiple influences and possibilities each word is. It is important to take time with people, asking questions, reflecting with them about what they mean by certain words, since words only partially signal what is meant and also contain implications that are absent or lacking (like the example of complaining about "disrespect" while not being aware that this implies an understanding and prior experience of "respect").

We have also indicated the ethical responsibility of therapists to at times introduce language tentatively that will assist people consulting them in further understanding the choices available in their situations. This can also involve supporting concept development. It is as if someone is holding their hand out needing assistance. We want to temporarily lend our hand until they have a better understanding of their next steps.

It is important to consider carefully how to write about people and their stories. Although organizations and associations require that we keep written recordings of our work with people, we need to remember our ethical commitment to the individual and so be aware of the long-lasting effects of how we describe people in these contexts. These recordings clearly come from our conversations with people and it is also important that we keep in mind what is required of an ethical conversation with "others." This involves engaging with each person as an individual with differences from ourselves and others, but also demands of us that we are purposeful in our conversations. We do not want to inadvertently keep the person constrained to one territory (like the nomad, wandering, but never escaping through a line of flight to another territory). We need to find ways to be creative and playful with our use of language, reflecting always on the taken-for-granteds in order to open up new possible ways of understanding for those people who come and consult us.

A favorite example of one of Michael White's questions that moved beyond taken-for-granted assumptions was when he asked someone who was crying, not what she was feeling, but rather, "If you could take that tear and open it up, what would be inside it?" Answering about a feeling state might have led to her saying she was "sad," but then it would have also been important to have unpacked the word *sad*. Every single word we utter is packed full of many traces of other experiences and influences. In order to more ethically engage in a useful and hope-inducing conversation with people, we must remember this and foster an ability to examine those influences and make their own decisions about their preferences, values, and commitments.

Questions for Reflection

1. How can we become more reflective and aware of the "taken-for-granteds" within language?
2. How can we ensure we do not jump to conclusions and close down discussions? How can we become more playful and poetic with our use of language so as to open up more possibilities for those people consulting us?
3. What skills do you use to tentatively introduce new language into a therapeutic conversation?
4. How do you think the use of language relates to the issue of ethics?

5. How would you describe the difference between Levinas's description of an ethical engagement with an individual versus a professional code of ethics?
6. Is it possible to write professional recordings (assessments, progress reports, closure summaries) in such a manner that highlights the provisional quality of language and keeps open the space for the voices of each person involved in the therapeutic process?

CHAPTER 4

Pivotal Moments

In this chapter we will introduce the concepts of pivotal moments, katharsis, and transport. We will discuss how pivotal moments move people to reconnect with their hopes and renew a sense of intimacy with themselves and others. We will also discuss how the therapist posture contributes to this movement in ways that are revitalizing for both the people seeking consultation and the therapist providing the consultation. In addition, we will describe some philosophical ideas that have contributed to a paradigm shift in our understanding of time and the significance of pivotal moments within therapeutic conversations.

Pivotal moments, which are situated in the present moment of the therapeutic conversation, are perhaps the most fertile ground of change for people. Although the characteristics of pivotal moments are distinct, similar phenomena are also known as present moments or now moments. As Daniel Stern stated, "The only time of raw subjective reality, of phenomenal experience, is the present moment" (2004, p. 3). The previous 100-plus years of psychotherapy have surely been more preoccupied with the past and the future, providing much less consideration to these pivotal and present moments. Ironically, the therapeutic conversation can only transpire in the present. "How would psychotherapy and therapeutic change look if the present moment held centre stage?" (p. 3).

Although many of us have been trained to join with people in their therapeutic process, developing a relationship—which occurs in the present—more often we have spent our time diligently working in therapeutic models that overemphasize the past (i.e., former present moments) and the future (i.e., imagined present moments). Of course, the past does express itself in the present through memory, although our present condition powerfully affects how and what we remember. And although the future can hold anticipated and imagined present moments, indeed, this temporal state also can only be experienced in the present. Psychotherapy, through the medium of moment-to-moment, intersubjective dialogue, can only occur in the present. "Although memories are about the past and hopes are about the future, both are situated in the present and often tell us more about the present than they tell us about the past or future" (Duvall & Béres, 2007, p. 232).

Morson described ways of understanding the present within his description of the four diseases of the present, or "unwise ways of understanding one's moment in time" (1994, pp. 12–13). He offered two of these ways of understanding the present in the following manner:

> The first disease desiccates the present by placing all value on either the past or the future. Either the present is felt to be a mere continuation of a completed sequence or it is regarded as a needlessly prolonged transition to the time that really matters . . . crucial events are already over and the present becomes a sort of posthumous life. . . . The second disease, the isolated present, is the opposite of the first. Here the present is felt to be the only time that matters and the only time that is truly real. (pp. 12–13)

Morson pointed out this issue as a primary concern within psychotherapy. On one hand, lingering and remaining in the intersubjective present moment of the therapeutic conversation is crucial. At the same time, the purpose of accomplishing therapeutic change in the present is to help people prepare for actions and increased personal agency, which lies in the future.

Although it is crucial to focus on the present moment in the therapeutic conversation, it is also important to understand that all present moments are not equal. Some of these microspans of time are, in fact, *pivotal moments*, in which people experience realizations, katharsis, and transport (White, 2007a) as they are drawn toward strongly-held values and preferred ways of being in the world.

These pivotal moments carry with them significance of resonate meaning and potential for movement.

DEVELOPMENT OF OUR CURIOSITY IN PIVOTAL MOMENTS

In the early 1990s the faculty of Brief Therapy Training Centres-International (a division of the Hincks-Dellcrest Centre, Gail Appel Institute) had a growing concern that the therapeutic models with which we had been affiliated were, in fact, distracting us from engaging with a wide range of influences that could contribute to meaningful change with people. We experienced the therapeutic models as limiting and constraining. Ironically, in an effort to obtain "fidelity" to the models, we became overly focused on having people fit the models, rather than remaining sensitive to people's stories as they were articulated right in front of us. There were times when we had noticed that powerful responses in our work with people were not necessarily situated within our therapeutic orientations. We finally came to the conclusion that our adherence to the procedures and practices of these models was not only preventing us from engaging as well as we could in dialogue with people, but the practices were also eclipsing people's expressions of their stories. Once we were on to the importance of responding to people's stories, we became aware of the need to further engage with people through the moment-to-moment dialogue. Paré and Lysak referred to this issue as follows: "it is not the therapist expertise per se, but the failure to engage in a relationally responsive manner, that constrains the possibility of therapeutic dialogue" (2004, p. 60). As a result of this concern about our response-ability, we decided to temporarily step back from our immersion in therapeutic models, avoiding what we referred to as "schoolism," and reflect on our practice more purposefully. We were interested in studying our work with people with a phenomenological view, while remaining true to the guiding assumptions of postmodern therapy. The history of this transition is more fully described in Chapter 1.

As most therapeutic models had favored past or future orientations, we decided to rely on the people seeking consultation to orient the conversation and choose to speak about the past, the present, or the future.

We then organized and developed the advanced training and research project to address these concerns. Integrating training, research, and clinical practice within the project made it possible for us to develop a heuristic approach, employing trial-and-error practices, while constantly evaluating and adjusting our work with people.

The project operated within an overall backdrop of reflective practices, as fully described in the Introduction. Within this reflective context, Michael White spoke to developing a basic mistrust in our own work, questioning everything we do (Duvall & Young, 2009).

We watched countless hours of live therapy sessions from behind one-way mirrors. Two teams worked concurrently morning and afternoon. We also reviewed countless hours of videotapes of sessions, noting what stood out and what seemed to be contributing to therapeutic movement and preferred outcomes. We slowed the tapes down and studied segments of therapy sessions in minute detail, making possible the microanalysis of the dialogic process. This minute studying of the dialogue made it possible for us to link what we were doing to the quality of people's responses. We were able to track the step-by-step movement of the conversation, illustrating the work between the person seeking consultation and the therapist, as difference was introduced and incorporated. This movement that occurred during the consultations "is absolutely impossible for one person, but . . . becomes a reality for two" (Vygotsky, 1986, p. 256).

As we observed the dialogic phenomena, it was striking how many times people appeared to be moved (e.g., looked away, silently paused). Many times this visible shift was accompanied by some verbal expression that confirmed the shift.

Therapist: Paige, from what you are telling me, it sounds like you have been feeling despondent and "down in the dumps" for a number of years. Can you tell me about a time when things were different? A time when your life wasn't down in the dumps and you were more the person that you want to be?

Paige: You know (*pauses and gazes off to the right*), now that you mention it, there was a time when things were very different. (*Another pause.*) Whew! This takes me back to a time when I was about 17. Those were the days. I was actually very assertive and clear about what I wanted out of life at that time. I had good friends, I was in really good shape, and I was on a mission. It's like the penny just dropped. (*Metaphor that makes the strange and different familiar.*) I think I need to get back in touch with myself. How did I lose sight of this? That was one of the best times in my life. I can see it clearly as I think back. We used to meet at the drive-in hamburger place on Friday nights. We were really on top of our game. (*Rich with imagery and metaphor.*) You know, like we were unstoppable. We would all hang out and talk about what we really wanted out of life and what we would be doing when we're like 35.

This memory challenges Paige's assumptions about the way in which she is experiencing herself in her present life. A shift in her perspective occurs in which movement becomes possible.

Michael White described this movement as follows: "These epiphanies are in harmony with what is precious to people that's beautiful that they want to rush towards. It's not a task" (Duvall & Young, 2009, p. 18). People were able to produce these realizations and epiphanies partially due to our efforts at providing space through a slower conversational pace and a respect for silence. Once the pivotal moment occurred it was crucial that the therapist respond by acknowledging the epiphany, providing an audience to it. Michael White spoke to the sustainability of these epiphanies when he stated:

> What makes them stick is how they are responded to in the outside world. We need to talk about these. There might be a way to recruit an audience to these in a way that acknowledges these epiphanies. That acknowledgement is authenticating these epiphanies and helping them stick in these circumstances. We need to assist with this idea of stick-ability. (Duvall & Young, 2009, p. 18)

Therapist: (*Slows the pace down significantly.*) Paige, this moment seems important. Would it be useful to talk about this a bit?

Paige: Well, yeah . . . (*Long silent pause.*) . . . I think I just realized that I was "on track." I already was the person that I want to be now. I was inspired in those days. I want to be that person again!

Therapist: I really have to say, it's exciting watching you get in touch with this powerful memory of your former self. I'm curious about what it's like for you as you're experiencing this memory and reconnecting with yourself in this way.

Paige: When we first started talking today I was feeling totally lost at sea. I was really feeling like "what's the use?" I live a lackluster life and I'm not even sure of what I want for myself. Then, somehow I remembered, there was a time when things were different and I was feeling vital and inspired about my life.

These mutually influenced experiences were often energizing and inspiring for both the therapist and the family members. As people described realizations, aha moments, and epiphanies, therapists would acknowledge these responses, expressing curiosity and carefully questioning them about what they were experiencing during those pivotal moments. More often the conversations would shift and refocus on what people realized during the moment, what difference that made for their view of their situation, and what they were drawn toward as a result of the pivotal moment experience.

When we began the project, we viewed these in-the-moment expressions of movement as powerful, rare phenomena. We thought these arresting and pivotal moments were anomalies, occurring only in a small number of sessions. We continued to watch endless hours of videotapes of sessions, in an attempt to identify what was occurring in the conversation between the therapist and the family members that led up to these pivotal moments. By doing so, we were hoping to create similar conditions for further epiphanies.

Early on in this process of observing sessions to better understand the quality of conversations that made pivotal moments more possible, we noted some of the following characteristics:

- The conversation had a slower pace.
- The therapist was often "mindful" regarding his or her use of silence and time in the moment.
- There was a relational attunement among the therapist and family members whereby the therapist expressed interest and curiosity about multiple aspects of the person(s).
- There was a use of particular types of questions and metaphorical language that seemed to invite transportive phenomena.

Then we became aware that the more we were committed to noticing these moments, the more they occurred in almost all subsequent therapy sessions. I (JD) tentatively named these "pivotal moments," to capture the element of movement and change inherent in them. Hoyt (1995) at a similar time was also writing about creating pivotal moments in single-session therapies.

Ironically, this was a big pivotal moment for me (JD). As we were letting go of the influence of other therapy approaches in order to more clearly notice and observe what was occurring in therapy sessions, we became aware of shifts in our work. We started to think about how to, in a sense, stay out of people's way, while at the same time facilitating the therapeutic conversation, in order to make space for pivotal moments to occur.

People were forthcoming with feedback regarding the quality of the therapy they received. They were routinely invited to offer thorough feedback through every step of the therapeutic process, both during and after the sessions. Following each session people were asked to comment on what stood out the most for them. What was useful? What could we have done differently to improve their experience of therapy?

Consistently people commented that it was useful having the time to think about things differently (a shift occurring). They appreciated being asked questions that were somewhat different and even a bit difficult to answer, as this helped them think about their situation differently. They also expressed an increased sense of confidence and hopefulness as the therapist focused the conversation more on what was important for them to talk about. Although, people may not have yet "solved their problem," they often reported a sense of being "on track" and moving in a preferred direction. Overall, the average number of therapy sessions that people attended decreased as they became more in touch with a stronger sense of what was important to them. Their feedback and increased involvement was critical in the process of guiding us in the reshaping of our therapeutic approach.

Coincidently, this was the first year that I (JD) sponsored Michael White to provide a two-day workshop in Toronto. After years of family therapy and systemic training, his ideas about people and how people change were fresh and inspiring; they significantly influenced our thinking even further. His narrative therapy approach fit like a glove with the ideas and practices that we were currently developing in our project. We were inspired and prepared for the shift to narrative practices. We became interested in including Michael White's narrative ideas with the ideas developed from our own project, which included our study of pivotal moments. Michael was supportive of our intentions to include our own innovations into what is commonly understood as narrative practice.

WHAT ARE PIVOTAL MOMENTS?

Pivotal moments are measured units of experience that exist within the present moment of the therapeutic dialogue. Stern (2004) described pivotal moments as experiences originally lived. They are produced in the intersubjective exchanges within the dialogue as a response to reflecting on something that was said or done, either inside or outside the therapy session. These moments are considered "pivotal" because people undergo a shift in meaning during the experience. More often they view themselves, others, or their situation differently as a result of the experience, which opens a range of new possibilities for consideration.

The emergence of a pivotal moment occurs over a short span of time, occupying only a number of seconds. "The present moment lasts between 1 and 10 seconds, with an average duration of around three to four seconds" (Stern, 2004, p. 41). While they can contain powerful expressions and epiphanies, pivotal moments are also vulnerable and risk disappearing quickly if they go unnoticed and are not acknowledged. Ironically, as Daniel Stern described present moments, "they are hidden in full view" (p. 32). "It is too evident, like oxygen in the air we breathe" (p. 33). Pivotal moments turn up partially formed, as they pass through a therapy session in linear *chronos* (clock) time (which is primarily concerned with reaching the future). However, in order to respond firmly to pivotal moments, linear, *chronos* time must give way to subjective time. Linear time, which is a taken-for-granted understanding of time, leaves little space to linger and dwell in the subjective, directly lived experiences of pivotal moments. (Concepts of time and how it can be used to sustain the life of pivotal moments will be discussed fully later in this chapter.) Mindfulness practices may also assist a therapist in developing comfort with lingering within this subjective time and in staying fully present to the other (Béres, 2009).

In a sense pivotal moments are like ministories, that we experience *as they are being lived.* They provide a calling, an ambiguous journey, and invite a reincorporation of identity. Subjective time makes space for people to express their ministory, or narrative, as it is being lived and for others to witness and participate in it. These pivotal moments as ministories are not structured as a more traditional and linear understanding of narrative or story (i.e., events in a sequence over time that form a theme or plot). These stories are associational and are expressions of people's subjective, internal experience, and what William James (1981) referred to as the language of inner life and *stream of consciousness.* James referred to this type of consciousness as that of a bird alternately flying and perching. The evoked associations that people experience in the pivotal moments represent the perchings. During these times people may experience an increased sense of personal familiarity and intimacy, as they become more in touch with a sense of themselves that may have previously been lost or relegated to the shadows. These moments can also provide a foundation for people to relate more closely to others, as they are often drawn to highly resonate times and places in their backstory that are inhabited by significant others.

Therapist: Paige, can you tell me more about that time? Can you introduce me to your former self?

Paige: Well, I think I was more in touch with myself then. I was more genuinely who I really want to be. I wa's confident, but not arrogant. I had really strong connections with my friends. I think because I was more confident and sure of myself, I was able to relate to people more easily. I've become a bit reserved as I've become older. I think because I don't feel as confident about myself that I'm a bit reserved with my friends.

Another important phenomenon to consider as it relates to pivotal moments is the experience of katharsis. As Michael White (2007a) pointed out, it's important to understand the concept of *katharsis* as it relates to transport and as it is distinguished from the more commonly understood notion of *catharsis*:

> I spell this with a *k* to distinguish it from the contemporary notions of catharsis associated with metaphors of discharge, release, abreaction, and so on. By katharsis I am referring to what I understand to be a central classical understanding of this concept—katharsis as a phenomenon that one experiences in response to witnessing powerful expressions of life's dramas, a phenomenon particularly associated with one's response to the performance of Greek tragedy. According to this classical definition, an experience is kathartic if one is moved by it—moved not just in terms of having an emotional experience, but in terms of being transported to another place . . . the phenomenon of katharsis relates to specific expressions of life that strike a chord for us, that we are drawn to, that most capture our imagination, that fire our curiosity, and that provoke our fascination. (pp. 194–195)

As Michael White implied, katharsis provides the innermost energy of pivotal moments, inspiring people to associate to powerfully resonate themes, memories, and associations. As people begin to experience these pivotal moments, meaning is "in-formation," ambiguous, and more cryptic.

Therapist: Tell me more about how you were more in touch with yourself then. How did this contribute to a stronger connection with your friends?

Paige: (*Pauses again and gazes to the right.*) Well . . . I think I just realized that we knew how to live more in the moment. I actually enjoyed the life I was having at the time. I wasn't just thinking and planning about the life I might have some day. When I think about it, I don't really do much now. I just plan and prepare for the life I might have tomorrow. I sit in front of my computer or sit in mind-numbing, boring meetings all day. Back then, every day was packed with action. (*Looks at the floor and smiles.*) . . . You know I used to have this best friend, Fran. We were connected at the hip. We would nudge and egg each other on to do things and take risks all the time. That made every day an adventure. We still talk about once or twice a year. She's still the same ol' Fran. She's an anthropologist now and travels all over the world. When I think back to these times, it really puts me in touch with what I really want for myself.

Therapist: Paige, even as you're describing these time to me it seems more connected and energized. When you think back to the relationship you had with Fran during those times, what clues are you finding that you could import from the past into your relationships in the present? Would that be useful to continue to explore as you are revisiting these cherished times?

Paige: Actually, this is the most inspired and hopeful I've felt in a long time. I'm enjoying my trip down memory lane. Yes, let's keeping talking about this. Hey, you know what else I just realized?

Therapist: What's that?

Paige: I think it would be a really good idea to phone Fran when I get home. I could always count on her to nudge me.

HOW THERAPIST POSTURE CONTRIBUTES TO PIVOTAL MOMENTS

The therapist plays a significant role in both creating a context in which pivotal moments are more likely to occur and, then, helping to sustain them when they do. A number of choices are available to them when they take up a therapeutic posture. We will propose ideas and skills for therapists to consider when intending to engage in dialogue that inspires the generation of pivotal moments with people.

Welcoming and Inviting Attitude

The therapist adopts a welcoming attitude and an openness to hear the concerns that people bring to the therapeutic conversation. "Committing yourself to dialogue with people is more than just recognizing their inherent dignity and defending their rights; it's being willing to allow their voices to count as much as yours" (Frank, 2004, p. 44). In doing so, the ideas, interpretations, expressions, and voices of people who consult us are privileged. The therapist invites dialogue and develops a shared sense of purpose and intention. There is a sense of "we are in this together," give-and-take. However, as Arthur Frank stated, "no reciprocity is required, for indeed none may be possible" (p. 2). He described this as "an act of generosity. . . a promise of consolation. . . . Generosity implies the host's trust in the renewable capacity to give; the generous person feels no need to measure what is given against what is received" (p. 2). This idea is similar to those expressed in the previous chapter regarding ethics. The therapist removes herself from center stage, acknowledges the distress the person is experiencing, and offers a promise of support. The clear expression of support from the therapist is a critical initial step when inviting people to express their stories.

Lingering in the Present Moment

There is significant value in lingering in the present moment. The longer the therapist can stay with the present moment and explore it, the more pathways will emerge. Engaging with *people* in the present moment with *presence* (Morson, 1994) requires a sensitive attunement to their unique beliefs, preferences, and language. The therapist cannot predict the direction of the therapeutic conversation. She builds on each facet of the dialogue as it is told, gradually scaffolding the story into focus. The scaffolding inherent in these conversations allows for associations with preferred identities that would not be possible otherwise. As it is told, the words and phrases used by people are precisely noted and routinely presented back to them through reflecting summaries. (This idea of noting people's words and phrases precisely is discussed fully in Chapter 3.) As stated in Chapter 2, deconstructive listening and deconstructive questions are used to elicit the person's story. "The process of constructing preferred stories almost always goes hand in hand with the process of deconstruction" (Freedman & Combs, 1996, p. 89).

Ambiguity, Tentativeness, and Curiosity in Dialogue

During this detailed scaffolding conversation the therapist conveys curiosity and interest and is open to surprise as the dialogue unfolds. In adopting this posture the therapist develops a tolerance for ambiguity, a respect for mystery, and a willingness to doubt, risk, and be humble. She listens obsessively, paying close attention to what people are saying, while avoiding inference and interpretation. She responds tentatively, often with partially formed sentences, leaving spaces for people to reflect on emerging possibilities. The curiosity, tolerance for ambiguity, and tentative responses aren't just inherent traits that the therapist possesses, but skills that are learned and developed. This is also discussed in Chapter 3 as we suggest the need for therapists to use language creatively. These skills make it possible for therapists to focus on people's hopes, desires, meanings, and attributions, rather than merely facts and information. This subjunctive dialogic experience brings forth involvement, evokes resonance, and creates an atmosphere for the occurrence of pivotal moments.

Supporting Pivotal Moments and Developing a Receiving Context

The therapist's attunement not only creates an atmosphere in which pivotal moments can occur, it also makes it possible for the therapist to pay attention, noticing, acknowledging, and supporting them when they do. Pivotal moments emerge through the details of stories as they are expressed. The telling and retelling of epiphanies and realizations holds them in the direct experience of the present. We assist people in giving voice to realizations, which helps them face up to previous notions of being mere passive recipients of life's events. We ask questions that generate experience. These questions invite people to speculate about their realizations and ideas. As people's realizations are supported, a receiving context is developed and they are able to come up with a plan for some initiative, or some step that they can take. The realization or epiphany becomes concept and theme oriented through the therapeutic dialogue and rich story development.

THOUGHTS ON TIME AND ITS RELATION TO MOMENTS IN THERAPY

Since a pivotal moment occurs within a moment in time, we began to realize that we could not think about pivotal moments without also thinking about our taken-for-granted assumptions about time. This is an aspect of critical reflective practice, contemplating how mainstream conceptions (within this chapter, mainstream conceptions of time) might affect our thoughts on what is possible in therapeutic conversations.

Morson (1994) pointed out:

> For better or worse, people tend to think of time in spatial terms. We speak of passing through it, of its flow, and of its vast expanse. Events are said to happen at specific points in it. These metaphors are so natural, so commonplace, and so widely shared among languages that we often do not reflect upon the fact that they *are* metaphors. (p. 17)

Hoffman (2009) commented that she has noticed different cultures (countries in Eastern Europe following World War II, as well as the United States and England more recently) talking about and experiencing time differently from one another. She suggested that for people in the United States "time is money," and they experience time moving quickly as they feel pressured to make the most productive use of every moment. On the other hand, in England employees attempt to show their employers that they do not need to work so very hard, but that they are rather naturally able to work efficiently without the flurry of busyness. Morson (1994) agreed that different cultures may think of time in different ways, saying:

> Time may be thought of as a cycle, which repeats as the seasons do; thus the past may be repeated as ritual, or people may be chained to the wheel of fate. This picture is usually opposed to that of time as a directional arrow. In the latter case, time is infinite in both directions. It never repeats and regret is irremediable. Some models are linear—a time line—and may allow for no alternative paths. Others

> have time ramify, with each moment having many possible future directions, depending on unforeseen contingencies and on countless free choices. Although in such models only one possibility will be actualized in any future instant, *many could be* [our emphasis]. (p. 18)

What Morson was highlighting was that our taken-for-granted conceptions and metaphors of time can affect how we think about life, and of course our beliefs about life can affect how we think of time. For instance, he went on to talk about the relationship between the linear model of time and beliefs in determinism, predetermination, and even different ideas about creativity. If we are more willing to adopt the model of time as ramifying and believe that in each moment there are multiple possibilities, then the significance of choice, and specifically choice in each moment, is opened up as a consideration. A pivotal moment in therapy makes the most sense within this second notion of time, as a moment where shifts in awareness bring about recognition of choices and personal agency becomes more apparent.

For example, Paula had been referred to counseling because she was experiencing grief following her mother's death six months earlier, combined with stress regarding her commitment to "be there for her dad." She had been married for little over a year. At the end of her first session she had expressed relief that the therapist had not told her that she had to stop spending time with her father, but she continued to experience stress as she juggled all the demands in her life.

Paula: I dreamt of my mother almost every night last week. I wake up missing her and thinking what big shoes she left for me to fill. My dad is lost and I feel I really have to be there for him as much as I can.

Therapist: When you say that your mother left these big shoes for you to fill, what do you mean by that?

Paula: She was always there for everyone. She was a wonderful mother. She worked but she also was always there for me and my sisters. She baked and made toys and played with us. She looked after Dad too. He doesn't seem to know how to look after himself now.

Therapist: Have you been thinking that this was how you were raised then? To be like her and take care of others?

Paula: Exactly, but she also asked me on her deathbed to look after Dad, and I have to.

Therapist: So that sounds like it is really important to you, to fill those shoes and do as she asked as well. Have I got that right?

Paula: Mmm hmm.

Therapist: How's that going? How does that affect you and affect you and Josh?

Paula: Well, we're hardly ever alone and almost never at home. Dad calls and he sounds so lonely, so we go over. I can't seem to say no . . . to anyone.

Therapist: Is that good, or not so good, or a bit of both?

Paula: Well, it feels like the right thing to do, but I get worn out and then I got so worn out that I was really sick and I couldn't be there for anyone for that one week a while back.

Therapist: And what happened then, when you were sort of forced not to look after anyone other than yourself because you were sick?

Paula: I guess I realized that I don't make everybody's world go around. Actually, it's really freeing to realize. My mother did everything for everyone—maybe she liked being needed, and maybe I like being needed, but you know, the world didn't end, it kept on spinning.

Therapist: So, if you could hold on to that realization, what difference would that make?

Paula: I could start focusing on my dreams. Josh and I could spend more time alone. I could find some balance.

Whereas Paula had described her situation as if she felt she was in a particular storyline that was unfolding in a linear manner, having been raised to be a certain way, she came to a point of realizing that she did not have to remain within that predetermined way of being. She experienced a shift in her thinking and realized she could interact with others differently. She had choice.

Morson drew upon Bakhtin, saying he was concerned by how dominant cultural models of time closed down time "by thinking away its processual nature. In so doing, they leave no space for creativity or choice" (1994, p. 21). Bakhtin called this type of thinking "theoretism." His descriptions of this way of thinking are chillingly similar to how many therapists have previously been taught to conduct assessments. What various schools within theoretism have in common, Bakhtin would suggest, is the belief that any phenomenon, or problem, can be explained by finding the causal rules. So, a theoretist would examine human action and attempt to find all that is generalizable, thus creating rules or laws.

Morson pointed out that the problem with these perhaps well-meaning theoretists is that their view "leaves time essentially closed" (p. 21). He went on to explain the problem with thinking of time in this closed fashion:

> There are no real alternatives, for everything has already been given in the rules or chains of causes. People act out of patterns or do what the laws have prescribed. . . . What people do not do is genuinely choose, even though they might imagine otherwise. . . . It was evident to Bakhtin that with the loss of choice, ethics also suffers, for ethics depends on the sense that what I do at this moment truly matters. (p. 21)

In noticing and working with pivotal moments within therapeutic conversations, we are truly noticing an event in which there are shifts in meaning; the path that perhaps previously would have been seen as naturally unfolding to a previously determined end seems to open up to a range of possibilities because of some sort of change that occurs within the person (thinking, feeling, privileging of values) in that moment. This is an example of what Morson described as time ramifying, as a variety of possible paths are opened up and choices become available. What people do and choose does matter if there are a variety of possible paths and outcomes. As we've already described, however, it is not as though every moment in a therapeutic conversation is pivotal—we've attempted to describe what we noticed and what stood out to us as defining a moment as pivotal. This may share something in common with what Bakhtin called "eventness." Bakhtin's ideas about eventness have been fully described in Chapter 2 as we have described the significance of events to the development of a storyline. His ideas are also useful when considering the impact of conceptions of time to pivotal moments: "Time ramifies and its possibilities multiply; each realized possibility opens new choices while precluding others that once could have been made. . . . Choice is *momentous*. It involves *presentness* [emphasis in the original]" (1994, p. 22).

This certainly sounds as though it shares something in common with what we were noticing as pivotal moments. There is something out of the ordinary about them, there is a sense of truly being "present" or "in the moment," and for those people coming to engage in therapeutic conversations there is perhaps the sense of relief that they are not stuck in the problem story, which would unfold in a linear manner, but that they have choices and agency. This was certainly true for Paula, as shown in the above transcript. I (LB) also remember working with Vivian, who had described having experienced childhood sexual abuse, but also had reported having been assaulted by two previous partners. At one point she asked with frustration, "What's the problem? Do I have 'V' for victim stamped on my head? How do these guys pick me out?" We worked together for a few years as she moved away from the "victim" storyline. She certainly experienced a great sense of relief from realizing she was not stuck in that victim storyline, which would have continued to unfold with her being victimized. She chose another path and applied for and received victim's compensation, enabling her to move out of the city and to buy a small home in the country in order to start a brand-new life. Believing that time ramifies and that choices open up makes very real differences in people's lives.

White (1994) spoke about the importance of filling the agentive gap that seems part of some people's stories at times. Some people's descriptions of events over time suggest that they have not experienced a sense of agency but have been more victims of circumstances. Even if those circumstances were judged as good, the people might have trouble acknowledging any role in their good fortune. The story might be told as having just been in the right place at the right time or having been lucky. White suggested that it was useful to ask how the people had been able to notice the opportunities and take advantage of them, to assist them in beginning to recognize their agency. Agency and choice are surely important within a therapeutic setting or else there really is no point in having a conversation. What can be done if there is no perceived agency and no perceived choice and someone is trapped within a determined or predetermined plot?

Morson's work (1994) assisted greatly in our critical reflection on time, bringing about a pivotal moment for us; we have experienced a paradigm shift regarding time. We had not previously considered how important our concept of time is on how we think of ourselves, others, and what is possible. Morson described foreshadowing, backshadowing, and sideshadowing, particularly drawing upon the way in which Russian novelists have thought through notions of time, and the consequences on people of thinking of time in certain ways, in their writing.

Morson (1994) began his discussion of various ways of thinking about time by describing different manners of considering foreshadowing. What they all share in common, despite their differences, is the lack or severe limitation of agency and choice and the implication of determinism. One way of representing time generally, as we have already indicated, is as one straight line with an arrow at one end, suggesting that time is like a line unfolding. One event brings about another and then another (determinism). Morson pointed out the questions that this notion of time raises in terms of creativity. How can we be considered truly creative if there is only one path ahead of us and it unfolds out in front of us like this? It would imply that we just discover rather than create.

> Determinists and fatalists often argue that even though people may sense themselves as free, these sensations themselves are entirely controlled by unseen forces; no matter how much people might imagine they have alternatives, their choices are, in principle, as predictable as so many entries in a logarithmic table. (p. 43)

Some people request counseling, suggesting they believe they are experiencing negative effects from childhood, as if these current effects are a natural consequence of these past experiences. This approach to considering causes of problems would depend on a notion of time unfolding in a determined manner. Ironically, this notion of time would also limit agency and possibilities for the future. The person would be stuck in the predetermined unfolding story, whereas notions of sideshadowing and time ramifying open up the possibility of multiple storylines and of choice.

Morson went on to say that the time line arrow can point in one direction, with events unfolding in a determined manner, with no alternative paths, or can be drawn in a straight line, but in the other direction. Everything that is going to happen is fated to happen and those events can trigger warning signals or events that foreshadow what will happen. Then he added in another image, which he called "fate or destiny as a vortex" (1994, p. 65). In this image there is still movement from one moment in time and place to another destined end, but there are several possible paths to that same end. "Destiny or fate specifies the end point, not the intermediate ones" (p. 65). Whereas the first two representations reduce a person's ability to take responsibility and make choices, here a person has multiple paths to choose but will be pulled into the vortex of that final predetermined endpoint. The classic story of Oedipus is used to explain this last example. An omen foreshadows that he is doomed to kill his father and marry his mother, and so it is decided he should be killed as a child in order to make sure this will never happen. But it is impossible to outwit fate, and Oedipus survives and, having never met his parents, as an adult kills the person he did know was his father and marries the person he did not know was his mother.

However, what is most interesting and useful to assisting us in understanding our experiences with pivotal moments, and our interest in ethics as discussed in Chapter 3 regarding the circulation of language, is Morson's (1994) descriptions of sideshadowing.

Morson began his description of sideshadowing by reiterating that foreshadowing "robs a present moment of its presentness. As we have seen, foreshadowing lifts the veil on a future that has already been determined and inscribed. . . . Wisdom in such a world consists in the appreciation of inevitability" (1994, p. 117). Time is closed if you believe in foreshadowing. Morson then went on to say that authors like Dostoyevsky and Tolstoy, on the other hand, believed time to be genuinely open and so had to invent ways of telling and writing a story that would not rely on literary foreshadowing techniques. Morson said that in attempting to represent time as open, they had to make use of the device of sideshadowing:

> Sideshadowing conveys the sense that actual events might just as well not have happened. In an open universe, the illusion is inevitability itself. Alternatives always abound, and, more often than not, what exists need not have existed. *Something else* [emphasis in original] was possible. . . . Instead of casting a foreshadow from the future, it casts a shadow "from the side," that is from the other possibilities. Along with an event we see the alternative; with each present, another possible present. Sideshadows conjure the ghostly presence of might-have-beens or might-bes. (p. 118)

Prior to taking up a full-time academic position I (LB) worked for many years with adults who had experienced childhood sexual abuse. I was often asked, during the time that this was my main work, how I could manage to hear these painful and traumatic stories over and over again. From early on in my work I have been directly influenced by narrative ways of thinking and so I thought of there being much more to each person and each story than just the painful events of abuse. This not only protected me from experiencing secondary or vicarious trauma but also kept me hopeful that each person would also be able to locate and string together events that were outside of the story of abuse or victimhood, that might have more to do with survival, or might have something to do with another plot altogether. If I had not had the experience of witnessing people moving from problem storylines of abuse to alternative stories, then I think I would have been more vulnerable to burnout and it would have been far more difficult to have done this work. (This is consistent with comments Michael White [2006a] made about his belief that working from a narrative perspective protected him and could protect others from vicarious trauma.) But as I read Morson, I realized that also believing in a field of possibilities for every person, rather than believing that they were each doomed because of their past, or predestined in some way, implied that I also was able to maintain an open conception of time. "Sideshadowing relies on a concept of time as a *field of possibilities* [emphasis in original]" (1994, p. 119).

An open concept of time, allowing for time ramifying, cannot be drawn as a straight line because at each moment choices are possible and action could take off in multiple different directions. So this opens up possibilities for the present and for the future, but interestingly enough it also opens up other ways of looking at the past, which are also consistent with narrative practices. Morson (1994) said:

> The actual is therefore understood as just another possibility that somehow came to pass. It was perhaps not entirely accidental, but it came without guarantees. . . . Sideshadowing therefore counters our tendency to view current events as the inevitable products of the past. Instead, it invites us to inquire into the other possible presents that might have been and to imagine a quite different course of events. *If only* [emphasis in original] that chance incident had not happened, if only a different choice had been made, . . . what would have happened then? Sideshadowing constantly prompts questions of this sort. . . . In permitting us to catch a glimpse of unrealized but realizable possibilities sideshadowing demonstrates that our tendency to trace straight lines of causality . . . oversimplifies events, which always allow for many possible stories. . . . What happened did not have to happen, and whatever exists, including ourselves, might not have existed. Sideshadowing therefore induces a kind of temporally based humility. (pp. 118–119)

It is interesting that this above quote from Morson fits closely with descriptions of how previously unstoried events (or possible imagined events) in someone's life can be put within a storyline structure. Once an alternative storyline has been developed, people can then imagine multiple possibilities opening up into the future. This may bring about what we noticed as being a pivotal moment. What is also interesting is that as Morson described this further, his ideas about open time and sideshadowing began to also fit with some of Derrida's notions of *différance*. Morson said, "It is as if one possibility out of many became actual but carried another as a sort of recessive gene . . . a present somehow grows partly out of an unactualized as well as an actualized past" (1994, p. 120). This suggests again the need to be careful with how we use language, how we speak of events, so that the space is kept open for what is implied but not fully present, for the shadows and the cinders (as discussed in the previous chapter).

The following transcript from a third session offers an example of how even a brief acknowledgment of previous possible storylines (sideshadowing) allows for time to ramify as choices become more available. Annie had been referred to counseling due to overwhelming feelings of anxiety, having recently finished a contract position and therefore being between jobs. She also told the therapist that she had been diagnosed with attention deficit disorder (ADD) as a small child, but her parents had not told her about this diagnosis until she was a teen. As a young woman, finding herself unemployed, she initially wondered whether her current difficulties were related to ADD.

Therapist: Why do you think your parents didn't tell you about this diagnosis at the time?

Annie: Well, we've talked about it since and they were really aware of the possible negative reactions I could have had from people in the school system. Some people would've treated me like I was stupid or slow, but they helped me, when they told me later, see it more as a gift. I had this energy and creativity.

Therapist: So, it's kind of like there were some possible different paths that you might have ended up following. Do you think if they had told you, and, um, if all your teachers had known, you might have felt differently about yourself or ended up having more difficulties in school?

Annie: Exactly. But as it was, like I said, I used my energy as a gift. I was great at sports. I was creative. That could have been all stifled. I might have dropped out. You know, that's why I think I might be really good at working with kids. I could help kids who think they're stupid.

Therapist: So if you think of this energy you have now as a gift instead of a problem, what difference might that make? What might that encourage you to do?

Annie: Instead of thinking I'm a loser for not having a job right now, I'll see this as an opportunity. I'll drop off my CV next week at a whole bunch of places. I'm not stuck. And, in the meantime, I can hang out with my family more. This does not have to be a bad thing.

CONCLUSION

In this chapter we have described how our interest in pivotal moments began in reflecting upon our therapeutic conversations with people. We have described a pivotal moment as being a short duration of time in a conversation where a shift in understanding occurs in a manner that can be experienced as quite startling and surprising to the person, like an aha moment. A pivotal moment may evoke a sense of katharsis as people experience transport through association with a preferred sense of "self" located in another time and place. This can open up possibilities and choices regarding how to respond to situations and act in the future.

We went on to discuss the skills that a therapist can practice that increase the likelihood of a pivotal moment occurring and increase the chances of the therapist noticing that a pivotal moment is occurring. It is necessary to acknowledge pivotal moments as they occur and provide sufficient time to unpack them to ensure their sustainability within the therapeutic conversation so that their significance is highlighted and supported.

Finally, we discussed some philosophical conceptions of time that are significant to how we approach and respond to people's stories and the therapeutic conversation. We stressed the importance of moving away from mainstream conceptions of time as unfolding in a straight line, because this could have the effect of limiting people's agency and choice. We suggested that in order to ethically engage in a purposeful conversation that opens up possibilities for a person, we need to hold on to the notion of time ramifying, since this concept of time allows people to make choices in each moment of their lives. Their lives are not predetermined and they are not caught in a linear cause-and-effect storyline. As therapists we are not merely helping people manage their lot in life, but rather we are assisting them to step outside of mainstream discourses and constraints and make freewill choices about how to live.

Questions for Reflection

1. Are you able to remember any aha moments that you have experienced in the past? Can you remember what these were like and how they brought about shifts in your thinking?
2. Thinking back now, how would you describe how you have previously thought of time? Have you found it difficult, easy, exciting (or some other word) to think about conceptions of time? Does it feel like being pushed to think about the air we breathe?
3. What are your thoughts on predeterminism, determinism, and fate? Do these affect your thoughts and ways of working with people?
4. How able are you to be truly present to another person, and not distracted by your own thoughts and reactions ("I wonder what I'll eat for dinner?" "What should I ask next?")? Do you think that practicing mindfulness techniques might assist you in developing skills of being present?

PART 2

Extending Learning: From Theory to Practice

CHAPTER 5

When All the Time You Have Is Now: Re-Visiting Practices and Narrative Therapy in a Walk-In Clinic

The purpose of this chapter is to introduce the use of narrative ideas and practices within a walk-in therapy clinic environment.[1] The walk-in therapy clinic is a unique way of offering therapeutic conversation opportunities to children, youths, and their families that is truly client centered, as it is there for people to use when they choose, with no more required than to walk in. In addition to briefly explaining the processes of this relatively unusual service, I will bring together many key aspects of narrative practice, clearly demonstrating their influence in the work in the clinic. Through stories and actual transcripts from the walk-in clinic, I will outline and demonstrate ways of thinking and practices that create therapeutic conversations that are not rushed, are slow paced and deeply meaningful, and are informed by a narrative "posture." These examples further highlight the ideas discussed in the chapters regarding the circulation of language and pivotal moments. This chapter expands on the work of the re-

1. This chapter was written by Karen Young.

search team described in the Introduction of this book by including comments and reflections from clients about what was meaningful and useful in sessions at the walk-in clinic, bringing forward information that allows for reflection on practice. This chapter introduces "brief narrative" as developed by a narrative therapist within the context of a walk-in therapy clinic.

THE WALK-IN CLINIC

Walk-in therapy clinics are a relatively new phenomenon in clinical service delivery (Bobele, Servin-Guerrero Lopez, Scamardo, & Solorzano, 2008; Harper-Jaques, McElheran, Slive, & Leahey, 2008; Miller & Slive, 2004; Slive, McElheran, & Lawson, 2008; Young, 2008; Young, Dick, Herring, & Lee, 2008), the first referenced clinic being in Minneapolis in 1969, which was the only known walk-in clinic until 1990 when Eastside Family Centre began a walk-in clinic (Slive et al., 2008). Since 2001, ROCK (Reach Out Centre for Kids) has opened the doors of three walk-in clinic sites (Young et al., 2008). Each site has one 8-hour day a week designated to walk-in, thereby offering the communities an opportunity for immediate access to a single session of therapy at times when people are most in need. The clinics function as the "front door" to ROCK's services, eliminating the traditional telephone intake and instead inviting people to attend the clinics. Although people can use the clinics more than once, approximately half of the people do not need any further services. This provides families with help when needed and reduces referrals into further services, thereby reducing waiting lists.

In each geographic site there is a range of three to six staff working at the walk-in clinics each week, usually with a number of students and therapists-in-training also assisting. There is a supervisor available for consultation and a receptionist in each site. When people arrive, they are given questionnaires that were designed in ways that reflect important brief-therapy concepts (DeJong & Insoo, 1998; DeJong & Miller, 1995; Friedman, 1994; Rosenbaum, Hoyt, & Talmon, 1990; Walter & Peller, 1994) and narrative therapy concepts (Epston, 2003, 2009a). These presession questionnaires (see Young et al., 2008) set the stage for conversations that strive to understand the problem and to find hope, new ideas, and knowledges about how to proceed. They help people to shift into paying attention to their abilities, skills, and accomplishments, and how to use these in relation to the current problem they are experiencing (Epston, 2003, 2009a). After the questionnaires are completed the receptionist brings them to an available therapist who then sees the person/family for a session that usually lasts about 90 minutes.

Therapists work alone some of the time, but more often they have a cotherapist or sometimes an outsider witnessing group (White, 2000). During the session the therapist takes notes in an open and transparent way onto a summary report form that is photocopied and given to the family at the end. This method of documentation was inspired by Michael White's style of note taking as discussed in Chapter 3 as "acting like a scribe." Prior to leaving the walk-in, people are given an evaluation form and asked to complete it and leave it with the receptionist.[2]

Both time limitations and high numbers of people at the clinic can create a risk for rushed and "thin" therapy conversations. The terms *thin description* and *thick description* are borrowed from cultural anthropologist Clifford Geertz (1973). A "thick description is one that is inscribed with . . . meanings" and finds linkages between "the stories of people's lives and their cherished values, beliefs, purposes, desires, commitments, and so on" (White, 1997, pp. 15–16). These descriptions are generated through eliciting people's stories in ways that facilitate a "double-storied telling" and are achieved by listening in ways that White termed "doubly listening" (2004, p. 53; also see Chapter 2). A thin conversation lacks detail and rich meaning. I have found that narrative ideas and practices are an antidote to the risk of thin conversation. They assist me to bring people's stories to the foreground and to work with them in ways that create possibility. The use of narrative therapy in a walk-in clinic environment is unique (Young, 2006; Young, 2008; Young et al., 2008), although White wrote, "The distance that can be traveled in one therapeutic conversation from the starting point . . . to destinations in new territories of life and identity is often truly remarkable"

2. The details of the walk-in clinic process and paperwork have been published in two papers:

Young, K. (2008). Narrative practice at a walk-in therapy clinic: Developing children's worry wisdom. *Journal of Systemic Therapies, 27*(4), 54–74.

Young, K., Dick, M., Herring, K., & Lee, J. (2008). From waiting lists to walk-in: Stories from a walk-in therapy clinic. *Journal of Systemic Therapies, 27*(4), 23–39.

(2007a, p. 250). He also wrote, "I do believe that narrative conversations . . . can play a significant role in such outcomes, even when these conversations are restricted to a single consultation" (p. 260).

Narrative ways of working lend themselves to "brief but deep"—deep not referring to deep assessment and information gathering but referring to deeply meaningful conversations that are likely to be sustaining of new ideas, conclusions, visions, and hopes. As suggested in Chapter 2, these are conversations that are guided by a storied approach to therapy, departing from information seeking to establish truth and instead engaging in a meaning-making exercise. I have been developing a narrative way of working in a very time limited setting by standing within the ways of thinking and being that are referred to in this book as a narrative "posture" (Young, 2008) and maintaining a commitment to strive for rich conversations. Over time I have come to believe in slowing down to move to new places more quickly. As discussed in Chapter 3, I believe it is important for therapists to slow down enough to listen for "lines of flight," traces of the absent but implicit, and to zigzag and weave back and forth among various possible meanings. This listening and the questions that arise from this approach assist the conversation to move into new territories or places. This creates a journey as suggested in Chapter 2.

This idea of moving to new places relates to the concept of "katharsis" as discussed by Michael White (2004) and also explained in Chapter 4. White explained that classical understandings of katharsis are linked to a view of:

> the performance moving the audience to another place in their lives . . . to become other than who they were at the outset of the performance . . . [to] think differently about their life . . . a new perspective on their personal history . . . [to] become newly engaged with certain precious values and beliefs, or [have] new ideas about how they might proceed in life. (p. 52)

It is this sort of "movement to new place" or transport (White, 2007a) to which narrative practice, even within brief contexts, is oriented. Within the walk-in therapy session I am presented with the current telling of a story by the person(s) present and must act in response to this story in a way that creates a multiplicity of possibilities (see Chapter 1). I want to create an experience that invites the people present into a "sense of traveling from here to there" and then being transformed through this journey. This can occur in a single session at the walk-in clinic.

I have always believed that therapy conversations and process just "take as long as they take," and have therefore been opposed to positions that attempt to situate narrative practice within "number of sessions expectations" and outcome measures that orient success to "less time is better" ideas. However, we never know if the people with whom we consult will ever come again. Therefore it is important to make the most of each conversation—creating opportunity for "katharsis" and a "journey." This has led me to discoveries about which aspects of narrative practice are especially useful within these potentially time-limited conversations.

STORIES

The stories shared throughout this chapter are both descriptions of and actual segments of conversations with people who have come to consult at the walk-in clinic. They are meant to illustrate and "bring to life" the narrative ideas and practices that have been so important in the work at the walk-in clinic. People have enthusiastically consented to be a part of this chapter as they believe in contributing toward the learning of professionals.

RE-VISITING PRACTICES

I joined the research team described in the Introduction to this book in 2005, bringing a strong interest in adding the voices of the people consulting us to our developing understandings of what was occurring within narrative conversations. I was interested in having them review videotaped sessions and hear from them about what they considered useful and meaningful. This connects to preferences in narrative therapy for centering the knowledge and expertise of those who consult us, as discussed in the Introduction of this book. It added to the "laboratory environment" of the research project by adding their voices to assist in answering the question, "What would make a useful conversation?"(see the

Introduction to this book). Research team members provided consultation around developing the process that we called "re-visiting." Scot Cooper and I participated in the project data collection, analysis, and writing up of the findings (Young & Cooper, 2008).

The Narrative Therapy Re-visiting Project utilizes narrative ways of thinking to shape research in ways that strive to center the voices of those who consult us in therapeutic conversations. This moves away from solely interpreted understandings of professionals and toward cocomposed understandings among professionals and therapy participants (Epston & White, 1992; Gaddis, 2004; Rennie, 1994; St. James O'Connor, Meakes, Pickering, & Schuman, 1997). It uses the notions of taking precise notes of people's exact words, acting like a scribe—as discussed in Chapter 3—into the area of research. The project recognizes that people's knowledges and perspectives should serve to inform ongoing practice and research.

Most of the participants in the research were people who had attended the walk-in clinic and were seen by myself as I provided narrative therapy consultation. Therefore the research provides information about what is important in a single session of narrative therapy. People who had attended previous therapy sessions at the walk-in clinic later returned and watched the entire videotapes of their earlier sessions with a research assistant. We called these "re-visiting sessions." I was not part of this feedback meeting, to ensure that my presence did not influence the participants' commentary. They were asked to stop the tape at any time they noticed a significant moment and were then asked a series of set questions meant to elicit their thoughts and understandings of the moment they selected. Their descriptions of these meaningful moments were audio recorded and later transcribed. The transcripts were then reviewed and analyzed for themes, a similar methodology to that described in the Introduction of this book regarding the team's initial research project.

These same session tapes were reviewed for another research project (Ramey, 2007; Ramey, Young, & Tarulli, in press) where they were analyzed and coded for the presence of White's scaffolding conversations map (White, 2007a). This research clearly demonstrated the presence of the scaffolding conversations map in all sessions, thereby confirming the presence of narrative practices in these walk-in sessions.

THERAPIST POSTURE

According to the Merriam-Webster's New Collegiate Dictionary, 8th edition, *posture* is defined as "a state or condition at a given time especially in relation to other persons . . . a conscious mental pose . . . to assume or adopt an attitude." This concept of posture invites reflection on preferences about "how to be" in therapeutic conversations. As discussed in Chapter 2, the therapeutic posture of a therapist who is practicing within a narrative framework is strongly influenced by poststructuralist ways of thinking and being. My posture at the walk-in clinic is one of respect, collaboration, and transparency. I step back from the taken for granted or what is routinely thought, and am guided by poststructuralist curiosity (Young, 2008). This curiosity is one that is in search of meaning, of people's conscious purposes (values, commitments, preferences), and of what the unspoken stories within the words might be. I employ a "double listening" as described in Chapter 2, where I am listening for traces in conversations that reflect people's hopes, values, preferences, knowledges, and skills.

The questions that arise from this curiosity are aimed at development of thick descriptions and rich meanings within conversational territories that are not often spoken of in the everyday. We are asking questions that invite people to be "like a foreigner in one's own language" (Deleuze & Parnet, 2002, p. 4; see Chapter 3) and, in fact, like a foreigner in one's own life stories, and thereby engage with their stories with new curiosity and new eyes. It is within these unusual conversational territories that I attempt to navigate at the walk-in clinic. These are not technique-driven, fast-pace therapy conversations, but instead they have the appearance of a slower pace. This may seem counterintuitive in the context of single sessions, but it does create an experience of "slowing down to speed up." In other words, highly meaningful, "thicker," and therefore potentially useful conversations happen in a single session when I stand within this practice posture.

SUBORDINATE STORYLINE DEVELOPMENT

At the walk-in clinic I want to create conversations that move into new territories and create "katharsis" and a sense of "journey." As discussed in Chapter 1, the medium for eliciting people's stories is the therapeutic conversation. As stories about the problem unfold, I will employ "double listening" (White, 2004) throughout. People will begin to tell their stories in the "usual" ways, but as I listen carefully and ask questions about some of the more neglected but potentially significant events of their lives, the meaning of these events can be developed. I remind myself that stories are "constructed and sustained between people" (Chapter 1) and that I need to elicit new tellings that assist the potentially "trapped storytellers" to move away from the reality created by the current and familiar problem-saturated telling. As I do this, I draw people's attention to the gaps in the storylines of their lives. Delving into the inevitable gaps that exist in the problem storylines opens up space for realizations, choice, and creativity (Chapter 1). These subordinate (or alternative, as described in earlier chapters) storylines include people's knowledges, skills, abilities, language, cultural beliefs, hopes, dreams, commitments, and preferences. This development of subordinate storylines is particularly important at the walk-in clinic as it may be the only time we will meet. As I ask questions to develop details of these stories, what had previously been subordinate storylines will begin to shift into a story of more prevalence in the person's life.

We can train ourselves to see and hear the openings into subordinate storylines. My first opportunity at the clinic to see glimmers of these storylines is on the presession questionnaire, and to then ask more about these clues in the session. The next opportunity is to consider the meaning that coming to the clinic may reflect, such as the person's hopes/wishes/commitments for their life and for their relationship with the problem. As the session begins with what people express an interest in talking about (the "agenda"), this says something about what is important to them, which again provides a possible opening into subordinate storylines. Later in the conversation, as I am listening carefully while they name and describe the problem, I listen for thoughts or actions that they have engaged in that stand apart from how the problem might need them to think or act. These represent initiatives that people have taken or considered taking and are doors into subordinate stories. The subordinate stories are about actions that have been considered or actually taken to attempt to solve or reduce the influence of the problem in their lives and represent preferences and longings for their lives. We can richly develop any of these stories through use of questions that seek details and meanings connected to the person's identity and their history. I can make these events more "meaning-full" by gathering the particularities around the event, giving the event "eventness" (as discussed in Chapter 2 and Chapter 4).

SETTING THE AGENDA

Setting the agenda is not a uniquely narrative therapy practice. However, given the importance of developing a clear understanding of what people want when they come to the walk-in clinic (Slive et al., 2008), I have developed ways of doing this that "fit" with narrative ideas. These agenda-setting conversations are different from "goal setting," perhaps more of a "postmodern contracting." The purpose is not a "goaling" process, but it is meant to be an inquiry into the person's hopes and wishes about what to converse about—to identify the conversational territory. This is act 1, points of the story; it is preparing for a journey (Chapter 2). I ask questions such as, "I am prepared to work hard with you for the next hour in relation to what it is that brought you here. What should we focus on in our conversation today so that you leave feeling it was useful?" or "What would you like to talk about for the next hour or so that is most important to you?" It is possible that the person may express this in a way that includes a goal-like outcome, but it is often true that people who come to the clinic are not sure exactly what "outcome" they are after, but are more able to identify a topic for conversation. My interest is more the latter, connecting to ideas in Chapter 3 that reflect the view that meaning and stories are changing as people converse with us, and that therefore even their hopes and desires for the consultation are changing while they explore and consider the questions.

In a conversation with Matthew, age 15, and his mother, Linda, we codeveloped an agenda for the meeting that was a reflection of the subordinate storyline suggested by both their questionnaires and their initial responses about what we should focus on in the conversation (Young, 2006). Linda indicated that her interest was to talk about "why Matthew makes bad decisions when he knows right from wrong." Matthew had a similar interest. Our negotiated agenda became to talk about what it is that Matthew knew about making "right" decisions—what values and commitments he has that assist him to do this. This subordinate storyline–focused agenda led to a rich and meaningful discussion that both son and mother identified as powerful and useful.

DOCUMENTATION

The paperwork at the walk-in clinic has been designed in a manner that stands within poststructuralist ways of thinking. The presession questionnaire that people complete upon their arrival at the clinic sets the stage for conversations that strive both to understand the problem and to find hope, new ideas, and knowledge about how to proceed (see Young et al., 2008, for these questionnaires). The summary report, along with any other therapeutic documents such as lists, declarations, and drawings, are completed within the session in a way that engages the people consulting us in the process, is transparent, and archives their own words and understandings. People's comments from the re-visiting research strongly support the importance of these writing and documentation practices (see the section "Development of New Language and New Knowledge" in this chapter, as well as Chapter 3).

Verbal reflecting summaries throughout the session serve as a way to check in about how the therapist's understanding of people's situation, ideas, and words is going. These summaries are derived from the notes taken during the conversation and are read back to people throughout the conversation. This "holds up their words as a reflecting surface" (White, 2005), allowing for any corrections and for the persons involved to "step back, and reflect" (Chapter 1) on their own words and to possibly expand on them. It creates the opportunity for people to step into the "landscape of consciousness," also discussed in Chapter 1. As language is circulating among us collaboratively, there is time and space for the meanings to become expanded and enriched (see Chapter 3). I can be listening for traces and clues to subordinate storylines and holding them up to the person through these summaries. The summaries are more regular and frequent as the conversation moves increasingly into act 3 and gathers up particularities or details of subordinate storylines.

Summarizing in this way slows the pace of the conversation and also creates a place from which the next question may be asked. It thereby allows therapists time to intentionally and carefully consider their next question. In taking away the summary report and other documents, people are provided with a record and a reminder of their own words, knowledge, and understandings that emerged within the conversation. This represents the practice of creating therapeutic documents, as shown in the third section of the concept map (see the Introduction to this book). People often share these documents with others who are not present, such as family members, friends, and schoolteachers or principals. This engages a potential audience and support team that assists in sustaining new ideas and commitments. This is a practice that is present in the story of Katie later in the chapter.

LOCATING PEOPLE PRESENT AS WITNESSES

The development of subordinate storylines is greatly assisted by locating people as witnesses to one another in their conversations with therapists. They can then be asked about the effects on them of witnessing these conversations. For example, parents may listen while therapists "interview" the children or youths, and then be invited to reflect on what stood out for them, what they heard that was unexpected/important/meaningful/useful to them, and so on, and why. Then the children/youths may be asked about what they heard from their parents' reflections that pleased, interested, or surprised them and why. This process was developed as a variation on concepts about outsider witnessing and repositioning family members as described by Michael White (2007a). It is a practice that furthers the creation of a "therapy of witnessing and acknowledgement" as discussed in the Introduction and also responds to concerns raised by trainees about how they might make use of outsider witnessing practices in their day-to-day work. It interrupts the usual back-and-forth responses among people, making a different sort of listening possible for them. This structure for conversation has been particularly useful at the walk-in clinic as people often come in immersed in misunderstandings and conflict; they blame each other and are therefore having difficulty really appreciating each other's experience, and are trapped in hearing and experiencing each other in the same usual ways. This witnessing structure creates the possibility for the therapist to spend enough time with one person to ask questions that can expand present understandings and develop new appreciations of situations, events, and one another.

Once again, looking at the conversation with Matthew and Linda (Young, 2006), we can find an example of locating a parent as a witness. As Matthew was asked to "think of a time when you made a decision that you are proud of and tell it like a story," Linda was positioned as a witness to this conversation. She was then able to hear a remarkable story from her son that reflected clear and strong values that guided his decision and to learn that her "words in his head" were with him in making this choice that he was proud of. The influence of Linda's teachings on her son was powerfully attested to by him in this conversation.

In the next story, of Katie's visit to the walk-in clinic, we can see another instance of locating a person as a witness; in this case Katie, age 13, was in a witness position.

GETTING TO KNOW THE PERSON AWAY FROM THE PROBLEM

This practice comes from the belief that the person is not the problem (White, 2007a; White & Epston, 1990). There is so much to know about the person that is different from only narrowly knowing the person in relation to the problem. David Epston's work has been particularly inspirational in this regard, as he often spent a great deal of time within these types of conversations with people who consulted him (Epston, 2003; 2009a). His work influenced two questions on the presession questionnaire that people complete before sessions at the walk-in clinic. The questions are: "Remember a problem that happened any time in your life that you resolved in such a way that left you feeling proud of yourself. What did you do that you felt proud of?" and "What would someone else come to admire and respect most about you if they had months or years to get to know you? It's okay to guess." The answers to these questions are often full of rich stories of people's lives and provide information that can be further explored in the session to develop subordinate storylines.

These conversations can explore a person's qualities, skills, ideas of how to live life, values, knowledge, know-how, and so on. This can lead to discovering just what it is that the person has got to put up against the problem (Epston, 2009a), which is something that the person is unlikely to be in touch with at the start of the session. This type of inquiry facilitates the development of links between stories of the person's identity and the possibilities that exist for influence over the problem and its effects. In fact, there are times when these conversations can stand on their own, in terms of being enough and sufficient for the person to find new places to stand in relation to the concerns the person came to consult about. This was certainly true in the instance of Matthew and Linda, who found the one conversation to be so powerful and useful that they did not see a need to return for further therapy. These conversations are most meaningful and useful when details are gathered that explore how these skills, knowledges, values, and so on show up in the person's life and where they come from in terms of the background development including past and present people of influence (White, 1997, 2007).

KATIE AWAY FROM THE PROBLEM

Katie came to the walk-in therapy clinic with her foster mother, Marion, and her foster care caseworker, Sharon (see Young, 2006, for a full description). During the initial agenda setting, the two adults indicated that they wished to talk about some recent self-harming by cutting that Katie had done, and Katie indicated that she had "nothing to say." Katie was then invited by me to stay in a witnessing position while I interviewed the others present about their agenda interests and about stories of Katie's life. Marion and Sharon, in response to my questions, guessed that the cutting was a reflection of distress from an argument with a friend and the fears Katie was experiencing that the relationship was over. This connected up with a history of loss Katie had experienced in her life. As she listened to Marion and Sharon speculating about how frightening and distressing the fear of loss might be, I checked with Katie about accuracy. She responded that it was "right on" and that the fears of loss that she experienced after such arguments were so intense that they were "unbearable." She agreed that the cutting was an expression of these unbearable fears. Marion and Sharon commented that Katie really liked to experience close connection with others and that, in fact, she had become close to her foster family.

At this point it was possible to begin to explore "getting to know Katie away from the problem" through questions such as "I'm curious about what's made it possible for Katie to become such a part of the family? What kind of qualities or things do you see in Katie that have made it possible for these well-connected relationships to develop?" Stories were then shared about Katie's kind and thoughtful actions toward her foster sister and her commitment to come back to "talk out" issues with Marion after arguments in ways that were open and insightful. I then asked Sharon questions that explored more about Katie away from the problem:

Karen: I'd like to ask you, Sharon, what do you think Katie has, like knowledge, or talents, or things she's figured out in life, that are going to help her next time when she's really distressed about an argument with friends?

Sharon: Well, I have seen Katie be incredibly compassionate at times, that's one. And I was just thinking about Katie's history of loss and that she has been in several foster homes, and has lost her family of origin in some ways. . . . I was thinking what it says about Katie that she was able to come to Marion's, after years of all these experiences, and still be hopeful that this could be a place where she could "be." So I was thinking about her hopefulness. In fact, one of the experiences I've had with Katie was that I took over as her caseworker from Sue, and Katie really loved her, but she didn't hold me at arm's length because I wasn't Sue—you know, again, there was a hopefulness. It's not: "because I'm having a loss, I'm going to hold it against the next person," you know.

Karen: Yes. You said she could have held you at arm's length. She could have not connected with you in any way, not allowed any relationship to develop?

Sharon: Yeah, and she could have done that in many ways—she could have said to herself: "How long are you going to be here? The last person I only had for a year. Are you going to only be here for a year?" . . . but I didn't get that from her.

Katie: There was Joan who left before, and then there was Sue. . . . But I think something that would help me would be to think about all the good times that I have with my friends and think about all those instead of thinking about me going to be losing them or something. And do things that I know will make myself feel better about myself instead of putting myself down and just sitting around doing nothing and waiting for them . . . just go off and do something, and not think that they are not going to be my friends or anything.

Katie, who had up to now been mostly quiet in the meeting, spontaneously came forward with ideas for initiatives she could take to help herself in these situations. This was now possible as Katie was "standing on" richer stories of her identity. It was possible because the conversation had stayed away from "interpreting" and "assessing" her, as described in the Chapter 3. I carefully documented all that she said along with the stories about her being told by the others.

I asked questions to develop more details about these possible initiatives and questions that discovered more about Katie's values and commitments. Katie told us that she believed in "looking for the better" in people and that she was a compassionate and giving person.

Karen: And you (*to Sharon*) were talking about compassion before. (*to Katie*) That was one of the things Sharon said a few minutes ago. Did that surprise you when she said that, or did you kind of know that?

Katie: I kind of know that.

Karen: What are some of the clues or reasons that you do know that about yourself?

Katie: Well, because I always want to just go and help someone else, and I'm always helping people at home and at school and everywhere.

Karen: Are you like a "giver"? (*example of tentatively suggesting a word*)

Katie: Yeah.

Karen: Is that a quality that you like in people generally, that you would strive for? Is that something that you want in life—to be giving?

Katie: Yes. I like helping people. It makes me feel better about myself.

Karen: I mean, this might be obvious—but why do you think that is a quality you want to have?

Katie: I don't know. I just think that the Agency has done so much for me—put me in a home that is great and does all these things for me, that I should do things for other people to make them feel good about themselves, so that they have a better life for themselves too. 'Cause there is this girl, named Michelle, and she was having a really hard time. . . . So I talked to her. And she is sort of like Lorrie, and so I wanted to get them to talk. So I gave Lorrie her phone number. Then they were always talking and it was really good that I could help them and have them knowing each other, so they could know somebody who was like each other, so that they don't feel so bad about themselves. And I thought, it really helped them and they seemed to feel a lot happier.

Karen: And you said that some of this has to do with you giving back? That you feel that you've been on the end of receiving and being given to, and that you want to give back. Is that right?

Katie: Yes.

Another rich story had been told, this time by Katie herself, about her values and commitments. A conversation then unfolded about many ways in which Katie had been giving to others in her family. I wondered about what she might be able to give herself in times of fear and she suggested "reassurance." We went on to discuss details of the ways Katie could reassure herself and also who was in her life that could make up a "reassurance team" to help with reassurance.

Katie agreed to be a part of the re-visiting research. The comments that she shared with the researcher suggested that the most important aspects of this interview for her had to do with the witnessing position she was in and with the "away from the problem" conversations. Katie told the researcher, "She was asking a lot of questions and seeing what everyone thought." The practice of asking others who are present to guess, speculate, and comment on what the person may be unable to express yet, or not know yet, places the person in a witnessing position to the speculations and stories from the others present. This is providing horizontal scaffolding (White, 2007a) to make it possible for people to know what they have not yet known (an example of this was also provided in Chapter 3). Katie was in a position of witnessing other people's responses to questions, and she was able to sit back and reflect on what they were saying. This led to her having an "aha" or pivotal moment: connecting loss and fighting with friends, an idea which she previously did not "know," and to having realizations about initiatives she could take to reduce her distress and fear.

Katie also told the researcher, "Well, she kept asking my mom and Sharon things, the abilities that I have to do things." The "getting to know the person away from the problem" practices were central and deliberate in this session. I interviewed others present about skills, talents, know-how, and so on that Katie had with her. I believed that the problem had Katie separated from stories of her own skills and competencies and that reconnection with these would make it possible for her to respond to her distress in different ways. She confirmed this in saying to the researcher that this helped her to "figure out strategies."

DEVELOPMENT OF NEW LANGUAGE AND NEW KNOWLEDGE

As discussed fully in Chapter 3, language is both a reflection of and shaping of our interpretations and meaning-making of the events in our lives. I am mindful of this during walk-in sessions and try to codevelop new, sometimes unusual language with people to open up new possibilities for meaning and actions. I strive to develop meaningful, experience-near, externalized problem descriptions (White, 2007a). I want to collaborate with people to develop language for the problem that makes sense to them and I do this from the philosophical stance or posture that sees people and problems as separate as discussed in the Introduction. I develop my questions guided by the statement of position map 1 as outlined in Chapter 2. So, for example, "I am anxious" or "I have an anxiety disorder" (experience-distance medical description) becomes "the fears" or "the worries." The person and problem become separated as we explore the effects of the problem on the person. The conversation deconstructs the person's identification with the problem and thereby separates the problem from the person's identity.

I ask children questions such as the following: "Would it be okay with you if we get to know some things about the worry?" "What kinds of things does this worry do to you?" "Does it put some thoughts in your head sometimes?" "Like what ones?" "Does it ever try to get in your way of doing things?" "Like what things?" "Does the worry cause some troubles for you?" "What kinds?" "If this worry/fear looked like an animal or a creature, what would it look like?" "How big is it, what color, shape . . . ?" "What do you think the worry wants for your life?" "Is that different from what you want for your life?" "What are those things you want?" (For more details on these questions, see Young, 2008).

Parents are often in a witnessing position for parts of these conversations and have told me how surprised they are about how much knowledge their child actually does have about the problem. Mothers of two different 8-year-old boys who attended the walk-in clinic agreed to participate in the re-visiting research. One mother told the researcher, "What Karen was doing, in terms of how she was phrasing things, 'The worry puts thoughts in your head' . . . I was feeling hopeful, because he was immediately saying, like echoing back what she was saying. He was saying, 'The worry does this' and 'The worry does this thought in my head,' so I was starting to feel . . . that this was looking good!" Engaging her son in an externalizing conversation about the worry appears to have been hope-generating for this mother. She began to see him stepping into the conversation and making some "discoveries" about what he "knows" as he responded to the questions.

This same mother also said that the externalizing conversation about worry "gave me a tool." Even though no homework or explicit statements about talking like this at home were given, she had a realization that this way of talking could be a useful tool outside of the session. She was learning something new by witnessing the back-and-forth questions and answers between her son and me. She became a "learner," as discussed in Chapter 2.

Another mother participating in the re-visiting research told us, "She's asking him questions . . . getting at information. She's starting to dissect it and compartmentalize it. . . . Not only is it about fears but what they look like. . . . She's going through the process of allowing him to describe the fears as these monsters . . . allowing space and time to describe them fully to his satisfaction. . . . She's writing down what he says and so he's quite happy about that."

It is interesting that the words this mother is using to describe what she is seeing are "dissect it" and "compartmentalize it." This seems to relate directly to deconstruction-of-the-problem practices and externalizing practices. She is referring to the fears as "they," which again seems to reflect that the separation of the person and the problem in this conversation was visible to her. She has noticed that the conversation is not rushed, that there is enough "space and time." She comments about a moment during an externalizing conversation: "This is a significant moment because (he) is laughing at his fears for the very first time . . . he actually thinks it's funny." (It is possible that this was a pivotal moment for her son.) This, his mother said, was a "hopeful moment" and one that she said had the effect of "developing trust. I guess I've developed enough trust that I am actually staying out of it, and letting them actually go through it." This development of trust assisted her to actually place herself in the witness position, which, I believe, was very useful to her son and to her own learning.

Relating back to the importance of documentation, this same mother tells us: "She's writing down, making note of what's important but making him part of that process. . . . It's respectful of him as a human being, it's not, but you're a kid. She gives him equal footing . . . letting it be about him. . . . I'm learning in this moment . . . (it's) making me understand him better . . . so I can be more effective in helping him at home and also more sympathetic as well. . . . It's huge things I'm learning in this."

The narrative practice of documenting people's words, writing down what people say during the conversations in an open way, checking with the person about accuracy and reading out loud, has always seemed to me to be a very collaborative, respectful, and engaging process. This mother is noticing the collaboration—she uses the words *interaction of the two of them* and him as a *participant*. It was because she was in a witness position to the conversation between her son and me that she was able to see from a distance, creating "learning" for her and building "confidence" in her ability to use the new learnings outside of the session.

CONCLUSION

Staying committed to practicing therapy at the walk-in therapy clinic in ways that are strongly influenced by narrative therapy has created the experience of "slowing down to speed up" in terms of the effects of these conversations. More than half of the people who attend the walk-in clinic find that the one conversation is enough and do not go on for further therapy services (Young et al., 2008). It is quite possible that these effects are happening due to the brief but deeply meaningful conversations that are had at the walk-in that assist people to "move to new places," providing a "journey" over a single session. This is achieved through the practice of a "brief narrative" therapy at the walk-in clinic.

The narrative posture and the development of subordinate storylines—with the practices of setting the agenda, documentation, getting to know the people away from the problem, positioning people as witnesses, developing new language and knowledge, externalizing conversations, and exploring people's preferences and position in relation to the problem—all create conversations that make it possible for people to know what they could not have known about their lives, their knowledge, and their skills if not for the meanings generated in these conversations. The re-visiting research has created a practice that invites us to step back and reflect on the narrative therapy conversations at the walk-in clinic. My best teachers have been the children, youths, and parents who attend the clinic and teach me about what is important and meaningful to them in therapeutic practices.

Questions for Reflection

1. What do you think it is about narrative conversations that make it possible to travel such a distance in a one therapy session?

2. What roads might we travel in a single conversation to discover the subordinate storylines of people's lives? How might we develop the details of these stories in one conversation?
3. What are the possible effects of these newly developed storylines on the concern that brought the people to the walk-in clinic?
4. What practices can we use in one therapy session to assist people to stay connected to new knowledge discovered in the conversation?
5. If we consider the re-visiting feedback, such as the importance of a collaborative, respectful posture; documentation practices that are done in partnership; use of language that separates people and problems; locating people as witnesses; horizontal scaffolding practices; and getting to know people away from the problems, how might therapists make use of this information in a variety of therapy approaches?

CHAPTER 6

Journey From the Underworld: Working With the Effects of Trauma and Abuse

Many people consult therapists in their efforts to address the effects of trauma in their lives. The conversational map and the three-act-play metaphor, described in Chapter 2, are particularly relevant when working with people experiencing the effects of trauma and abuse. As we have previously described (Duvall & Béres, 2007):

> Through the therapeutic conversation, this map provides a structure for therapists to introduce scaffolding to the person's story, helping him or her to move from the despair inherent in the knowable and taken-for-granted dominant story to the hope that is inherent in what is possible to know in the emergent alternative story. (p. 234)

Through the rites of passage (journey) analogy (Campbell, 1949; Turner, 1977; van Gennep, 1960; White, 1999) that is invoked within the three-act play, we understand people's responses to the effects of trauma as part of an intense life transition. In this chapter we will illustrate how the conversational map and the three-act play provide frameworks for addressing the complexities of people's experiences as they journey through life transitions. In doing so, key events that are located in the problem-saturated story are called into question, reinterpreted, and deconstructed with others, making it possible for neglected experiences to come into awareness. Realizations and pivotal moments are acknowledged and linked together, producing chains of association, which develop into preferred storylines. These emerging preferred storylines make it more possible for people to consider necessary actions. As Michael White (2007a) pointed out:

> People become curious about, and fascinated with, previously neglected aspects of their lives and relationships, and as these conversations proceed, these alternative storylines thicken, become more significantly rooted in history, and provide people with a foundation for new initiatives in addressing the problems, predicaments, and dilemmas of their lives. (p. 62)

Although the effects of trauma and abuse may eclipse people's strongly held values or previous initiatives, they are still there. Inevitably, there are gaps in the problem story. Like panning for gold, one may need to sift through a lot of sand until the sparkles appear. As the sparkling moments appear, they become entry points into preferred storylines.

JO'S STORY

This chapter will focus on one woman's story of her experience of significant trauma, resulting from ritual abuse that was perpetrated against her 23 years earlier. While focusing on her story we will map her journey. We will show how she ultimately freed herself from the debilitating effects of the trauma and revised her life to one that she strongly prefers and now inhabits much more fully.

Jo's name has been changed for purposes of confidentiality. Her desire to express her story is heartfelt. She wishes to inspire hope for other women who are also struggling with the effects of trauma and abuse, reassuring them that it is possible for them to create the life they long for. Jo hopes her story will move therapists to see women who have experienced ritual abuse as who they really are, allowing them to be seen, and not hidden by the abuse. She would like therapists to maintain a "human" connection, generously (Frank, 2004), supporting women's efforts as they journey through uncertain and challenging territories while reclaiming their lives from the effects of trauma and abuse. To this end, "Jo" participated in and consulted directly toward the creation of this chapter, regulating the accuracy or inaccuracy of her journey in order to tell her story and protect her privacy.

Like many women who have endured the effects of significant trauma, Jo experienced a sense of desolate inner and outer isolation. She also experienced regular periods of dissociation and a diminished sense of identity. This was related to a loss of a sense of personal agency and a sense that she was able to affect the shape of her life.

She believed that the problems associated with her abuse were a reflection of her own identity and that even as a young child she was somehow responsible for her own abuse. "This sort of understanding shapes their efforts to resolve problems, and unfortunately these efforts invariably have the effect of exacerbating the problems" (White, 2007a, p. 9). Her isolation had developed into a double-sided experience. It provided a "cavelike" refuge from the fears connected with the abuse and, at the same time, prevented her from being fully present in her relationships with her friends and her family and from enjoying the routine pleasurable activities of life. She spoke of living in a profound loneliness and a loss of a sense that the world was in some ways responsive to the truth of her existence.

Time after time she would dissociate from her immediate surroundings, retreating to a shadowy cavelike world in an effort to escape from her fears. Ironically, the isolation left her more vulnerable to fall victim to the intrusive memories of the abuse. Over time, her life became a bleak existence as she increasingly questioned her sense of "reality." She spoke of hope becoming increasingly inaccessible, trapping her in what she referred to as the "ever present," frozen in the ubiquitous time between the past and the future.

ACT 1: THE BEGINNING AND THE SEPARATION PHASE

When Jo first contacted me, I (JD) answered my telephone only to discover silence on the line. I guessed that the silent call was a friend playing a prank on me. Following what seemed like a huge span of time, I was just about to hang up the phone when her faint voice finally spoke. We scheduled our first session.

Session One

For a large portion of our initial session Jo and I sat together in an awkward silence. She struggled hard to find the words to express herself and often looked away from me. Right away, I sensed that she was going to teach me a lot about managing silence and ambiguity. I had no idea what the purpose of our session was, but I did sense that it was very important. After sitting together for some time we tentatively started our conversation.

Jo: Maybe I shouldn't have come. I'm probably wasting your time.
Jim: Jo, this is your session. I hope you use it in whatever way that works best for you. Take the time you need.
Jo: It's hard for me to find the words. It's hard to talk, but I know I need to do it.
(*Jo then described how over time the isolation had become a refuge from her fears and over time it had become easier to hide in the "cave" and avoid being with people.*) The isolation has immobilized me. Sometimes I just feel frozen.
Jim: So, it's become easy to hide in the cave, but it leaves you feeling immobilized and frozen? If the isolation has cut you off from people, what ideas does that leave you with about getting free from isolation? Do you ever have ideas about reconnecting with people? Given what you have been through, would that be something that you are interested in doing?
Jo: Oh, I need to reconnect with people. I know that. But that's easier to say than to do. I just feel so immobilized.

At this point in our conversation, which was spent in a great deal of silence (approximately 45 minutes), I was experiencing a growing awareness that I needed to manage my expectations for this initial conversation. There was a strong possibility that I would not understand the purpose of our meeting by the end of this session. There was other work that needed to be done first. We needed to move at a very slow pace and carefully set the stage in order to have a useful therapeutic conversation.

Jim: So, you do know that reconnecting with others would help to break free from the isolation.
Jo: Yes, I want to finally deal with this. But I feel like I'm probably wasting your time.

Jim: Jo, I'm pleased to be part of our conversation. So let me ask you: What do you think would be the effects of getting free of the isolation?

Jo: I won't feel so overwhelmed expressing my opinions to other people and feel so shut down. I won't feel overcome by fear and start to get images. I'll be able to literally speak, without worrying so much about if I'm right or wrong. I will start to get my voice back.

Jim: You will start to get your voice back. Jo, given all that you just said, would you like another session so that we can have further conversations about getting free of the isolation and getting your voice back?

Jo: Yes, I would like another session.

Jim: Okay, and given that you would like to talk more after this session, I wonder if it might be useful sometimes to view these challenges that you are facing as a project. Like any project, it makes it clearer how to approach it if you name it. You know, like the "blank" project. What name would you give this project that you are undertaking?

Jo: Well, how about I call it the "Getting My Voice Back Project."

Jim: As we move along through the process you can continue using this name, or if you think of something more fitting you can change the name to suit where you are at that point in time. But for now, let's call it the "Getting My Voice Back Project."

"The notion of providing space for the 'voice' of the person is the first of three important aspects of our philosophical positioning when in conversation with someone who has experienced trauma" (Duvall & Béres, 2007, p. 231).

Reflecting summary: This is a primary summary that is offered at the end of a therapy session. It helps to clarify the alternative storyline as it is emerging. The reflecting summary is described fully in Chapter 2.

Jim: (*Looking at notes and using Jo's words*) Jo, we've talked about a number of things so far today. First, I want you to know that I appreciate that it was hard for you making the telephone call and then coming in for the session today. It seems like this was a big step for you. You said how difficult it was even finding words to start our conversation. You also talked about experiencing significant isolation, so much that at times you were immobilized and felt frozen by it. You also said that you know you need to reconnect with other people. Finally, you said that you want to "get your voice back" and be able to express your opinion without getting so overwhelmed that you can't speak. You named this the "Getting My Voice Back Project." How does this fit with your understanding of our conversation so far?

Jo: Sure, that's what we talked about. It is hard finding words and being with people wouldn't be that easy to do.

Jim: Oh, of course not. Of course it wouldn't be easy. But, you know, it's got me thinking about an idea. But first let me ask you a question. Because "it wouldn't be easy," would it be useful to practice with being with others, in preparation for reconnecting with others for "real"?

Jo: Well, I guess. But I don't know what you mean. How would I do that?

Jim: Well, this is just an idea and I want you to feel free to reject it without needing to explain why. You said that you know that one way to break free from the isolation is to reconnect with other people. You also said that you would like another session. I could arrange our next session to occur with a team. The team would listen to our conversation and then, at some point during our session, they would offer their impressions about what they heard us talk about. These impressions would include what stood out for them and what moved them in our conversation. They may also talk about how what you have talked about affected them and how they may take those ideas into their own lives. The team members do not offer judgments or evaluations or tell you what you should do. After they talk for a few minutes, we would resume our conversation without the team. At that time I would ask you what stood out for you as you listened to the team's conversation.

I wonder if we worked with the team in this way if it may be one way for you to familiarize yourself with reconnecting with people in a way that doesn't count, like in "real" life. It would be a safer environment to practice, trial and error. In that environment we could make adjustments and talk about things as we do them, in preparation for reconnecting with other people in your life.

Jo: To be honest with you, it sounds pretty scary. But, I need to do it. Yes . . . I will do it.

Jo had entered the first stage. She clearly wanted something to be different in her life. She wanted to distance herself from her fears and isolation. She has heard the "calling" (Campbell, 1949) and has accepted it, for now.

We still had some road to travel in act 1. I still did not clearly understand the point of Jo's story and what was most important to begin talking about. I also needed to understand her backstory. What was the relevant history of her story and who were the significant people who populated and influenced her life, both past and present? We needed to address these lines of inquiry before Jo began the middle phase of her therapeutic journey.

Session Two

Point of the Story

During the second session we were able to further clarify that Jo wanted to focus the therapeutic conversation on "getting her voice back," but that ultimately she longed to inhabit her life more fully. A focus on getting free of isolation and getting her voice back would prove to be a solid start for the process.

An outsider witnessing team was present for the second session and continued to remain present for a number of sessions afterward. Jo commented that the influence of the team was a key and important aspect of her therapeutic journey. In some ways the team mirrored the structure of the group that had ritually abused her. Their "watching" and "witnessing" her in the therapy sessions initially made her apprehensive. However, as the process continued, she experienced the influence of the team as being powerfully therapeutic. Not only was the team validating of her efforts, they also made it possible for her to understand that she could have an effect on others. She said that prior to being with the team she had felt invisible. She talked about beginning to feel more visible because she could see the team and they could see her. She learned about connection as she moved from feeling objectified by them, to experiencing a sense of mutual subjectivity with them. Through the acknowledgment of the outsider witnessing team Jo began to reclaim her ability to trust herself and others.

Backstory

Jo's history was pervasively influenced by trauma and abuse. She spoke of being ritually abused by a group of people in Africa 23 years earlier. The members of the group wore robes, which concealed their identities. Because of that, she was afraid to trust anyone in the small village where she lived, fearing that anyone could be a member of the group. Therefore, she was unable to disclose the abuse or confide in anyone. As years passed, the images of the abuse frequently invaded her thoughts, causing her to dissociate from her daily life and trapping her in what she referred to as the "ever present." Jo described the invasive memories of the group as shifting shadows that constantly moved, and said that it made it difficult for her to get emotionally grounded.

Because she felt there was no one to whom she could safely disclose the abuse, she became isolated and without support. She lived in a rural area and was able to find comfort from a huge oak tree that was located in the back of her family's property. For years to follow Jo would find sustenance from trees and nature.

Years later Jo immigrated to Canada where she married her husband, Rick. He firmly denied Jo's experience of the abuse and accused her of concocting the story of it. He spent many hours searching the Internet for information to support his claim. In many ways Rick reproduced the imposition and imbalance of power that Jo experienced from the group that originally abused her. In a response to his disqualification of her experience, Jo retreated further into isolation, creating a distance and a dissonance in their marital relationship.

She had friendships that she developed over time. Many of these friends lived in her surrounding neighborhood and a few lived farther away. She considered many of them good, supportive friends.

At this point we were reaching the separation point of the initial phase of Jo's story. We now had a sense of the point of her story. She said she wanted to "get her voice back," and she wanted to more fully inhabit her life. This was her "calling" (Campbell, 1949). This was what was important to talk about. This began Jo's process of separation from an "aspect of identity or role that is determined to be no longer viable" (White & Epston, 1990, p. 7) for her.

We gained a better understanding of Jo's backstory. We had a clearer sense of the events of her history of trauma and abuse that were located in the past, as well as her current social context, including her present day-to-day life, all of which formed a story that influenced how she viewed herself and how she experienced others viewing her.

Jo had begun naming the problems as fear, isolation, and self-doubt. She had also named her "quest," as stated above, to "get her voice back" and more fully experience her life. She had accepted the calling and was compelled to move forward.

This was a very important beginning step for Jo. Because of that, it was important for me to be aware of my own reflexivity, taking care to go slowly, inviting Jo to express what was most important for her talk about. Although she had moved this far into the process through considerable effort, it was sensible to remain open to the likelihood that Jo could stop at the threshold of her therapeutic journey and return to the refuge of the "cave." A response of this sort would not be understood as "failure" or "resistance," but rather the use of good judgment and the need for further preparation. A journey such as Jo was facing should not be approached lightly. It proved to be a significant, life-altering process that required perseverance, thorough planning, and careful readjustment of previously held commitments as Jo moved toward more fully inhabiting her life.

ACT 2: THE JOURNEY PHASE

A second reflecting summary was provided at the end of the second session and act 1, as an invitation to Jo to cross the threshold into act 2, the journey and transitional phase of the therapeutic process.

Session Three

In the previous session Jo had talked about how she didn't know who to trust in her immediate surroundings and because of that she would find strength in a 300-year-old oak tree that was behind her house on the farm where she grew up. She would sit under the tree and gather strength from that proximal association. There was a large tree outside the therapy room where we met. Starting at session three and at the beginning of every session afterward, we routinely opened the curtains and lifted the blinds in the therapy room, revealing the large oak tree just outside the window. Jo could turn her chair so that she could see the tree during our conversation, accepting support from it when needed.

During this journey phase of the three-act play Jo would revisit, reflect on, and reconsider numerous events in her life. She would experience setbacks when fear and self-doubt would threaten to regain control of her. She would also experience progress as she moved toward getting her voice back and inhabiting her life more fully. More and more, recent events reflected Jo's initiatives, the accounts of her responses to trauma that were in line with her project of getting her voice back. These events formed chains of association and the development of Jo's emerging preferred story. She began to realize what was possible as hope began to reappear in her life. The recent events that began to create the preferred story were rich with *eventness*, "indispensable for real creativity and choice . . . the sense that what I do at this moment truly matters" (Morson, 1994, p. 21).

She also revisited a significant and central distant event, which was where her abuse originated. Of course, this event was emotionally loaded, laden with imagery and meaning and profoundly challenging. The outsider witnessing team played an important role as Jo recounted the events of her abuse in detail. The ability of the outsider witnessing team to respond to Jo's telling of her abuse had an effect of moving her experience from "the old to the new." The outsider witnessing team helped to deconstruct the myth of what the original abusers had said and helped Jo consider reinterpretations of the events.

In Chapter 2, the betwixt-and-between phase (Turner, 1977) of the journey was described. As Jo was entering this phase she was invited to reflect on the effects of the problem on her life, through revisiting and reinterpreting those experiences located in the various events. In this evaluative aspect of the journey, we engaged in an exploration of the relativity and multiplicity of meanings. Meaning was generated through the scaffolding of the therapeutic conversation, side shadowing her experiences to reveal options for creativity, choice, and possibility.

Jim: Jo, you had said in the last session that you were ready to voice the details of the abuse. But you wanted to know it was okay to talk about it. So I want to be clear with you. Of course it is okay to talk about it. On the other hand, it's been 2 weeks since I've seen you. So other things may have come up that are also important to talk about. What would you prefer to talk about right now?

When Jo experienced the abuse, her choice was taken away from her. She was a child. In later life her husband reproduced the influence of her abusers by removing a significant amount of choice from Jo's life. Therefore, I wanted Jo to experience clear choice in everything that we did together in therapy. We were on a mission together to restore choice. My purpose was to create space for Jo to experience that she had a choice about the topic of discussion and when to choose the time to talk about the topic. She had indicated in a previous session that often she preferred to work up to difficult topics more slowly, beginning with less intense discussions. Therefore, this is a form of pacing whereby Jo directs the speed of the conversation. Through incremental questions I invited Jo to reflect on various events and evaluate the effects of her actions within them. "The therapist facilitates the development of these alternative storylines by introducing questions that encourage people to recruit their lived experience, to stretch their minds, to exercise their imagination, and to employ their meaning-making resources" (White, 2007a, 62).

Jo: It's all kinda connected anyway.
Jim: Okay, so can we connect it up as we go along? Do you want me to be more passive or more active during this session?
Jo: Probably more active because I tend to avoid things.
Jim: Okay, so where would you like to begin?
Jo: Well, apparently I'm wallowing in everything and it's definitely making things worse, according to Rick.
Jim: According to Rick?
Jo: He said that therapy in general makes things worse. I said, well, you only know two people in therapy. That's you and me. What he was saying is he's not seeing results.
Jim: How would "results" be defined?
Jo: If we were having sex every single night. He just wants everything to be "nice."
(Initiative #1.)

In the previous session Jo described an event where she attempted to discuss an issue with Rick whereby he abruptly dismissed her. Once again she became overwhelmed, shut down by fear, and retreated. The following example is her second attempt to initiate having a voice with her husband. This attempt is loaded with significance.

Jo: Actually, I challenged Rick on a couple of things this week.
Jim: Can you tell me more about that? How did you challenge Rick?
Jo: I told him I don't like it when he overrules my decisions and I want him to stop doing that. He just bullies his way through. It's always his way.
Jim: So what was that like for you in the moment, challenging Rick? Can you describe what you were experiencing at the time?

Jo: My heart was pounding when I was doing it. I was scared and excited at the same time. It felt better. I told him that it wasn't open for discussion. Then I just walked away. I was just telling him. You should have seen the look on his face. He looked surprised. At least now he's listening.

Jim: Okay, so is this different? Would this be a start to getting your voice back? At least he's listening now?

Jo: Yes, it could be a start.

Jim: Jo, you said, "It felt better." What are the effects of feeling better when you have a voice?

Jo: Well, I felt more confident.

Jim: What did that get you in touch with about what you said you want for your life?

(*Initiative #2.*)

Jo: That I matter! That I'm not invisible. That I have influence. It got me thinking about other things I could do (*i.e., side shadowing, other initiatives are possible*) For example, there is this journal that I've had for 23 years. I took it out and I thought, maybe it's a good time to start writing, In that way, if something came into my head, I could just write it down.

Jim: Twenty-three years! You have had this journal 23 years and you just took it back out? So, could the fact that you have retrieved your journal and that you are writing in it, after all this time, be another way to have a voice? I don't mean to overstate it. Those are my words, not yours. But what do you think?

Jo: No, I don't think it is overstating it. I think the journal is part of the bigger project.

Jim: Jo, I would like you to place this on a scale of 1 to 10. Let's say that 10 is a very significant rating that you give yourself for retrieving this journal and to start writing in it again, and 0 is not really very significant at all. Where would you place the significance of retrieving the journal and starting to write in it on this rating scale?

Jo: I would say an 8. It's like what we were talking about last week about getting things out of the eternal present. Jim, it's been kind of like a black hole of stuff up until now, so it helps to write things down. But the hard part of writing it down is that you have to look at what it means.

Jim: Sure, it helps to write things down and at the same time it may be hard to look at the meanings of things that you are writing. Yet, you're doing it anyway. So are both of these things ways to start having a voice?

Jo: Yes, I suppose they are. But, you know, the ways that I've been dealing with things over the past number of years have helped me function until now. Otherwise, I wouldn't have been able to do what I do every day. But then there was also a down side, which is by keeping stuff separate and not putting it into words and talking about it, it just stays there in the constant present. Then the fears keep getting in the way.

Jim: So, are you saying that if you could talk about it and, in a sense, put your fears out in front of you and face them, that would help you get free of them, or not?

Jo: Absolutely, I want to get free of the fears and in order to do that I need to stop avoiding them. I need to face the fears head-on.

Jim: Tell me more about how you're dealing with things that help you function.

Jo: Well, I think the way I have been dealing with them helped me to get by and just cope, so that I could do what I needed to do every day. But since I've been starting to talk I've noticed the positive side of connecting with different aspects of myself. I'm starting to understand more about what's going on, because I have started to have more connections with people. My connections with people seem to be giving me more strength and clarity. Things don't just come out of the blue. *(The social construction of identity.)*

> People can move their identities from defining themselves only in relation to the traumatic experience to having identities that also involve other elements of their lives . . . toward a context that makes it possible for people to experience themselves as being able to overcome the effects of trauma. (Duvall & Béres, 2007, p. 233)

Jim: You say you're finding strength and clarity through reconnecting in your relationships. What are the effects of experiencing more strength and clarity?

Jo: Well, I'm starting to feel more stable. It's like the floor isn't moving as much. I'm realizing that words have an effect and that sometimes I need guts and courage to have a voice.

Jim: You're now realizing that words have an effect and that sometimes you need "guts and courage" to have a voice. Can you tell me a bit more about what this new realization makes possible for you?

Jo: Well, I realized that just because I have a voice doesn't mean that people will agree with me. Sometimes I need to have the guts to say what's important to me. It also means that having a voice doesn't have to depend on people's response to it. (*Reflecting summary.*)

Jim: (*Looking at notes of Jo's words*) Jo, I need to know I'm understanding you correctly. What I have heard you say is that you told Rick that you didn't like it when he overrode your decisions and that you would like him to stop doing that. Then, you said that you felt better afterwards and as a result you had more confidence. Then you said that it got you thinking about other things you could do, so you started writing in a journal that had been put away for over 23 years and that you would rate that as an 8 out of 10 in terms of the significance of that initiative. You went on to say that speaking up to Rick and writing your thoughts into your journal were both examples of getting your voice back and were part of the bigger "Getting My Voice Back Project." Then you said that talking about it and writing about it helps you to face up to your fears so that you can break out of the "ever present." You also said that reconnecting with people has given you more strength and clarity and that as a result of that, you are experiencing a bit more stability. You also said that you are realizing that words have an effect and sometimes you need guts and courage to have a voice. I'm understanding you to say that you are experiencing more confidence, stability, and courage. Have I understood you correctly so far in this conversation?

It would not have been possible to predict the many events and realizations that Jo experienced that are recounted above. This relates to the metaphor of rhizomes that is fully described in Chapter 3. Jo's rhizomes have spread from standing up to her husband, to writing in her journal, and so on. "There is no hierarchy of root, trunk and branch, but a multiplicity of interconnected shoots coming off in all directions" (Deleuze & Parnet, 2002, p. xi).

Jo: Well, yes. It sounds like a lot when you put it like that.

Jim: How does this connect up with where you are headed in your life?

Jo: I think it connects with the conversation we had in the last session about as I start to get my voice back, I will start to be more visible and be seen. While I want that to happen, it's also a bit scary.

Jim: Yes, we talked in a previous session about if you were to be seen, how you would want to be seen. Have you come up with any other ideas about how you want to be seen?

Jo: Yes, I want to be seen with respect.

Jim: So, what does that say about you that you know you want to be seen with respect? How are you different with people now that you know you want to be seen with respect?
(*Initiative #3.*)

Jo: It says that I know that I matter. I no longer let myself get pulled into situations with people who are disrespectful. I want to be more like I was before. Things mattered. I had a voice. I've started to come back again. An example is last week I went to a restaurant with my friends and the owner was very rude and disrespectful to all of us. After we left the restaurant my friends and I were talking about it. Then I thought to myself, this just isn't good enough. I said to my friends, "He was really inappropriate." So I went back in and told the owner that he was rude and disrespectful and that he needed to improve the way he treats his customers or we wouldn't be returning. He genuinely apologized for his actions. My friends said that they couldn't believe that I had the guts to go back in and deal with him.

Jim: So Jo, you talked about needing to face your fears and have a voice. Then you shared this example of a social situation in which it would have been easier for a lot of people to just walk away. But instead you took a stand against disrespect and faced up to the owner. Would you say it made a difference to the owner? Do you think he may have been appreciative or not appreciative that you took the effort to speak to him?

Jo: Yes, I think he was appreciative. I got the sense that he genuinely didn't realize that he had come across that way.

Jim: So, this is an event in which you did something that, to use your words, took guts and courage to have and use your voice. It also sounds like you had a moving effect on a number of people, which are your friends and the owner. Is this more how you want to be? How does this connect with what you want in your life?

Jo: Well yes, it connects strongly with what I want in my life. I don't want to lose that. Like when I got really emotional a couple of months ago and I just got lost and then I had no access to that. I just got lost in this black hole again where there aren't any words. For years I've been trying not to look at stuff, but when I do that it keeps coming back. When I first talked to you I made a decision that I need to look at this. Sometimes it's still hard and I get scared. But I've decided that I really need to face my fears and figure out how to deal with it in that way.

Jim: Given all that we have talked about, all these examples of recent times that you have faced your fears, what are you appreciating about yourself that's different?

Jo: I'm noticing that just putting things into words helps. I can't just keep wallowing in this and avoiding things. Actually, there's one thing that's been sitting there for a long while that I need to talk about (*leg vibrating, looking out the window at the tree*). It's standing in the way of me being more connected to myself. Sometimes I can get so fragmented that this thing shuts me down and takes my voice away.

Jim: Would you feel more connected to yourself if you talked about it, or would you prefer not to talk about it?

Jo: I need to talk about it. Then I can look at it and understand it. But I have such a love-hate relationship with words. It's just been sitting there. It's something that happened. It has such a strong effect and it's so tied up with power. I was a victim. I had no power. (*sobbing*). They really played with my head. I had nowhere else to go. I had no idea how to deal with the pain of it. Sometimes it's been so hard. Part of the way I dealt with it as a kid was to find ways of resisting. So right now talking about it is another form of resistance and a way of being visible. Now that I'm writing in my journal again, it's also another way of resisting it and being visible. It's like I'm reappearing.

Jo continued to describe details of the ritual abuse that happened to her 23 years prior. She faced her fears "head-on." This represented a significant undertaking for Jo in moving her story forward.

Jim: Like your reappearing on the pages of the journal. (*Reflecting summary.*) Jo, in our last session you said it is just really important to say "it" and get the words out. Then you came in today and talked about two challenging examples that occurred over the past 2 weeks in which you took initiative to have a voice. Then you went on to speak in very powerful ways about a traumatic and abusive event that took place in your life that you had never "told anyone about." It's got me wondering: What do you think the effects of hearing you give voice to the abuse were on me? What kind of word would you use to describe that experience?

In this way Jo can have an in-the-moment experience of her effects on others and that it matters.

Jo: Happy? That you would be happy and thought it was a good thing that I talked about it?

Jim: So, your word is *happy*. The word that comes to mind for me is *joy*.

Jo: I'm really glad that I finally talked about it. It feels different. I'm finding out that talking is a good thing. It's not wallowing in it. It feels like moving forward.

Session Four

Jim: So, Jo, where would you like to start with our conversation today?

Jo: I like the idea of putting boundaries around the fears so they don't just roam free. Sometimes it's easy to leave images inside my head, so they're not real. In my head they remain ghostly figures. It's like science fiction. I have my life now and then there's my life before, which I refer to as the underworld.

Jim: We've talked before about the effects of the underworld. Some of the effects were that in the underworld you didn't have a voice, the perpetrators had power over you, and you were very isolated. How is it that in spite of it all that, you are drawn more toward having a voice, forming connections, and bringing your voice into relationships with other people? How is it that instead of fear, courage is taking up more space in your life? These are your words.

Jo: Just the process of talking it out helps the fear to ebb away. Sometimes it feels like the tide ebbing and flowing. But the tide has to come in, in order to go out.

Jim: So talking about it seems to ebb the fear away and make more space for courage and connection. When do you notice this courage and connection the most?

Jo: I'm most in touch with it when I'm in the country. That's where I feel most present and connected to life. Also, when I listen to music it really helps. In fact, I've taken my guitar out of the attic and started playing it after many years. I'm a bit rusty, but it's great to be connected to it again. I'm thinking of taking lessons.

Jim: After all these years you're starting to play your guitar again. Is this yet another way to reconnect to your life? This gets me wondering if these recent developments are examples of becoming reconnected to meaningful things that you had to leave in your past, and at the same time connecting to new initiatives and possibilities in the present (*the beginning of reincorporation of identity*).

Jo: I'm starting to experience the difference. Each time I talk about it and face my fears, it gets a bit better. I've learned that it's possible to experience courage and that it's possible to have a voice and a life. Now it feels like there is much less of a choice to avoid things. That's so isolating. I'm much more comfortable having a voice now.

Jim: What does this say about possible next steps?

Jo: Well, finally actually putting words to all those images helps. I can't tell you what a difference that makes. It frees the energy up. I'm not always trying to use the energy to hold things back, so it's available to do other things. I'm interested to see if the tidal-wave feeling of the ebbing and flowing gets smaller. I think it will, because it already has.

Jim: Would you mind keeping track of those waves until we meet again? (*Reflecting summary.*)

An overall summary of the therapeutic processes was offered to Jo, inviting her to cross the threshold into act 3. In this reflection Jo was able to comment on the overall process and talk about any new learning and realizations that resulted from it. She was asked if these new developments fit with her purposes for her life. The experiences were strung into themes, chains of association, and then recognized as alternative storylines. All of these initiatives spoke to a progressive movement in identity. Jo was in a different place at this point in time than she was at the beginning of her journey.

ACT 3: THE REINCORPORATION STAGE

Jo attended six more sessions. During that time she continued to break free from the grip of the problem-saturated story of the abuse. She made many more changes in her life, bringing forth preferred aspects of her identity that had been left dormant in her past and incorporating those aspects with her new learning and skills that she acquired on her therapeutic journey.

Jo brought courage, passion, ingenuity, and imagination from her past life forward to her present to continue serving her. She would incorporate these aspects with learning and skills that she picked up during her therapeutic journey, some of which were newfound abilities to take risk, make connections with people, and experience empathy and concern for others. She also developed an ability to have fun and be funny, something her friends strongly validated as she reconnected and reclaimed her relationships with them. Jo had now experienced a new sense of personal intimacy, which provided a basis for relating intimately to others, and a foundation upon which to proceed with her life.

Jo began her therapeutic journey with a foreshortened sense of future. She felt trapped in the "ever present" and unable to connect with future aspirations. She now rushes toward her future, imagining a multitude of possibilities. She is no longer afraid to be visible and, in fact, wants to be noticed. She now knows how to take care of herself and has learned skills that have contributed to a restoration of a sense of personal identity and personal agency. Jo knows that there will be many trials and possibilities awaiting her on her continued journey. She now has the confidence that she will live her life fully and with purpose. She describes her life as having walked from a gray and bleak, thin existence into the light and fully inhabiting a life that is lit up with color.

As we completed this chapter Jo reminded me that if this was truly a collaborative project between herself and me, then I needed to also describe the effects that traveling alongside her through her therapeutic journey had on me. She is right. As her therapist I was not exempt from the effects of being with Jo through the process. I was often moved. I experienced many powerful emotions and realized new learnings through the process. My therapeutic relationship with Jo taught me to sit with people through their pain and discomfort. She taught me not to "rescue," but to remain steady. She taught me that these painful moments often produce powerful learnings. My relationship with Jo also helped me understand my use of language in conversation with her. I learned to use less words, unfinished sentences and half-baked ideas. In this tentativeness there was more space for Jo to step into the conversation and remain the primary author of her story.

One of the most powerful things I learned in my relationship with Jo was to question my assumptions about who people are and what is possible for them to do. Jo accomplished far more than I thought was possible when we began our work together. Witnessing her as she faced terrifying fears, one after another, taught me how to face my own fears and how to be useful to other people in similar situations. I could list volumes when describing the effects of being a passenger with Jo on her therapeutic journey. Finally, as this response demonstrates, Jo taught me to be more transparent and accountable. Truly we changed together as we moved through the therapeutic process. Just as the changes resulted in fitting better with Jo's purposes with her life, the changes I experienced as a result of working with Jo through this process fit better with my purposes as a therapist and as a person.

CONCLUSION

In this case we have illustrated the use of the conversational map and the three-act-play metaphor in narrative practice. More specifically, we have further described how these frameworks are particularly useful when addressing the complexities of working with people who are experiencing the effects of trauma and abuse. We have done so through the experience of a woman who consulted with us in an effort to separate from the problematic effects of trauma and abuse. These two frameworks move away from categorically identifying people as containers of problems. Instead, we propose the notion that through the rites of passage (journey) analogy (Campbell, 1949; Turner, 1977 van Gennep, 1960; White, 1999), people's responses to the effects of trauma can be understood as contextual and part of an intense life transition. These conversational maps help therapists provide scaffolding within a therapeutic conversation that draws upon rich lived experience and local knowledge that supports people in separating from problem-saturated identities. They are then free to progressively move toward a reincorporation and restoration of preferred identity and personal agency.

Questions for Reflection

1. Can you remember an intense transition in your life that strongly affected how you experienced yourself and how you perceived others experiencing you? Can you remember your responses to the effects of the experience and what skills you used to journey through it?
2. Have you ever found yourself dissatisfied with your circumstances, and think-

ing that your way of being was no longer viable? As a result of that have you ever experienced a calling, a sense of being drawn toward a preferred way of living?

3. What are times in your life that you have had to face your fears? How did you do that? Where did you draw support and sustenance?
4. How did this contribute to your sense of being in touch with yourself? How did this contribute to your ability to connect with others?

CHAPTER 7

Working With the Languages of Addictions: A Story With Pivotal Moments

A case study, with reflections about working with addictions from a narrative therapy perspective, will be presented within this chapter. Becky decided she did not want her name changed for the purposes of this chapter because she is comfortable sharing her story and hopes that it will be helpful for others who will be working with the effects of addictions in their lives and other people's lives.[1]

As we have described in previous chapters, narrative therapy has a particular philosophical and political stance that is committed to moving away from totalizing and pathologizing accounts of those people who come and consult us (White, 1995a). This can be viewed as being in direct opposition to certain approaches to working with addictions that use a disease model framework and expect people to label themselves as addicts or alcoholics for their entire lives.

This chapter will review some key ideas related to narrative therapy that are particularly important for a narrative therapist to keep in mind when working with people attempting to gain control over addictions in their lives. Reference will also be made to the ideas presented in earlier chapters of this book, re-

1. Another, introductory version of this work and case study was included in Csiernik and Rowe's (2010) *Responding to the Oppression of Addiction*.

garding storyline structure, the importance of the careful use of language, and the movement associated with pivotal moments. The theory and innovative ideas that we have developed in the first half of this book are contextualized using a case example, privileging Becky's descriptions of her journey through an inpatient rehabilitation program, various eclectic social work interventions, attendance of Alcoholics Anonymous (AA) meetings, and finally a combination of AA and individual narrative therapy conversations with me (LB) as her primary social worker.

Becky's insights provide some interesting thoughts as to how she has been able to supplement her AA support with what she calls the more empowering and liberating ideas she has received from narrative practices that do not limit her identity to that of an addict, or even a recovering addict, but rather provide further choices regarding her story and her future. She describes how this has not been experienced as contradictory, but rather as hopeful.

MOVING AWAY FROM TOTALIZING AND PATHOLOGIZING ACCOUNTS

As we have indicated earlier, Michael White suggested that people who seek counseling often believe that the problems in their lives are due to some problem associated with their identity. They may begin to believe that their problems are "internal to their self or the selves of others—that they or others are in fact the problem" (2007a, p. 9). White worked against these tendencies for people to see themselves as the problem by developing externalizing conversations, as described in Chapter 2.

> This makes it possible for people to experience an identity that is separate from the problem; the problem becomes the problem, not the person . . . the problem ceases to represent the "truth" about the (person's identity), and options for successful resolution suddenly become visible and accessible. (p. 9)

Conversations that externalize the problem from someone's internalized account of their identity also involve externalizing internalized discourses to a certain degree (White, 1995a). Nigel Parton (in Healy, 2000) presented a useful definition of discourses:

> Discourses are structures of knowledge, claims and practices through which we understand, explain and decide things. In constituting agents they also define obligations and determine the distribution of responsibilities and authorities for different categories of persons such as parents, children, social workers, doctors, lawyers and so on. . . . They are frameworks or grids of social organization that make some social actions possible while precluding others. (p. 39)

Internalized discourses, therefore, would be frameworks of understanding the world and how to behave in the world that have been incorporated and have become "taken-for-granteds." These internalized discourses can be externalized so that people can reflect upon where they have learned these ways of being and can make decisions about whether they wish to continue to be influenced in these ways. Many discourses are supported and circulated through popular cultural texts (Bennett, Mercer, & Woolacott, 1986; Béres, 1999, 2002).

In discussing the circulation of language in therapeutic conversations in Chapter 3, we described the need to assist people in unpacking all the traces of meanings and influences within the words that circulate in those conversations. Sometimes this means also examining the influences from various discourses to which the people in the conversation have had access.

There are therapeutic discourses as well as discourses that influence how we interact socially. This is an area of narrative therapy that has been particularly influenced by Foucault (1965). White also challenged the normative cultural practices that have developed over the last 300 years in Western culture that contributed toward the objectification, totalization, and pathologizing of modern-day subjects. Psychologies and psychotherapies have also contributed to the reproduction of these tendencies that arose with scientific classification and labeling through disorders and dysfunctions that occur when an individual is given a diagnosis from one of the editions of the *Diagnostic and Statistical Manual of Mental Disorders* (*DSM*) (White, 1995a). However, White stated, "we can render transparent many of the taken-for-granted practices of the culture of psychotherapy that are reproductive of problematic aspects of the dominant culture" (p. 46).

A person is objectified, totalized, and pathologized when she is labeled, or referred to, as a "victim" or even a "survivor," as "depressed" or as "an alcoholic" since each of these terms has the tendency to limit the person's identity to only that descriptor. Having worked for many years with adult survivors of childhood sexual abuse, I (LB) was struck by the fact that many people with histories of having been abused would often commence counseling feeling as though they were merely victims, would move to a point of viewing themselves as survivors, but would then move on to a position of not wanting to think of themselves in relation to their history of abuse at all, so not as victims or survivors, but just as people. Dolan (1998) made reference to this need to move beyond both trauma and therapy to a life of joy.

Having worked for many years with men who had used abusive behaviors toward their female partners, it also became clear that it was important to not totalize the men as "abusers" (Jenkins, 1990). If we call a man an "abuser" or a "perpetrator," we may inadvertently limit his potential to choose to be anything other than that. A full discussion of this will be presented in the following chapter, in which we present the structure and results of a case study of group work with men who have used abusive behaviors.

It was due to my experiences of realizing the importance of moving away from totalizing and pathologizing accounts in relation to childhood sexual abuse and family violence that I was particularly careful about the use of language that could label in these ways in my work with people struggling with addictions. Although there is a history of AA expecting people to take responsibility for their lives by saying, "I am an alcoholic," I have been worried by the possibility of this approach limiting people's options and preferences in their lives. I was interested in asking Becky how she was able to manage this difference in our work together versus her experiences with AA.

Becky has reported that recently she has found it much more empowering to be able to introduce herself at her regular AA meetings as someone who has struggled with addiction, rather than as an addict.

This commitment to opening up possibilities for a person's identity through therapeutic conversations also necessitates a commitment to using language tentatively and reflecting on how it is circulating within the conversation. White suggested that it can be much more useful to develop descriptions of problems and situations that are more relevant to the person than the diagnostic label (White, 2007a, p. 20). This means moving away from the types of diagnoses that people sometimes bring with them to a therapeutic conversation and asking them to describe their personal experiences with "addiction," "depression," "anxiety," "ADHD," or whatever their professional or self-proclaimed label is. As described in Chapter 3, Frank (1995) suggested this is also part of the postmodern agenda, privileging personal stories and personal voice over the professionalized general account.

RE-AUTHORING FROM DOMINANT TO ALTERNATIVE STORYLINES

In Chapter 1 we described how White and Epston (1990), building on the work of Bruner (1986a), Geertz (1986), and Gergen and Gergen (1984), began considering the "proposal that persons give meaning to their lives and relationships by storying their experience and that, in interacting with others in the performance of these stories, they are active in shaping their lives and relationships" (White & Epston, 1990, p. 13). We have also described how White and Epston went on to build upon Goffman's (1961) idea that there are "unique outcomes," or events in people's lives that may have previously been ignored, which can be built upon to develop an alternative storyline. Moving from a problem storyline to an alternative storyline is described by White as a "re-authoring" (2007a, p. 61) conversation.

As we have suggested already, people usually begin counseling due to a problem, which they often describe as being due to their identity. They go on to tell the history of the problem, telling the story of the series of events that have happened over time that prove their problem. This was particularly clear in Becky's accounts. When Becky began counseling with me (LB), for example, she told me she had been clean and sober for a few years but that she was still struggling with low self-esteem and relationship difficulties. She labeled herself as an alcoholic and told me of the series of events over the course of her life that, when strung together, could be labeled as having the plot of alcoholism and low self-esteem. She had met with several therapists and trainee therapists who believed in the importance of uncovering the details of these painful experiences in order for her to understand herself better, deal with her emotions, and not make the same mistakes again. As described in Chapter 4, when we discussed the role of time in pivotal moments, these approaches she had experienced previously would have been based on Morson's (1994) descriptions of time, which assumed "foreshadowing," as if Becky's condition in the present was caused or predetermined by past events. This is often a taken-for-granted belief in mainstream discourses about mental illness and addictions. As Becky began meeting with me she indicated that she was worried that she would be required to go over everything with me again and that she was never going to be better and able to move on from these events.

Although it is not necessary to explain the theory of re-authoring conversations to people in order to assist them in moving into an alternative storyline, I decided to explain the idea to Becky in one of her later sessions with me. I explained that people often think of themselves and describe themselves to others in a storyline. However, of all the events that have occurred in a person's life, only a fraction of those events are given enough importance to be linked together in the story. Becky had spent many years thinking of all those painful events over the course of her life and all those times when she smoked pot and drank beer to excess and lost control. She had thought and spoken of those events and that story as having the overriding theme or plot of addiction. However, there are many more events in Becky's life that have occurred that may have previously seemed insignificant, had not been privileged (or in fact given any attention at all), and had not become part of a story. As she is able to look at those events when she has been taking care of herself, enjoying her time with her son, reading and journaling and generally feeling relaxed and happy, she can see that there is more than one truth or one storyline in her life. If she steps into the re-authoring of her life, looking for those events that can be linked together into a preferred and healthier storyline, she is better able to make choices about her future life that are consistent with that alternative storyline rather than consistent with the problem storyline. Becky was fascinated by the notion of multiple storylines and that there were other possible storylines present in her life if we together spent more time looking for those events that had previously been unstoried. I drew these ideas out on a piece of paper as we talked about this and she was keen to take this home with her. When we look back on that conversation now, it seems as though this was a pivotal moment for Becky as she began to experience opportunities opening up for her; time ramified. She was not stuck in a storyline of addiction because of past events, but she could see "side-shadowing" (Morson, 1994, p. 118) of her current story. She could have made different decisions in the past and within each moment of her present she is able to make decisions that contribute to whichever storyline she now wishes to pursue. Becky has said that she thinks everybody should be told about this idea about multiple storylines and she has been explaining it to as many people as possible.

I (LB) remember when I first began working from a narrative framework. I would become excited when we would discover a unique outcome or event that stood outside of the problem storyline and showed a victim of sexual abuse that she was not only a victim but also a survivor. I was initially surprised by the fact that finding this event did not make as much of a positive impact as I might have hoped. It took a while for me to truly comprehend that it takes more than one event to make a new story; it takes a series of events over time to make a story. One unique outcome or event is susceptible to being argued away as having been a coincidence or fluke. The more events that can be discovered that fit in to the preferred storyline and the more details that can be shared about those events and story, the more robust the story will be.

These ideas that people make meaning of their lives by storying the events, and that there are multiple stories available and possible from the multitude of events in a person's life, are consistent with Foucauldian, postmodern, and poststructuralist thinking. Irving pointed out that "Foucault draws us away from Enlightenment ideas of a universal history, atemporal truth, and human nature that is fixed and timeless. He looks to pluralities, provisional truths, and many changing practices of knowledge" (1999, p. 43). Healy indicated that while poststructuralists highlight the power of language and discourses, they also "are concerned to move away from the notions of 'essential' meanings or beliefs in a fixed, singular, logical order" (2000, p. 39). Poststructuralists and narrative therapists do not look for one singular truth but rather believe there are multiple and fluid truths. Thus, this encourages us in moving away from assessing and labeling someone as an alcoholic, which can be experienced as totalizing and limiting of alternate possibilities, and toward a curiosity in the multiple possibilities present in the person's experiences and in their interpretations. This is not to be misunderstood as a relative stance. It is not a matter of anything goes and it is all relative. It is true that a victim of sexual abuse was victimized and it is true that someone has experienced negative effects from alcoholism. However, these are not the only truths, or the whole truth. They have also resisted, survived, and been sober at other times. This is another example of needing to keep language tentative and open to examination. If we can keep the image of a spiral, instead of a circle, in our minds, as discussed in Chapter 3, then Becky is not encapsulated by the word *alcoholic*, but rather has room to move in and out of the label, recognizing she is far more than just that experience of alcoholism.

VALUES, HOPES, PREFERENCES

The re-authoring conversation involves two distinct landscapes, as also described in Chapter 1, where we discussed storyline structure. White developed the re-authoring conversation in such a way that it can be visualized or "mapped" over time from remote history, distant history, recent history, to the present, and imagined into the near future. However, as well as involving this time line, it also zigzags back and forth between what he has called the "landscape of action" and the "landscape of identity" (2007a, p. 81). White's use of these "landscapes" has been influenced by Bruner (1986b). Asking questions within the landscape of action would illicit concrete details of things that have occurred, actions ("just the facts"). Asking questions in the landscape of identity involves inquiring about the person's understandings, meaning-making, preferences, and hopes. By being careful to ask questions in both landscapes, a richer and more complex story is developed. Thinking about a favorite novel, it is possible to think about the richness that is needed to make a good story versus a list of events.

In fact, we have begun to think that one of the unique contributions of narrative therapy to the field of counseling is its focus on people's values and preferences. In many of the conversational maps that White has developed (2007a), there is a component of asking about why a person has judged something a certain way. This is done in order to center and privilege the client's interpretations and judgments versus the therapist's assessment as to whether the effects of a behavior are good or bad.

As a therapist or addiction counselor it might seem sensible to assume that alcoholism is "bad" and has negative effects in someone's life. This would perhaps lead us to assist a person in problem-solving a way out of the problem of alcoholism or addiction. This can inadvertently be an act of silencing the person's preferences and hopes, as the therapist judges what is best for the person. On the other hand, if a person struggling with an addiction is asked to think about and describe why they have judged the effects of their addiction as negative, and what that therefore means they give value to, then the person is better able to develop more individualized strategies for developing behaviors that are in line with their own preferences, values, and dreams. White (2007a) has suggested that this can lead to "problem dissolving" rather than "problem solving."

This commitment to asking the people who are consulting us to judge the effects of the problem in their life is also similar to the commitment to never take language and specific words at facc value. As discussed in Chapter 3, it is useful to think of the rhizome nature of language and the helpfulness of using even our first language as if it were our second language so that we remember to ask what the other person means by using those particular words. When did Becky begin using the word *alcoholic* or *addict*? Who and what has contributed to her use of one word over the other? How has she negotiated those words and begun to use them more tentatively? Has the use of these words been helpful? Is there another word that might also be helpful? What does this imply is important to Becky?

David Epston (personal communication, February 11, 2010) mentioned what he sees as being the difference between certain problem-solving approaches to counseling, which imply a "let me teach you what to do" stance, versus a narrative therapy stance, which asks the other to teach us what they know already about their life. It is through our questions that we assist people in coming to realize just how much "insider knowledge" (Epston, 2009b) they already have and they become clearer about their own preferences, values, and commitments, contrary to what others might suggest for them.

RE-MEMBERING CONVERSATIONS

Re-membering conversations follow a particular structure within narrative practices (Russell & Carey, 2004; White, 1995a, 2007a). They develop conversations, with those people who consult us, that focus on the impact of other people in their lives. (These re-membering conversations have also been discussed in Chapter 2 in regards the storyline structure as a three-act play.) White developed re-membering conversations based upon the "conception that identity is founded upon an 'association of life' rather than on a core self" (White, 2007a, p. 129). He also described this "association of life" as a club, as if our club of life is made up of many members. We can review membership of our club of life and make choices regarding revoking membership from those people who are not supporting our preferences, and perhaps giving honorary life membership to those who have been particularly significant in positively shaping who and what we are.

Our experience with re-membering conversations with many people, with a range of presenting problems, is that they are profoundly moving. The steps of re-membering conversations (see Russell & Carey, 2004, or White, 2007a, for a complete description of the steps) provide people with the opportunity to closely examine and richly describe not only other people's contribution to their lives and identity, but also their own contributions back to those people.

This idea of examining the effects of people in someone's life and making changes so that people will support sobriety as opposed to addiction is not new. What is new about this within narrative practices is how these re-membering conversations focus on how people affect one another's identity (White, 2007a). This focus allows for the people consulting us to reflect on how they in turn have shaped the identity of the people who have been so supportive of them. For those people who cannot remember any positive person in their life, these conversations can be based upon people whom they admire from a distance, fictional characters, pets, and even toys. These conversations would flow into discussions of how they imagine the other people might be affected if they knew of their importance to them.

Re-membering conversations can be facilitated for a number of reasons. They can be facilitated when someone is grieving the loss of a person they love, and so be used to examine the importance of that relationship and how the effects of that relationship will continue. They may be facilitated when people talk about how much they admire and respect someone who is helping them, so that they can see that they also are contributing something to the other's life and identity. They can also be used when there is a new tentative skill, like sobriety or abstinence, developing and we ask who might support the person in continuing to develop this new skill, or ask about who would be least surprised to know that this new skill was developing.

In one of my (LB) earlier conversations with Becky, she was telling me about how important her sponsor of the time was to her. Going through the steps of the re-membering conversation, I asked her about those activities that they had pursued together and then had her explore how those events and activities had contributed to how she thought of herself and the development of her identity. However, the final two steps of the conversation involved having Becky recall and describe in detail how she had contributed to her sponsor's life and then how she would have impacted her sponsor's sense of self. These last steps of the conversation need to be prefaced with a comment about how difficult it often is for people to answer these types of questions, because we are not usually asked to reflect in this way. Answering such questions as "How do you guess your acceptance of your sponsor's help has affected how she thinks about herself and her purpose in life?" "How has knowing you, and you being part of her life, enriched her life and what she holds dear?" and "The fact that you have continued with her as your sponsor, what is your guess about how that has reinforced what she values?" all brought about a shift in thinking for Becky where she was able to begin to think of her own value as well as her sponsor's value. She left the session telling me that this was a completely different conversation from any she had previously experienced and could be the beginning of helping build back some of her self-esteem. One way of looking at the shift in thinking that she experienced would be through the concept of a pivotal moment that occurred during this re-membering conversation as she began to think about herself differently. She no longer was only lucky to have that sponsor in her life, but was also more aware of her agency, of what she had done to accept her sponsor's help, and she started to feel better about herself as she realized how she had also contributed to her sponsor's life.

BECKY'S STORY

Becky consented to be audiotaped while she was interviewed about her story of healing for the purposes of this chapter (and the chapter that appeared in Csiernik and Rowe, 2010) and then later read and approved the written versions. She was given the opportunity to make changes and corrections.

Becky indicated she first realized she might have a problem with addictions and alcoholism shortly after the death of her mother. She noticed she was drinking a lot. She was seeing a social worker at that time who suggested that she try to slow down the amount she drank, by drinking a glass of water in between each alcoholic beverage. Becky says this seemed to reduce her hangovers, but it did not slow down her alcohol consumption.

She then decided to attend an addiction center in the area. They *told* (our emphasis) her she was an alcoholic but that she should be able to drink socially. They were hesitant to give her a list of local AA meetings because they did not encourage the AA approach. They made a follow-up appointment for her 2 months later, but she canceled it because she did not think they were going to be able to help her. She continued to drink for another 18 months. This indicates how unhelpful it can be for the professional to make judgments that do not involve reflections and contributions from the person requesting assistance. How does it help to diagnose someone ("you are an alcoholic") and then tell them not even to try AA while they wait 2 months for a follow-up appointment? No wonder Becky decided they were not going to be able to help her.

Becky went on to say that when a friend of hers at work told her about how her husband had attended a residential treatment center for addictions and alcoholism, she realized she needed to also look for more serious treatment and assistance. She went to her general practitioner to ask for a referral and she was told by her doctor that only 10% of alcoholics and addicts can recover (a totally incorrect fact), but that she should start by attending a "detox" center. She went to the detox center, not knowing what to expect, and was told that she would have to stay for a week right away. She said she found the staff rude and unpleasant and unwilling to assist her in juggling her work responsibilities and so she left. (Here is an example of how social workers or other professionals not listening to the complexity of a person's life situation and her preferences and values related to maintaining her job resulted in them being unable to be truly of any assistance.)

At this point Becky says she was given the name and number of a doctor who specialized in assisting people in preparing for withdrawal symptoms and referred her to the residential setting. She was given the time necessary to negotiate with her employer in order to have the 21 days necessary to move in to the residential program setting.

She says she found the residential program very helpful. The first week provided her with time to "dry out," and she was expected to begin attending three AA or NA (Narcotics Anonymous) meetings each week. She remembers being physically sick and also struggling with "paranoia" in her second week there.

Becky says that the hardest part of the program was the daily morning check-in groups when each person was expected to talk about how they were feeling at that moment. She says this was a very great struggle for her. Her 21-day program became a 28-day program since she was having difficulty sharing her emotions in the group setting. She says she ended up staying for 6 weeks because she was nervous about leaving and going home, where there was no one to support her in her new sobriety.

Becky describes the residential program as having promoted healthy living and a routine that could support health. Residents were encouraged to eat breakfast, lunch, and dinner regularly, to take walks, and to attend recreational groups as well as the therapeutic groups. She says the therapy groups were similar to AA groups but were facilitated by a professional counselor.

After the 6 weeks in the residential setting, she was offered a 9-month aftercare program, which involved attending a counselor-led group each week. Although she was also encouraged to attend AA meetings five to seven times a week during this time, she remembers "relapsing" (Becky's language) several times during the 9 months of the aftercare program. Considering the rites of passage and migration of identity metaphors discussed fully in Chapter 1, we can visualize how Becky departed from the preseparation identity that was linked to addictions and set sail into a liminal phase as she began to develop other skills. White (2006b) suggested that we can assist people in normalizing how difficult it is to make changes and fully commit to new skills by talking about the migration of identity map and clarifying how very long it can take to reach that postseparation stage, with confidence in those new skills. In this way, we might talk less about "relapsing" or even "lapsing" but would consider these natural events within the journey.

About 18 months after completing the residential and aftercare program, Becky says she met her son's father. This was a difficult relationship and during this time a cousin of Becky's, who was working as a social worker, suggested she begin individual counseling. At this point she began receiving individual counseling at a small counseling agency and she says that this, combined with AA, "saved her."

Becky says that she greatly values the one-on-one professional environment that individual counseling provides. She says that as many as 25 people may attend her usual AA meeting, and there is not time for everyone to talk and share their feelings and thoughts each week. As well, she finds there can be concerns regarding trust at times within these AA meetings. She explained that although there are ground rules regarding confidentiality, many members of AA recognize that they cannot always rely on this. She believes many members also attempt to work with individual therapists where they can trust in the safety of being able to discuss their thoughts more fully, knowing there are professional codes of ethics to guarantee privacy.

Becky says that she met with three different social workers in individual counseling appointments prior to being referred to me (LB). Two of these three were social work students. She says that she would describe this as a time of "having to go back to move forward." Each time she was transferred to another social worker, she says she would spend lots of time again looking at the history of her problem. She says she believes that she learned to be flexible during this time, as she was transferred from one person to another.

Becky has now been attending individual appointments with me for approximately 4 years. She schedules appointments about once every 4 weeks and attends weekly AA meetings. She also has begun attending church from time to time. She says this is what is supporting her right now.

I asked Becky to describe her reactions to working with me and the approach I use. She says that it feels natural and that what she has understood from my approach is that she has several stories, whereas for so many years it felt like there was only one story, which was of addiction. She says she has found it freeing to be able to pick out the more positive ways of being. In more mainstream counseling approaches she was told she had to go over the painful parts of her past in order to try to figure it out and make it better. This seemed to her to be consistent with step 4 in the AA 12 steps where she had to make an inventory of everything, including all the hurts to herself and others. She says this can be quite involving if you do it right, but the idea is to move on and she has found that a narrative approach to counseling has helped her more in the moving on.

Having to say, "Hi, I'm an alcoholic," is helpful for many people in AA as far as she can see because maybe it helps people become more accepting of themselves. It seems to make people think of themselves as always being an alcoholic and so helps people stay committed and involved in AA. We recognize that despite our commitment to move away from diagnostic labels because of the danger of their limiting the person's identity and possibilities, some people seem relieved to be given a diagnosis. We believe that this is because sometimes a diagnostic decision can feel better than the unknown at times. For instance, I am currently working with a man who received the diagnosis of ADHD as an adult. He appreciated this diagnosis because it has given him an understanding of some of his previous behaviors that formally confused him. He admits that it was probably beneficial that he was not provided this diagnosis as a child in the school system because it might have affected how others thought of him and treated him. As an educated adult he makes use of the label when and how he wishes. However, considering the need to reflect on language and also the role of migration of identity, we continue to be committed to holding on to any diagnosis tentatively, unpacking all the significance and meaning of that word to the person and highlighting the possibilities of movement from one identity (the known and familiar identity) into a liminal, betwixt-and-between phase, and then on to what is possible to know.

Becky also reports that it feels very good within narrative conversations to begin to feel separate from the alcoholism and to think of herself as having a relationship with the alcoholism as opposed to being an alcoholic. These types of externalizing conversations do not in any way minimize the seriousness of the effects of alcoholism. Becky and I continue to have discussions about how "sneaky" alcohol and pot can be in her life. They still have the power to try to convince her that just one joint or just one drink won't hurt her, but having had a recent lapse, she knows the effects of giving in and knows that she and her son are both much healthier and happier when she continues to choose healthy routines.

What Becky suggested in her final comments was that the group and community aspects of AA are extremely helpful, even though she has moved away from embracing all of AA's practices. She was interested in the possibility of narrative therapy being able to provide group support and said that she would be able to fill a group with interested people should we ever want to begin such a narrative therapy group for people wanting to take control over their addictions.

REFLECTIONS

Becky's stories raise interesting considerations for working in the area of addictions. She has attempted various treatment options and has found the greatest success for her from a combination of approaches. We cannot argue that one approach is the best approach, even though we clearly have our preferences. Becky has also experienced the frustration of lapses, but these seem to be shorter and less dramatic than her experiences with drug and alcohol prior to initiating treatment. Perhaps this implies we examine more carefully our preconceived ideas about what success and health look like. Success does not have to be based upon never having a lapse or a relapse. It can be based upon constantly moving forward, having fewer lapses, and making more choices that fit within a person's preferences and dreams for her life. It is useful to have these discussions with people, so that they are prepared for the challenges and for what they will need to do to help themselves move back into their preferred storyline.

Although Becky had been clean and sober for many years, had recently been baptized (considered a threshold marking a rite of passage within many cultures), and had become more involved in a local church, which she reports as significant positive changes in her life, when her sponsor told her that she thought she was ready to begin dating again, Becky jumped at this suggestion. She says that she had been happy as a single mom, raising her son alone and focusing on her health and her son's health, but she became distracted by this suggestion. She says she was thinking she might not need to continue individual counseling for very much longer since things appeared to be going so well in her life. However, she became happily excited by her sponsor's suggestion and began using a telephone dating service. She met and attempted relationships with several men. This has not gone well and has negatively affected her self-esteem again, which prompted a short lapse, which also affected her self-esteem. In several appointments we decided together it would be useful if we examined how her use of the telephone dating service mirrored some of the other addictive thinking. The telephone dating service can be as "sneaky" as the alcoholism, attempting to convince her that "just one" call or just "one more" meeting with a man may bring her great happiness.

Becky and I examined her alternative storyline again, looking at how a fairly recent holiday with her son, when she was not tempted by addictions, fit within her preferences and hopes. She was able to step into the alternative storyline and begin to imagine what types of small changes she might bring about if she could hold on to her values and preferences.

Just as Becky was beginning to feel far more confident in her abilities to manage her addictions and the oppressive discourses that would have labeled her as an addict, it would seem as though she was challenged by another set of discourses that would suggest she needed a man in her life in order for her to be fulfilled. As discussed previously, narrative practices are positioned to examine internalized discourses. Although our conversations were earlier focused on externalizing those internalized discourses that labeled Becky an alcoholic, narrative practices keep open the space for shifting conversations and can later focus on externalizing other discourses. Our conversations may in the future focus more on gender and heterosexual romance discourses and the effects of these in her life. Where did she learn that alcohol and drugs might give her some release from stress in her life and where has she learned that a relationship will bring further happiness?

CONCLUSION

In the introduction to their book regarding narrative practices with people resisting anorexia and bulimia, Maisel, Epston, and Borden stated that their work was not a "how to" therapy manual, since the problem of anorexia and bulimia "is too cunning a problem for any one-size-fits-all approach. It is a moving target, sidestepping your shot and returning fire. Furthermore, blanket prescriptions, even if well-intentioned, often end up mirroring the prescriptive nature of a/b itself" (2004, p. 2). In much the same way it is important to maintain a flexibility in work with addictions for addiction, particularly alcoholism, has long been called both cunning and baffling.

Narrative therapists would argue that many various discourses, whether about addiction or about therapeutic practices, contribute toward the oppression of people. Given some of the commonalities among anorexia, bulimia, disordered eating, and alcoholism, we have been struck by Maisel et al.'s (2004) comments about how narrative practices can be seen as anti-oppressive. Maisel described himself as having been drawn to narrative practices because of his "longstanding desire to see psychotherapy used to address social injustice. . . . [White's] work illustrates how power can operate in an oppressive way in the therapist-client relationship" (p. 7). Borden goes on to say that:

> narrative therapy's focus on the external "forces" which shape people's lives was far more in line with [her own] sense of justice than the therapies which viewed problems as merely arising within families or in individual minds. Narrative therapy called upon [her] desire to not stand idly by but to actively challenge cultural discourses, including those of the culture of psychotherapy. (p. 9)

Within this chapter we have demonstrated the manner in which narrative practices have provided us with an approach that is sensitive to the effects of discourses in the lives of the people, like Becky, who consult us. The problem storyline of addiction or alcoholism may have been what initiated Becky's search for counseling, but "solving" or even "dissolving" that one problem does not necessarily mean she is immune to the effects of other discourses in her life. As Maisel and Borden suggested in their contribution to the introduction to their book with Epston (Maisel et al., 2004), it is important for narrative therapists to also be involved in a type of practice that does not re-create oppressive interactions among therapists and clients and which provides opportunity to deconstruct all the discourses that contribute to social injustice in a person's life.

We are particularly drawn to narrative practices because of their commitment to assisting people in reflecting upon the effects of internalized discourses that contribute to social injustice and the maintenance of problem storylines. As discussed in Chapter 3, examining internalized discourses also involves an examination of language and a great deal of care when using language that has the danger of labeling, pathologizing, and totalizing.

Within this chapter we have also provided a practice example of how Becky experienced pivotal moments, as described in Chapter 4. This had the effect of time ramifying as she recognized that she had choices about which storyline and identity to occupy. As she has indicated, she has found this empowering, since she has come to realize that she is not fated to be stuck within a certain problem storyline because of her past, but rather she can choose to move into a preferred storyline.

Questions for Reflection

1. Why is it so important to move away from labeling people as alcoholics or addicts? What pressures are there to continue to label?
2. What are your thoughts about "lapses" and "relapses"?
3. How do you think narrative therapy could be integrated with a harm-reduction model?
4. In what way would you explain the migration of identity or rites of passage metaphor to someone so as to provide reassurance that change takes time?

CHAPTER 8

Group Practices With Men Who Have Used Abuse

In this chapter we will present a case study of a narrative therapy group that was facilitated for men who had used abuse.[1] In particular, we will present transcript examples of narrative therapy group work that came from an exploratory research project that took place in a family counseling agency in the area of Toronto, Ontario, Canada, in 2005. We will explain the earlier influences in working in the area of violence against women, describe some of the most relevant contributions to this important work from a narrative therapy perspective, and indicate how this then was translated into actual practice within this research project. We hope this will encourage people to begin to incorporate narrative practices into the work they might already be doing. Narrative ways of working are very much influenced by feminist theory and so may be integrated well within the field of responding to violence against women and children.

Students with whom we have worked in the past have sometimes wondered

1. Melissa Page-Nicholas worked as a research assistant with Laura Béres reviewing transcripts and contributing to a version of the material presented in this chapter that was published in *Families in Society: The Journal of Contemporary Social Services* (2010).

how narrative practices could be used within group settings. In an attempt to address this concern, this chapter also provides an example of working in a group format with narrative practices.

Much of the work in the area of family violence has been influenced by feminist understanding but also structured by a cognitive-behavioral approach to practice. These influences have found their way into psychoeducational models, particularly when working with groups of women or groups of men. However, as practitioners have become more and more interested in narrative therapy generally, there has also been a growing interest in integrating narrative approaches into the area of violence against women and children specifically.

Due to the growing demands from funders, and therefore agencies and organizations, for evidence-based practice, cognitive-behavioral approaches to working with men have been privileged over those approaches that have not been researched to the same extent. Therapists and counselors who have become excited by learning and practicing narrative therapy would prefer to work from a narrative perspective and so have increasingly demanded research on narrative approaches. They have been requesting this so that they can choose to work with men in various ways that have been proven effective, rather than feeling pressured by organizations to only use cognitive-behavioral approaches.

In order to respond to some of these requests for research regarding narrative practices with men, we conducted an exploratory study of the practices involved in a narrative therapy group for men who had used abuse. Our main goal was to examine transcripts of group sessions to identify whether a commitment to use a narrative therapy approach to work with men actually did result in practices notably different from traditional psychoeducational and anger-management groups. The research project was intended as a first step toward researching effectiveness of narrative work with men who had used abusive behaviors, realizing that before we could compare the results of this work to other approaches to this topic, it was important to examine the actual process of a group that was purported to be a narrative therapy group. We were interested to see whether the ideas of narrative therapy would be evident in what the two group facilitators said and asked within the group sessions. However, reviewing the findings has also provided the opportunity to consider these narrative practices within the context of new ideas about storyline structure, the circulation of language, and pivotal moments, as described in the first four chapters of this book.

LITERATURE REVIEW: THEORY AND RESEARCH

Much of the work with men who have used abuse (Ganley, 1981; Mederos, 1999; Pence & Paymar, 1993; Shepard & Pence, 1999; Stourdeur & Stille, 1989; Yllö & Bograd, 1988)—including the Domestic Abuse Intervention Project (DAIP) of Duluth, Minnesota, in the 1980s—has relied heavily on cognitive-behavioral and feminist schools of thought.

The cognitive-behavioral model views abusive behaviors as socially learned, self-reinforcing, and reflective of social skill deficits, requiring interpersonal skills training, cognitive restructuring techniques, and "time-outs" in order to enact changes in behavior (Adams, 1988; Bandura, 1973; Edelson, Miller, & Stone, 1983). However, it has also been our experience in the past that unless issues of power are addressed fully, a "time-out" is not necessarily effective because it may still be used as a control tactic. Furthermore, it is the therapist's role to point out the damaging and detrimental effects of violence, providing education around alternative behaviors and the application of new life skills (Adams). This positions the therapist in an "expert" role, with expert knowledge about how the men should change. As stated in Chapter 7, this suggests the therapist take on a role of teacher rather than one of learner. This has the tendency to shut down curiosity, which is so important within narrative practices, and does not facilitate respect for the "insider knowledge" of the other person. In our experience, we have found that this is less likely to involve the men in developing a strong commitment to particular behavior changes because the changes are suggested to them more often than coming from reflecting on their preferences and values in life.

The feminist school of thought emphasizes the need for therapeutic interventions to flow from understanding the misuse of power and control as the fundamental root of abusive behavior, and it charges therapists with the responsibility of "persistently challenging . . . the abusive ideology . . . that might makes right" (Adams, 1988, p. 196).

Another critical component of the feminist school of thought is men's self-examination of their sexist beliefs in addition to men's confrontation of their own controlling behaviors (Pence & Shepard, 1988) and acceptance of the fact that they cannot control the actions and feelings of others (Adams, 1988). Adams went on to say that feminism has brought about a broader definition of violence, encompassing both overt and covert forms of abuse that cause the victim to be fearful, coerced, or inhibited. As with many anti-oppressive approaches to practice, this can at times result in positioning the therapist as the "expert" who is required to educate the client in order for the client to become more aware of these power dynamics in society.

Glancy and Saini, in reviewing studies regarding anger and aggression, found that the majority focused on "treatments containing components of cognitive and behavioral aspects or combination of the two" (2005, p. 229). They concluded that "the most pressing need is for more and higher-quality primary studies on the effectiveness of anger and aggression treatment programs using a variety of psychological treatment approaches" (p. 244). They particularly suggested that research needs to clearly indicate the interventions being studied. Our study was a first step toward more rigorous examination of narrative therapy approaches with men who have used abuse. Although we have provided anecdotal feedback from the female partners about their observations of the effects of the group, the main purpose was to examine whether a group being facilitated from a narrative perspective was, in fact, different in its content and process from a typical cognitive-behavioral-influenced group. The next step could involve more rigorous outcome studies.

Cranwell Schmidt et al. examined attitude and motivating factors to change in men who had used abusive behaviors. The researchers focused on men who had participated in a group based on profeminist and cognitive-behavioral approaches. According to Cranwell Schmidt et al., "research indicates that batterers hold rigid sex role stereotypes, or traditional, stereotypic views of masculine and feminine roles and male-female relationships" (2007, p. 92). They went on to say that there is limited research on the effectiveness in changing batterers' perceptions in this area and on linking these changes to ongoing changes in behavior.

At the same time that models to address woman abuse were developing out of cognitive-behavioral and feminist-based theories, Jenkins's narrative therapy approach was also emerging. His approach was based on the original theoretical work of Bateson (1972, 1980), White (1984, 1986), and White and Epston (1990). In Jenkins's model, developmental issues, sociocultural factors, family of origin, history of abuse, gender roles, personality characteristics, addiction, financial or marital stressors, and individual psychology are seen not as reasons for abusive behavior, but as influences that reinforce values and ways of thinking that promote abusive behavior rather than the acceptance of responsibility. Jenkins referred to these traditions, values, and paradigms as "restraints" that inhibit the establishment of respectful, mutual, nonabusive ways of being in and relating to the world. Lastly, Jenkins proposed that the key to facilitating men's acceptance of responsibility and accountability is to invite each man to "become preoccupied with his own competence in challenging restraining habits and ideas and discovering and practicing alternatives to abuse" (1990, p. 32). Assisting someone in becoming preoccupied with his own competence is another way of saying that we can assist someone in recognizing their own insider knowledge. This contributes to shifting the focus away from the expertise of the therapist and toward the expertise of the person who is consulting the therapist.

Narrative therapy takes into account discourses of stereotypical masculine and feminine roles as aspects of the restraints to change that must be reflected upon during the therapeutic work. This is one area that narrative approaches have in common with feminist approaches (Russell & Carey, 2004). As Russell and Carey pointed out, the philosophical and political underpinnings of narrative therapy have been very much influenced by feminist thinking. Narrative therapy strives to position the client as the expert on his life, while acknowledging that the therapist is an expert in the therapeutic process. This is also an opportunity to provide a role model for an alternative way of being for the men who have become accustomed to stereotypical uses of power. Rather than teaching men about discourses such as power and control dynamics, narrative practices are committed to helping men uncover this knowledge through self-reflection prompted by a carefully structured series of questions designed to scaffold learning across the 'known and familiar' to the 'possible to know' (White, 2007a) and throughout the therapeutic journey as described in Chapter 2. Narrative therapy suggests that when a man's expertise in his own life is centered and acknowledged, he will be more likely to commit to following through with changes that are congruent with a preferred way of being.

Within this context of developing different approaches to working with men, Buttell and Carney (2006) have critiqued the "one size fits all" mentality when addressing standardization within treatment groups for men who have used abusive behaviors, arguing that this approach provides no room for diversity in meeting the needs of specific minority populations. Levin-Rozalis, Bar-On, and Hartaf (2005) also discussed the lack of efficacy with traditional North American treatment models. In addition, it can be argued that standardization based on the traditionally feminist-informed, cognitive-behavioral group treatment approach (Buttell & Carney) inhibits the opportunity for research on the application of newer treatment models, such as narrative therapy, in an attempt to rectify the elements of the traditional model that have proven limitations.

Since the pioneering narrative work of Jenkins (1990), these ideas have been further developed. Katz (2006), Ericsson, Taneja, Jhally, Katz, and Earp (2002), and Nylund (2005, 2007) have particularly examined the impact of discourses of masculinity on men struggling with developing nonaggressive ways of being. Denborough (1995), Fisher (2005), and Augusta-Scott (2001, 2007) also further explored and developed narrative therapy and theory as applied to a group model of working with men who have used abusive behaviors toward their female partners and children. Despite all of this interest and work, narrative approaches with men continue to be very much underresearched.

STUDY DESIGN

Objectives

The main purpose of the study conducted with this group was to begin a process of studying narrative therapy practices with men who have used abuse because these practices continue to be underresearched. With this in mind, we began by focusing on this group in such a manner as to particularly examine whether a group designed to be facilitated from a narrative therapy point of view did, in fact, look and sound any different from a group run from a cognitive-behavioral or psychoeducational model. Because the theoretical framework and resulting interactions are shaped primarily by the therapists/facilitators, we were mainly interested in examining the kinds of questions and statements used by the facilitators in order to judge whether these were narrative in nature. There is little point in studying effectiveness if we do not, first of all, know what therapeutic process we are examining.

We included partner contact feedback because it was standard practice of the agency involved, but it resulted in only anecdotal feedback at this time.

Methodology

Guba and Lincoln (2005) suggested the following:

> Geertz's . . . prophecy about the "blurring of genres" is rapidly being fulfilled. Inquiry methodology can no longer be treated as a set of universally applicable rules or abstraction. Methodology is inevitably interwoven with and emerges from the nature of particular disciplines . . . and particular perspectives. (p. 191)

This study drew upon a variety of different approaches, such as a case study design and phenomenological content analysis, which we will describe further. Our hope is that more and more narrative therapists might begin to reflect upon, study, and write about their work. These simple case-study designs are a relatively simple way to begin this process.

Purposive Sample

Because our aim in this study was to examine whether a group described as a narrative therapy group for men actually demonstrated narrative practices, we needed to find a group to study that was reported to be informed by narrative therapy. We discovered only one group attempting this in our geographical area (southwestern Ontario, between London and Toronto in Canada).

The target population for participants in the group was men, aged 25 and older, who were referred to the agency due to having used abusive behaviors in their intimate relationships. The geographic catchment area included all of the greater Toronto area.

The group was not a mandated program. However, in most cases the men were strongly encouraged to participate by someone such as their partner, a family member, or a child protection worker. Referrals were made by third parties, but the individual men were also required to initiate contact by a phone call to set up a screening interview. The screening interviews lasted approximately 1 hour each. These interviews were comprised of semistructured questions related to such items as current living situation, family of origin, abuse history, legal involvement, mental and physical health, spirituality, substance use/abuse, suicidal ideations, coping, and goals for therapy. A behavioral checklist and a conflict tactic scale were both used as part of the screening and to begin the process of having the men reflect on their behaviors and possible impacts of their behaviors. These were fairly standard "screening" interviews and were not overly influenced by narrative practices, but did provide the opportunity for gathering a sense of the men's backstories and readiness for the journey to begin.

As the men were offered placement in the group, we explained the research component of this particular group and had the men sign consent forms if they agreed to participate in the group while the research was being conducted.

The group was a closed group comprised of 12 total sessions, each 2 hours in length. The 12 weeks were organized according to the following topics:

1. *Contracting to face abuse (safety guidelines/context of self-respect, preferences for relationships/social expectations for men, define taking responsibility for abuse/define abuse, define distractions)*
2. *Naming violence/beliefs (gender boxes, shame and sexism, men study their abuse/beliefs)*
3. *Impact of abuse (disabling shame and helpful guilt, internalized other interview—building empathy)*
4. *Demonstrating respect (define areas in which men want to demonstrate respect, demonstrating respect)* (Fisher & Augusta-Scott, 2003)

After the 12th group session, the facilitators conducted a final exit interview for each group member. Its purpose was for planning and referral, based on individual needs following the group experience, as well as to provide an individual opportunity for closure and feedback to the group facilitators. The group aimed to begin with a maximum of 12 and a minimum of 6 participants.

A total of 6 men participated in this particular group studied. There were two group facilitators—one male, who had been extensively trained in narrative therapy and was experienced in running this type of group, and one female, who was a recent graduate of a social work program and had cofacilitated this group only twice previously and was much newer to narrative practices.

The facilitator with greater experience had worked closely in the past with an experienced narrative therapist and trainer in another part of the country. The facilitator had attended numerous narrative conferences and training workshops and had recently begun graduate studies in postmodern and poststructuralist ways of working in social work.

The agency in which this study took place has long had the policy of ensuring that both a male and female work together in facilitating groups for men. There are two reasons for this. On the one hand, having a woman present adds an element of accountability to women, which would be consistent with feminist and narrative concerns. On the other hand, the participants are able to witness respectful interactions between a man and woman as a form of role modeling, which has its roots in more of a cognitive-behavioral framework.

Partner Contact Procedures

It is also standard practice at this agency to include partner contact as a necessary component of services to men who have used abusive behaviors. The men sign consent forms that give permission to a social worker on the Violence Against Women (VAW) team to contact their female partners/former partners to ensure that the women are safe and have access to any needed services. The women are contacted before the group begins, once during the group, and once following the group. From time to time, the women do not wish further contact from the VAW team because they have no further contact with the men who are attending the group. The social worker who contacts the women is not one of the group facilitators because this ensures complete confidentiality for the women and avoids any conflict of interest. The partner contact also allows for a more objective evaluation from the partner as to whether or not the man's behaviors have changed, rather than relying solely on group facilitator observations or the reports of the men themselves.

Data Collection

Each of the 12 group sessions was audiotaped and then transcribed. Both the primary investigator (LB) and research assistant (MPN) were trained in narrative therapy theory and practice. The primary investigator had previously cofacilitated this group at this agency. Both had also previously facilitated groups for men from a more traditional feminist, cognitive-behavioral standpoint prior to their training in narrative therapy. Each reviewed the transcripts for themes separately from each other and only then consulted and reviewed findings together.

Content Analysis

The analysis of the transcribed taped group sessions was influenced by a phenomenological approach because we were primarily interested in the general essence of the facilitators' questions and comments. However, we analyzed the whole text so that the resulting responses from group members could also be reviewed. We examined the texts deductively to see which of the utterances could be seen as influenced by narrative practices such as, perhaps, comments that engaged in externalizing the problem or developing an alternative storyline from unique outcomes. However, through immersion in the texts, it was possible for inductive themes to unexpectedly emerge.

We had originally thought that if we found a narrative group to be significantly different from other group approaches, the next step would be to incorporate more thorough analysis of the outcomes of narrative therapy compared with psychoeducational and cognitive-behavioral approaches in group work with men who have used abuse. However, we found in this study that this group was influenced by a range of approaches, including narrative practices. Therefore, we suggest that future studies could benefit from thoroughly describing what goes on in the group process as well as the outcomes because it may be unrealistic to expect any group to be facilitated purely from one approach. We also did not expect to see such a difference among the types of questions and comments made by the two facilitators; we now believe this was based on their level of training and experience.

Findings/Themes

We will focus on themes that derive from this particular narrative therapy group that was studied, although the actual quotes provided may share elements with other approaches. There was a great deal of discussion regarding socialization of men and women and power imbalances, but these would not be unique to a narrative therapy group and we have chosen not to present examples of this here. As a result, we have not referenced all of the group sessions.

The themes that emerged deductively from the data were externalizing conversations, challenging essentialism–totalizing accounts, centering client knowledge, dominant and alternative storylines, and preferred ways of being. An inductive theme that emerged was building empathy.

Externalizing Conversations

Externalizing conversations, as described in Chapter 2, assist in developing interactions that help people "experience an identity that is separate from the problem; the problem becomes the problem, not the person" (White, 2007a, p. 9). These types of conversations help shift from the internalization of blame and shame and, in the case of working with men who have used abuse, they decrease the chances of the men becoming defensive about their attitudes and behaviors. This then allows us to examine dominant discourses about masculinity that link masculinity with the use of violence and abuse, and also the development of responsibility for change.

If we can place the abuse outside of the men's identities, they can then gain insight into the abuse through examining where they learned these behaviors, who and what supported the behaviors, how the behaviors have negatively impacted them and the people they care for, and what they can do now to learn and implement alternative, nonabusive ways of interacting. This can also be achieved by creating some distance from the experience, so that the men have a sense of looking back at their situations from a new territory.

In session 1, page 15, Facilitator 1 said, "One of the things that we want to try to achieve is some kind of distance from your own experience, right? . . . So, part of what we want to do is set it up so that we can start to have a little distance from that experience . . . sort of like watching TV or a sports game or something like that . . . so that you can sort of guess what's going to happen next."

One aspect of an externalizing conversation is examining the effects of the problem. In session 2, page 34, Facilitator 2 said, with regard to their discussion about masculine and feminine discourses and expectations of gendered interests and topics of discussions, "The other part we were just going to talk about was the effects. What are the effects on men you know in regards the kinds of stuff that you are expected to talk about and what you are not expected to talk about . . . ?"

In session 9, page 18, when looking at effects again in more detail, one of the men in the group was able to identify as follows: "It's all related to her self-esteem. She just wants to feel good about herself and I ain't helping it." Facilitator 2 asked, "And do you want her to feel good about herself?" (This may seem like a simplistic question, but a narrative approach as described in Chapter 3, suggests the importance of asking about what might otherwise seem "taken for granted," providing the space to have the person "justify" his "evaluation" of the "effects" [White, 2007a].) The man replied, "Absolutely."

Challenging Essentialism–Totalizing Accounts

As discussed fully in Chapter 3, there is a need for caution in the use of labels and language that "totalizes" (White, 1995a) in any context. Even referring to a woman as a "victim" or a "survivor" can limit a woman's identity, as if that is all there is to know of her. If we call a man an "abuser" or a "perpetrator," we may inadvertently limit his potential to choose to be anything other than that. It is clear from the group transcripts that the cofacilitators were both mindful and intentional in their use of language; the purpose was to not totalize the male participants or limit them to a rigid identity of an abuser rather than a male who has used abusive behaviors but has the capacity for change. This is obviously a sensitive area because language is powerful, and there is also the need to help the men take responsibility for their abuse. We believe, however, that it is only through the careful deconstruction of the abusive *behaviors* that the men can choose to move toward other ways of being, and this needs to be done in a way that does not totalize them as abusers but rather opens space for preferred ways of being.

In session 1, page 14, Facilitator 1 attempted to set the stage for acknowledging the tendency for men to blame their partners, while suggesting the need for taking responsibility:

"When it all comes down to it, it's very likely the case that your partners do things that drive you nuts sometimes, and that's the way it is, and what we feel is helpful is to focus on what we can take responsibility for."

This is not only a narrative type of comment, but also consistent with shifting the men from blaming their partners and beginning to take responsibility for their own behaviors—which is necessary in this type of work, regardless of the approach used.

Having set the tone that the men need to take responsibility for their behaviors, Facilitator 1 in session 3, page 8, said the following:

> That doesn't mean that I am pathetic, or that you are pathetic . . . I think it's helpful to sort of not see it as something that is wrong with me . . . but to see there are patterns here that we are all living out and we've been indoctrinated into following from the time we were little boys, and these have an effect on how we are in our relationships. . . . I guess, for me, that's what gets really interesting about this stuff. It's how can we take responsibility and at the same time locate it outside of just me? How can I do something different than what I've been raised to do?

This comment would be consistent with an attempt to externalize the abusive behaviors and the discourses that support abusive behaviors. It moves away from totalizing accounts of the men while, at the same time, supporting the need for them to take responsibility for the behaviors. We believe it also is consistent with the narrative commitment to maintain a sense of curiosity.

In session 7, page 22, Facilitator 1 again said this:

> One of our assumptions is that no one in this room is *only and always* angry and abusive and violent and terrible and stressed out and all that stuff . . . part of this process is not to just come up with things that are new, but to come up with things that are actually really important but in other pieces of your life . . . it's about kind of noticing all the different things that are going on in your life all the time and making more of an intentional choice about what we want to sort of tap into.

We particularly like this comment that Facilitator 1 made at this point because it is a good example of how to move away from interacting with the men as if they were only "abusers." Rather, he makes it clear that he believes that the men are not always angry and abusive and that it is important to become interested in what is going on at other times in their lives in order to be better able to notice the types of behaviors they already enact that might provide them with other choices. This is also an example of looking for the unique outcomes, or events, that have not been storied into the dominant story line and that provide the clues and first steps for the development of an alternative (nonabusive) story line.

Centering Client Knowledge

As previously stated, a major tenet of narrative therapy is to center the client's knowledge and decenter the therapist's position as "expert." However, this does not mean that the therapist's knowledge and experience are minimized. The therapist is the process expert, but the man is always more knowledgeable than anyone else about the content of his life. Narrative therapy comes from a place of attempting to ask thought-provoking questions that elicit thicker descriptions and a fuller context of a situation, rather than coming from a position of diagnosing and teaching a client. It is evident from the transcripts that the group cofacilitators came from this mind-set, although at times there was more of a monologue from the cofacilitators rather than posing more questions to gain richer and more complete descriptions from the group members.

Despite some of these slips into monologues, there were numerous examples of the facilitators' attempts to center the men's knowledge. In session 1, page 17, Facilitator 1 said, "It's not about us introducing some, you know, revolutionary new technique. It's about noticing the stuff you are already doing that works and kind of stretching it out a little bit."

Each week, beginning with session 3, the facilitators began the process of distributing typed handouts created from the notes generated from the previous week's discussions with the men (notes were originally made on paper attached to the walls of the group's meeting room). This placed value on the men's insights. As we have indicated in previous chapters, narrative therapy often incorporates therapeutic documents (Speedy, 2005; White & Epston, 1990) as a way of supporting new initiatives, and these handouts were a nice example of how to do this within a group setting.

In session 5, page 2, Facilitator 1 said, "That's a good example of one of those things that you'll never see in a '21 tips for communication in a relationship,' . . . but it's important to notice what works in your relationship." This is a good example of looking for "experience-near" (White, 2007a) descriptions and centering the knowledge of the men in the group.

Dominant and Alternative Storylines

As we have stressed in the first two chapters, one of the unique aspects of narrative therapy is its focus on storylines. As we have pointed out, White and Epston (1990) argued that people talk about their lives as they would a story, linking together a series of events across time according to a plot or theme. Although people usually begin therapeutic conversations because of the effects of a problem storyline (e.g., abuse), White and Epston suggested that it is important to help people uncover those unique events that fall outside of that problem storyline and can be strung together under an alternative theme. Once a few different events begin to be uncovered and highlighted, they lead the way for further actions in the future that will also be consistent with that alternative storyline (e.g., one of respect rather than abuse). This also contributes to centering client knowledge because it reinforces that the clients may not need to learn a whole new repertoire of behaviors; they may already have some skills that they can use more often—skills that have previously gone unnoticed and unstoried.

In session 1, page 2, Facilitator 1 asked, "How did it subside in the end?" as a way of looking for a unique outcome that could be the first step toward developing an alternative storyline.

In session 2, page 4, Facilitator 2 asked, "How do you stay calm when you don't feel calm?" The man responded, "I just kind of catch myself, and I am catching myself more because I am kind of watching out for it. . . . I'm not saying I have control all the time, but I feel this way when I'm looking out for it. . . . If I stay calm, everything resolves."

In session 5, page 1, Facilitator 1 said, "This week, we would like to focus on some of the things everyone is already doing to have a different relationship . . . to look at some of the specific kinds of skills that people are using."

In session 5, page 8, Facilitator 1 supported an alternative storyline that a man shared regarding how he handled a situation differently than he would have in the past, and which resulted in a hug from his wife rather than a cold stare: "It sounds as though one of the things that didn't happen was 'dismissing her feelings,' but also [as was a concern in the first group session— our addition] you didn't just say, 'Yes, dear.' You didn't give in, the two of you talked."

In session 6, page 3, Facilitator 1 responded after a man described how his wife scraped the whole side of the car and he stayed calm, even though in the past he would have "lost it": "So, that's very different from what you might have done." The man replied, "Oh, absolutely. I thought it just doesn't make sense to belittle her, yell at her. It's already done. What're you going to do? Accidents happen."

Within narrative approaches, however, room is always kept to discuss the problem storyline when required. This is not only a strengths-based and solution-focused approach, looking solely at strengths and future solutions, but it also believes that clients wish to discuss the problems to a certain degree and learn from them. This contributes to the clients feeling understood by the facilitators. There is an attempt to make space for discussion of both the problem and alternative storylines. In discussing people's complaints and problems, using the absent but implicit conversational structure as described in Chapter 3, it is possible to also highlight people's values, preferences, and skills.

In session 9, a couple of the men brought up a few examples of previous attempts to change that did not work well in order to learn why those attempts were not effective. On page 8, Facilitator 1 said, "Well, one of the things you've noted is that what often happens if you go away and stew about something is that you end up blowing up later, right?" One of the men in the group continued:

> I was leaving it, and it was bugging the crap out of me. It was like I knew I should just forget it, but it was making me so mad—and I think that without letting it go, I couldn't find a way to express it, because I wasn't thinking straight. You know, by just letting myself sit there and stew and think about it, I didn't know a good way out of it, you know. I just was sitting there feeling nothing productive.

This demonstrates that a certain level of acceptance and safety had been generated in this group where men could discuss their attempts and struggles in this way.

Preferred Ways of Being

Many of the conversational maps that White (2007a) described using in his approach to working with people incorporate an element of assisting people to become much more articulate and aware of their preferred ways of being. This means describing those ideas and ways of being that they value. These conversational maps particularly allow for carefully crafted and structured questions. These specific conversational maps did not appear directly in the groups' transcriptions, but the ideas behind the maps were present.

The men in the group did not prefer to be abusive toward their partners. They did not want to be thought of as "abusers." In helping them provide thick and rich descriptions of how they would prefer their relationships with their partners and children to be, they were better able to talk about their values and dreams. This could then help them develop new behaviors within the context of what was important to them, which helped them commit to attempting these behaviors. This contributed to "problem dissolving" rather than "problem solving."

In groups that were previously facilitated at this agency, before shifting to the use of a narrative framework, men reported at the completion of their groups that although they might have finally begun to accept that their behaviors had previously been abusive, they felt they were still unsure of how they should behave instead. They were still uncertain as to what would constitute respectful, nonabusive behaviors. The decision was therefore made to spend the last two group sessions primarily focused on discussing the development of respectful behaviors. However, as early as session 2, the facilitators raised the topic of what the men's hopes and dreams for their relationships had been in the early stages of the relationships.

Narrative perspectives also use "why" questions fairly liberally. White (2007a) argued for the need to develop a further comfort with using this word because it can help people articulate their meaning-making behaviors, intentions, and hopes. It helps both therapists and the people consulting them to move beyond the "taken for granteds."

In session 3, page 27, a man talked about changes he'd made being noticed at work. He said that it was "a good thing, right?" Facilitator 1 asked, "Why is that a good thing for you?" This pushed the man to explore what his preferences were because he thought this might be a good thing. He said, "It just makes me feel better because I am actually getting a response without having to yell. I think ahead of time about how to present it."

In session 5, page 11, Facilitator 2 asked, "Why is that important to you? Why would you say that's important in terms of the relationship?"

Rather than make the men defensive, which some suggest is the potential problem with "why" questions, these questions assist men develop thicker and more detailed descriptions about their commitments.

In session 6, page 4, Facilitator 1 said, "So part of what we would like to look at today is what's that place that that's coming from? What are the values, or the things that are important to you that help you to sort of take a stand against belittling her or getting angry or against abuse?" Facilitator 2 said, "What do you stand for by coming here?" One man suggested that he stood for "family values and respect for his marriage." On page 8, Facilitator 1 asked, "Does anyone want to say anything about that? Maybe, like, why that point is important?" This was an attempt to thicken the storyline around preferences. Later, on page 31, Facilitator 1 also said, "This might sound like a stupid question, but why do you want a happy family?" This provided a way for the men to further examine those taken-for-granted assumptions and truly unpack their preferences.

In session 7, page 7, Facilitator 1 asked, "When you are trying to keep your children from seeing the argument, to try and keep the problems away from them, what are your hopes in that? What are you kind of hoping for your children, and what are you hoping for your relationship with your wife when you do that?"

A lovely example of how moving these conversations can be for the men occurred on pages 24 and 25 of session 7, when Facilitator 1 asked, "So if you have taken that as a kind of principle that's important to you, what would you call that?" The man responded, "I don't know if I can answer that, but I see it as important to have a strong, loving family where my son can grow up with confidence in himself and hopefully learn how to treat people well and not follow the same angry path I have." Facilitator 1 responded, "It always amazes me when people say they don't know if they can answer, and then they go on to answer beautifully." The man commented, "I don't know where that came from, I really don't." This exchange also highlighted the man's knowledge that he hadn't previously recognized.

Building Empathy

A focus on developing empathy has not been particularly emphasized by narrative authors, but the earlier work of Fisher and Augusta-Scott (2003) suggested incorporating internalized "other" interviews into narrative group practices with men who have used abusive behaviors. The group we studied also incorporated this technique; in sessions 9 and 10, one volunteer from the group was interviewed as if he were his wife. The facilitator repeated the man's wife's name numerous times while interviewing the man, so he began to tap into what her responses might be to certain questions about their relationship and his behaviors. Men have reported how different this experience is from traditional role-playing and how emotionally powerful this experience can be for them. This also helps them begin to realize that their partners may not be quick to trust their commitment to now interact in nonabusive ways. In session 9, page 27, Facilitator 2 wondered whether a man's wife was, in fact, still unsure of his wishes. Facilitator 1 pursued this on page 28 by asking the man, "What would it look like if you were able to demonstrate to her right now that you are going to respect and understand why she currently still has this wall built up?" This tied in with attempting to have the men stand within their new alternative storyline of respect and imagine how they would be and behave as a result of being in an alternative storyline.

Limitations of This Study

Given the fact that the family service agency committed to having two facilitators for this group, it would have been preferable to have more participants in the group in order to move away from centering the facilitators as much as possible. It was unfortunate that only 6 men joined the group for the sessions that were being taped and transcribed. However, this provided each participant with more "air time" in the group. Because we were primarily interested in examining the questions and comments of the facilitators, this was not as great a problem as it would have been if we had been focusing on outcomes for the men. Another limitation of this study was that we audiotaped and transcribed only one series of group sessions.

Although this study's intention was to examine the facilitators' behaviors rather than to examine outcomes, the VAW team supervisor who conducted the partner contacts provided some anecdotal comments. These are in no way rigorous, but they may be of interest and can be explored more fully in future studies. She reported an overall shift in the types of comments the women made from the time this agency first started facilitating groups for men, from a cognitive-behavioral approach, through the last 5 or 6 years, when they have been facilitated within a narrative framework. The supervisor said that approximately a third of the women reported positive improvements and that they remained with their partners. Another third said they did not see much of a change, and the final third said they would separate from their partners. Although she believed the overall proportions in each category seemed similar with both approaches, the women reported much more respectful conversations and dialogical interactions as a result of the narrative therapy group. The supervisor asked us to pursue further research now that we can see that a narrative therapy group does, in fact, integrate narrative principles. Further research would allow us to more rigorously examine the process, effects, and outcomes of the group involvement.

Implications for Practice and Research

It was satisfying to see in the group session transcripts that a commitment to interact within a group from a narrative therapy stance does, in fact, result in interactions that engage in externalizing conversations, moving away from totalizing accounts, centering the men's knowledge, supporting an analysis of dominant and alternative storylines, and the privileging of values and preferences as well as building empathy. Therapists wishing to facilitate groups from a narrative perspective may be interested in the examples from the transcripts of how the facilitators incorporated narrative practices in this setting.

It was also interesting to hear from the VAW supervisor that, through her partner contacts, she began to see a trend of the women reporting more respectful discussions as a result of involvement in the narrative therapy group. This aspect of this exploratory study can be developed much more thoroughly for future studies into the effects of these types of groups.

Since narrative therapy is oriented to a specific paradigm and grounded in postmodern and poststructuralist thought, it requires an adoption of a new therapeutic posture and a new way of thinking rather than simply learning a new set of practice skills. Thus, it is not surprising to find that while the transcripts demonstrated that the experienced facilitator of this group maintained a narrative therapy framework of practice throughout the group, the less experienced facilitator at times interacted with the men in the group in a manner that more closely resembled a didactic approach.

In future research involving the evaluation of outcomes of narrative therapy groups, it will be important to ensure that either the process is followed in a truly narrative manner or the process is much more clearly described each time a group is studied. This is because it may be common for facilitators to actually draw from a number of approaches rather than facilitate a group that is "purely" driven from one approach or another. Further studies will need to review larger numbers of groups and use multiple methods to incorporate more outcome results and feedback from the participants in the group and their partners.

CONCLUSION

Within this chapter we have presented the structure and results of a small case study of a narrative therapy group that was facilitated for men who had used abuse in their intimate relationships. We have presented this work to demonstrate how narrative approaches and the ideas inherent within the narrative conversational maps may be adjusted and practiced within a group setting. The themes that were discussed demonstrate the manner in which important concepts to narrative therapy, like externalizing the problem and moving away from totalizing accounts, continue to be possible within a group setting.

The work that the cofacilitators and men did also demonstrated reflection upon the taken-for-granted understandings inherent within language and discourses that circulate about masculinity and men's ways of being with women and children. This was consistent with our discussion regarding the circulation of language in Chapter 3.

Also, the structure of topics covered through the 12 weeks of group sessions shows a movement from reflecting upon their previous hopes for their relationships, an examination of the behaviors that damaged their chances of fulfilling those hopes, and finally a movement toward an alternative identity of nonabuse, which is consistent with the three-act-play metaphor and migration of identity. This would provide an answer to why men in previous groups that had not been facilitated from a narrative perspective had suggested that although they might at the end of group recognize they had been abusive, they did not know how to act instead. It is as if previous groups had taken men into the liminal stage of the migration of identity, but had not continued their journey any farther and had not arrived at their destination in the new territory with a new sense of identity fully explored. This reminds us of the usefulness of the three-act-play, rites of passage, and migration of identity metaphors for supporting people in their journeys all the way through to their preferred destinations.

Finally, within this chapter, we have also demonstrated the manner in which a case study can be used to examine practices within a group setting. We hope that more people will begin to write about their practices and so contribute to a broader base of practices from which therapists can choose to work within agency settings that are demanding the use of evidence-based practices.

Questions for Reflection

1. How comfortable are you in being able to talk about "men who have used abuse" versus "abusers"?
2. How have you experienced language as being used to label people?
3. What challenges do you experience regarding the commitment to move away from totalizing and pathologizing descriptions of people who have used abuse?

4. What do you think about Jenkin's ideas of "inviting men to responsibility"?
5. How would you describe the link between moving away from labeling and the possibilities that can open up for men when they are treated as more than just an "abuser"?
6. How will you respond to the invitation to write about your practices?

Conclusion

It has been an exciting process to work together on our narrative practice, training, and research project, and to finally experience it coming together as a book. We have spent endless hours combing through massive amounts of detail, grappling with new concepts, sometimes very inspired through the development of a new concept or practice and other times experiencing a crisis of faith, lost in a sea of ambiguity. Like any journey, we learned a great deal through trial and error and a lot about our own perseverance. To then be able to work together even further to organize our work into book form has truly been a gift. It has been a very great pleasure and privilege to have the opportunity to work together, reflecting upon and writing about narrative practices.

As we have indicated throughout the book, we are indebted to Michael White and David Epston for their groundbreaking and foundational work in developing narrative practices. Yet, one of the many qualities that we have admired in both Michael and David is their unquenchable thirst for knowledge, which incorporates openness to further developments in narrative practices. We have often heard Michael close his training sessions by saying he realized that as people began practicing narrative therapy this approach would continue to evolve and change. It has been with encouragement like this that we have brought critical reflective practices to our research and writing, in order to be able to further build upon and expand theory and practice within narrative approaches. In this way practice further extends and continually informs theory.

Having remained committed to the foundational philosophical and political underpinnings of narrative therapy, we have felt the confidence to reflect upon our teaching and practice in order to expand and develop new theory. We believe that this has resulted in a truly unique book in which practice, theory, and research have been woven together throughout each chapter. In the first section of the book, which primarily presents new and expanded theory, we have explained how the research brought these areas to our attention and we have provided practice examples to ground the theory. In the second section of the book, which primarily provides detailed descriptions of narrative practice in a variety of settings, we have demonstrated the use of simple case-study designs and linked these descriptions to the theories presented in the first section of the book.

Although we wrote this book together, we found that we were required to each write separately for a great deal of the time, bringing drafts of the work to each other in order for both of our voices to find their way more fully into each chapter. This resulted in the writing process being more of a solitary activity than either one of us initially imagined it might be. However, just as Deleuze and Parnet commented on the rhizome nature of their writing together, so that by the end they could not be sure who had contributed which word or thought, we have also found that not only have we influenced each other, but we are aware of all the various influences surrounding us. So, in some ways, it has not been an isolating process at all, because we can almost hear the community of scholars and practitioners all around us providing their thoughts and experiences.

Within the introduction we described the research project and research team that developed as narrative therapy practices were taught within an advanced-level program at the Hincks-Dellcrest Centre, Gail Appel Institute in Toronto. We described the manner in which narrative practices were taught and the manner in which field notes were generated. The tapestry of ideas and practices that have come from that research would not have been as rich or colorful without the contributions of all the team members at that time. As we have indicated in Chapter 3, for instance, we are particularly indebted to Adrienne Chambon for her interest in the circulation of language, which then energized us all the more to pursue further reading in this area.

In the Introduction we also presented a concept map as a structure to visualize the manner in which various concepts within narrative therapy relate to and support one another, including the new ideas that we have described in the first section of the book. We have presented this concept map at conferences early on in the research process and have received encouragement to utilize it in this way in this book.

Within the first section of this book the first chapter provided the historical and cultural background, which illustrated the significance of story within therapeutic settings. This provided a backdrop to understand how narrative therapy practices are situated within an ever-changing cultural discourse that is also embedded in story form, thus making it contextually relevant. Then in the following three chapters within the first section, we discussed in detail three innovative ideas about narrative therapy that came out of the field research described in the Introduction. In Chapter 2, the metaphor of therapy as a three-act play, which expands the rites of passage passage analogy, was introduced. The three-act play includes a conversational map, illustrating incremental steps for developing storyline. In Chapter 3, the significance of the circulation of language and the need to work both tentatively and creatively with language were presented. We also reflected within Chapter 3 on the need to consider the issue of ethics as we talk and write about others. Within Chapter 4 we presented new ideas about how to notice and work with pivotal moments, how these moments are transportive, and how they revolutionize the way in which we think about time and therapy.

In the second section of this book we have provided four practice chapters, all of which focused on one area of practice or another. Each chapter also demonstrated a method for reflecting upon or researching practice, and also provided practice examples of the new ideas presented in the first section of the book.

In Chapter 5, Karen Young presented her method of working from a narrative perspective with families as they request services within a walk-in clinic. She has invited families to return to watch copies of tapes and DVDs of their sessions of therapy in order to comment on those aspects of the sessions that were the most significant to them. This represents an innovative form of qualitative research, which we will be continuing to develop as we pursue further research at the Hincks-Dellcrest Centre, Gail Appel Institute in the future.

In Chapter 6, we presented a case study highlighting the process of working with a woman who was reclaiming her voice from many years of ritual abuse. We charted her story as she journeyed from the underworld to a vivid life filled with possibility and hope. This chapter came about from reviewing videotapes of sessions, transcribing conversations, and involving Jo in reflecting on her work with me (JD). She provided the title for the chapter and numerous comments on the process of our work together. The process of our journey together has been described using the metaphor of the three-act play. Our work together emphasized the notion that Jo's difficulties were situated in a social cultural backdrop and part of an intense life transition.

In Chapter 7, we presented a case study in which Becky's story of reclaiming her life from the effects of addiction was described. She shared her thoughts about how empowering she has found it to begin to talk about the effects of alcoholism in her life and to think of the multiple story lines that are available to her as she reflects on events in her life, rather than only think of herself as an alcoholic who needs to heal from problems in her past. Becky's story highlighted the manner in which language needs to be used carefully in order not to pathologize and totalize people. Examples of pivotal moments and the opening up of personal agency and choice in alternative storylines have also been described.

Finally, in Chapter 8, we have provided an example of how narrative practices can be used within a group format for men who have used abuse. In this chapter we have demonstrated the way in which a case study method may be used for researching a group. We have presented the themes that were found within the case study and have also pointed out aspects related to language and the three-act play metaphor.

We have begun to realize that the process of writing this book has also followed the stages of the rites of passage metaphor. A great part of the journey involved the liminal stage as we felt very much betwixt and between. As we readied ourselves for passing on the manuscript, we sensed that this was a transition that would involve some serious celebrating, even though we realized that this was only just the beginning of the third act and there would be much further work ahead of us in the way of editing, resubmitting, and then waiting patiently for the final hard copies.

References

Abrahams, R. (1997). Forward to the Aldine paperback edition. In V. Turner, *The ritual process: Structure and anti-structure* (pp. v–xii). London: Aldine Transaction Publishers.

Adams, D. (1988). Treatment models of men who batter: A profeminist analysis. In K. Yllö & M. Bograd (Eds.), *Feminist perspectives on wife abuse* (pp. 176–199). Newbury Park, CA: Sage.

Anderson, H. (1997). *Conversation, language, and possibilities: A postmodern approach to therapy.* New York: Basic Books.

Anderson, H., & Goolishin, H. A. (1988). Human systems as linguistic systems: Preliminary and evolving ideas about the implications for clinical theory. *Family Process, 27*(4), 371–393.

Atkinson, R. (1998). *The LifeStory interview.* Sage University Papers Series on Qualitative Research Methods, Vol. 44. Thousand Oaks, CA: Sage.

Augusta-Scott, T. (2001). Dichotomies in the power and control story: Exploring multiple stories about men who choose abuse in intimate relationships. *Gecko: A Journal of Deconstruction and Narrative Ideas in Therapeutic Practice, 2,* 31–54.

Augusta-Scott, T. (2007). Conversations with men about women's violence: Ending men's violence by challenging gender essentialism. In C. Brown & T. Augusta-Scott (Eds.), *Narrative therapy: Making meaning, making lives* (pp. 197–210). Thousand Oaks, CA: Sage.

Ball, D., Piercy, F., & Bischoff, G. (1993). Externalizing the problem through cartoons: A case example. *Journal of Systemic Therapies, 12*(1), 19–21.

Bandura, A. (1973). *Aggression: A social learning analysis*. Englewood Cliffs, NJ: Prentice Hall.

Bateson, G. (1972). *Steps to an ecology of mind*. New York: Ballantine Books.

Bateson, G. (1980). *Mind and nature: A necessary unity*. New York: Bantam Books.

Bennett, T., Mercer, C., & Woolacott, J. (Eds.). (1986). *Popular culture and social relations*. Milton Keynes, UK: Open University Press.

Béres, L. (1999). Beauty and the beast: The romanticization of abuse in popular culture. *European Journal of Cultural Studies, 2*(2), 191–207.

Béres, L. (2001). *Romance, suffering and hope: Reflective practice with abused women*. Unpublished doctoral dissertation. Toronto, Ontario, Canada: University of Toronto.

Béres, L. (2002). Negotiating images: Popular culture, imagination, and hope in clinical social work practice. *Affilia: Journal of Women and Social Work, 17*(4), 429–447.

Béres, L. (2009). Mindfulness and reflexivity: The no-self as reflective practitioner. In S. Hick (Ed.), *Mindfulness and social work: Reflective practice and interventions* (pp. 57–75). Chicago: Lyceum Books.

Bergin, A. E., & Lambert, M. J. (1978). The evaluation of therapeutic outcomes. In S. L. Garfield & A. E. Bergin (Eds.), *Handbook of psychotherapy and behavior change* (2nd ed.) (pp. 139–189). New York: Wiley.

Bird, J. (2006). *Constructing the narrative in supervision*. Auckland, New Zealand: Edge Press.

Bird, J. (2008). *Talk that sings: Therapy in a new linguistic key*. Auckland, New Zealand: Edge Press.

Bobele, M., Servin-Guerrero Lopez, S., Scamardo, M., & Solorzano, B. (2008). Single-session/walk-in therapy with Mexican-American clients. *Journal of Systemic Therapies, 27*(4), 75–89.

Bohart, A. (1993). Experiencing: The basis of psychotherapy. *Journal of Psychotherapy Integration, 3,* 51–67.

Bohart, A., & Tallman, K. (1996). The active client: Therapy as self help. *Journal of Humanistic Psychology, 36,* 7–30.

Bohart, A., & Tallman, K. (1999). *How clients make therapy work: The process of active self-healing*. Washington, DC: American Psychological Association.

Bruner, E. (1986a). Ethnography as narrative. In V. Turner & E. Bruner (Eds.), *The anthropology of experience* (pp. 139–155). Chicago: University of Illinois Press.

Bruner, J. (1986b). *Actual minds, possible worlds.* Cambridge, MA: Harvard University Press.

Bruner, J. (1990). *Acts of meaning.* Cambridge, MA: Harvard University Press.

Buttell, F., & Carney, M. (2006). A large sample evaluation of a court-mandated batterer intervention program: Investigating differential program effect for African American and Caucasian men. *Research on Social Work Practice, 2,* 121–131.

Campbell, J. (1968). *The hero with a thousand faces.* Princeton, NJ: Princeton University Press. (Original work published 1949)

Carey, M., Walther, S., & Russell, S. (2009). The absent but implicit: A map to support therapeutic enquiry. *Family Process, 48*(3), 319–331.

Chambon, A. S. (1999). Foucault's approach: Making the familiar visible. In A. S. Chambon, A. Irving, & L. Epstein (Eds.), *Reading Foucault for social work* (pp. 51–82). New York: Columbia University Press.

Cranwell Schmidt, M., Kolodinsky, J. M., Carsten, G., Schmidt, F. E., Larson, M., & MacLachlan, C. (2007). Short term change in attitude and motivating factors to change abusive behaviour of male batterers after participating in a group intervention program based on pro-feminist and cognitive-behavioral approach. *Journal of Family Violence, 22*(2), 91–100.

Csiernik, R., & Rowe, W. (Eds.). (2010). *Responding to the oppression of addiction: Canadian social work perspectives* (2nd ed.). Toronto, Ontario, Canada: Canadian Scholars Press.

D'Cruz, H., Gillingham, P., & Melendez, S. (2007). Reflexivity, its meanings and relevance for social work: A critical review of the literature. *British Journal of Social Work, 37*(1), 79–90.

De Jong, P., & Insoo, K. B. (1998). *Interviewing for solutions.* Scarborough, UK: Brooks/Cole.

De Jong, P., & Miller, S. (1995). How to interview for client strengths. *Social Work, 40*(6), 729–736.

Deleuze, G. (1994). *Difference and repetition* (P. Patton, Trans.). New York: Columbia University Press.

Deleuze, G., & Parnet, C. (2002). *Dialogue II.* London: Continuum.

Denborough, D. (1995). Step by step: Developing respectful and effective ways of working with young men to reduce violence. *Dulwich Centre Newsletter, 2 & 3*, 73–89.

Derrida, J. (1974). *Of grammatology* (G. Chakravorty, Trans.). Baltimore: John Hopkins University Press.

Derrida, J. (1976). *Of grammatology.* Baltimore: John Hopkins University Press.

Derrida, J. (1978). *Writing and difference* (A. Bass, Trans.). Chicago: University of Chicago Press.

Derrida, J. (1991). *Cindres* (N. Lukacher, Trans. & Ed.). Lincoln, NE: University of Nebraska Press.

de Shazer, S. (1991) *Putting difference to work.* New York: Norton.

Dolan, Y. (1998). *One small step: Moving beyond trauma and therapy to a life of joy.* Watsonville, CA: Papier-Mache Press.

Dooley, M., & Kavanagh, L. (2007). *The philosophy of Derrida.* Montreal, Quebec, Canada: McGill-Queen's University Press.

Duvall, J., & Béres, L. (2007). Movement of identities: A map for therapeutic conversations about trauma. In C. Brown & T. Augusta-Scot (Eds.), *Narrative therapy: Making meaning, making lives* (pp. 229–250). Thousand Oaks, CA: Sage.

Duvall, J., & Young, K. (2009). Keeping faith: A conversation with Michael White. *Journal of Systemic Therapies, 28*(1), 1–18.

Edelson, J. L., Miller, D. M., & Stone, G. W. (1983). *Counseling men who batter: Group leaders' handbook.* Albany, NY: Men's Coalition Against Battering.

Epston, D. (2003, December 8 & 9). *Inner-viewing of narrative interviewing.* Workshop sponsored by Brief Therapy Training International (a division of Hincks-Dellcrest Centre, Gail Appel Institute), Toronto, Ontario, Canada.

Epston, D. (2009a). *A new genre of a narrative therapy approach to the problem of young people and their families/communities.* Professional workshop notes. Retrieved February 17, 2010, from http://www.narrativeapproaches.com

Epston, D. (2009b, May 4–8). *Five-day intensive with David Epston.* Sponsored by Brief Therapy Training—International (a division of Hincks-Dellcrest Centre, Gail Appel Institute), Toronto, Ontario, Canada.

Epston, D., & White, M. (1992). Consulting your consultants: The documentation of alternative knowledges. In D. Epston & M. White, *Experience, contradiction, narrative and imagination* (pp. 11–26). Adelaide, Australia: Dulwich Centre Publications.

Ericsson, S., & Taneja, S. (Producers); Jhally, S. (Director); Katz, J., & Earp, J.

(Writers). (2002). *Toughguise* [Video recording]. Northampton, MA: Media Education Foundation.

Eron, J., & Lund, T. (1996). *Narrative solutions in brief therapy.* New York: Guilford Press.

Fisher, A. (2005). Romance and violence: Practices of visual map making and documentation in conversations about men's abuse to women. *Catching the winds of change: Conference proceedings* (pp. 115–123). Toronto, Ontario, Canada: Brief Therapy Network.

Fisher, A., & Augusta-Scott, T. (2003, May 28). *Innovations in practice: Working with men who abuse.* Workshop at the Brief Therapy Network 2nd Annual Conference: Theory, Practice and Practicality. Sponsored by Brief Therapy Training International (a division of Hincks-Dellcrest Centre, Gail Appel Institute), Toronto, Ontario, Canada.

Fook, J. (1999). Critical reflectivity in education and practice. In B. Pease & J. Fook (Eds.), *Transforming social work practice: Postmodern critical perspectives* (pp. 195–208). St. Leonards, Australia: Allen and Unwin.

Fook, J. & Gardner, F. (2007). *Practising critical reflection: A resource handbook.* Berkshire, UK: Open University Press, McGraw Hill House.

Foucault, M. (1965). *Madness and civilization: A history of insanity in the age of reason.* New York: Random House.

Foucault, M. (1973). *The birth of the clinic: An archaeology of medical perception.* London: Tavistock.

Foucault, M. (1980). *Power/knowledge: Selected interviews and other writings.* New York: Pantheon.

Foucault. M. (1997). *Ethics: Subjectivity and truth* (P. Rabinow, Ed.; R. Hurley, Trans.). New York: New Press.

Frank, A. W. (1995). *The wounded storyteller: Body, illness and ethics.* Chicago: University of Chicago Press.

Frank, A. W. (2004). *The renewal of generosity: Illness, medicine and how to live.* Chicago: University of Chicago Press.

Freedman, J., & Combs, G. (1996). *Narrative therapy: The social construction of preferred realities.* New York: Norton.

Freeman, J., Epston, D., & Lobovits, D. (1997). *Playful approaches to serious problems.* New York: Norton.

Freire, P. (2006). *Pedagogy of the oppressed.* New York: Continuum.

Friedman, S. (1994). Staying simple, staying focused: Time-effective consultations with children and families. In M. F. Hoyt (Ed.), *Constructive therapies* (pp. 217–250). New York: Guilford Press.

Gaddis, S. (2004). Re-positioning traditional research: Centring client's accounts in the construction of professional therapy knowledges. *International Journal of Narrative Therapy and Community Work, 2*, 37–48.

Ganley, A. L. (1981). Counseling programs for men who batter: Elements of effective programs. *Response to Victimization of Women and Children, 4*, 3–4.

Geertz, C. (1973) *The interpretation of cultures.* New York: Basic Books.

Geertz, C. (1986). Making experience, authoring selves. In V. Turner & E. Bruner (Eds.), *The anthropology of experience* (pp. 373–380). Chicago: University of Illinois Press.

Gergen, K. J., & Kaye, J. (1992). Beyond narrative in the negotiation of therapeutic meaning. In S. McNamee & K. J. Gergen (Eds.), *Therapy as social construction* (pp. 166–199). Thousand Oaks, CA: Sage.

Gergen, M. M., & Gergen, K. J. (1984). The social construction of narrative accounts. In K. J. Gergen & M. M. Gergen (Eds.), *Historical social psychology* (pp. 173–189). Hillsdale, NJ: Erlbaum.

Glancy, G., & Saini, M. A. (2005). An evidenced-based review of psychological treatments of anger and aggression. *Brief Treatment and Crisis Intervention, 5*(2), 229–248.

Goffman, E. (1961). *Asylums: Essays in the social situation of mental patients and other inmates.* New York: Doubleday.

Gredler, M. E., & Shields, C. C. (2008). *Vygotsky's legacy: A foundation for research and practice.* New York: Guilford Press.

Griffiths, M., & Tann, S. (1992). Using reflective practice to link personal and public theories. *Journal of Education for Teaching, 18*(1), 69–84.

Guba, E., & Lincoln, Y. S. (2005). Paradigmatic controversies, contradictions, and emerging confluences. In N. Denzin & Y. Lincoln (Eds.), *The Sage handbook of qualitative research* (3rd ed.) (pp. 191–215). Thousand Oaks, CA: Sage.

Guilfoyle, M. (2003). Dialogue and power: A critical analysis of power in dialogical therapy. *Family Process, 42*(3), 331–343.

Harper-Jaques, S., McElheran, N., Slive, A., & Leahey, M. (2008). A comparison of two approaches to the delivery of walk-in single session mental health therapy. *Journal of Systemic Therapies, 27*(4), 40–53.

Healy, K. (2000). *Social work practices: Contemporary perspective on change.* London: Sage.

Hoffman, E. (2009). *Time.* New York: Picador.

Holmgren, A., & Holmgren, A. (2009, July 8). *Foucault, Derrida and Deleuze: Their implications for narrative practice.* One-day pre-conference training for the European Conference of Narrative Therapy and Community Work, sponsored by the Centre for Narrative Practice, Brighton, UK.

Hoyt, M. (1995). *Brief therapy and managed care: Readings for contemporary practice.* San Francisco: Jossey-Bass.

Irving, A. (1999). Waiting for Foucault: Social work and the multitudinous truth(s) of life. In A. S. Chambon, A. Irving, & L. Epstein (Eds.), *Reading Foucault for social work* (pp. 27–50). New York: Columbia University Press.

James, W. (1981). *The principles of psychology.* Cambridge, MA: Harvard University Press. (Original work published 1890)

Jenkins, A. (1990). *Invitations to responsibility: The therapeutic engagement of men who are violent and abusive.* Adelaide, Australia: Dulwich Centre Publications.

Katz, J. (2006). *The macho paradox: Why some men hurt women and how all men can help.* Naperville, IL: Sourcebooks.

Kimball, S. T. (1960). Introduction. In A. van Gennep, *The rites of passage* (pp. v–xxii). Chicago: University of Chicago Press.

Labov, W., & Fanshel, D. (1977). *Therapeutic discourse: Psychotherapy as conversation.* New York: Academic Press.

Lambert, M. (1992). Psychotherapy outcome research. In J. C. Norcross & M. R. Goldfried (Eds.), *Handbook of psychotherapy integration* (pp. 94–129). New York: Basic Books.

Lambert, M. J., & Bergin, A. E. (1994). The effectiveness of psychotherapy. In S. Bergin & L. Garfield (Eds.), *Handbook of psychotherapy and behavior change* (4th ed.) (pp. 143–189). New York: Wiley.

Levin-Rozalis, M., Bar-On, N., & Hartaf, H. (2005). A unique therapeutic intervention for abusive men at Beit Noam: Successes, boundaries, and difficulties. *Journal of Social Work Research and Evaluation, 1,* 25–45.

Lindemann-Nelson, H. (2001). *Damaged identities, narrative repair.* Ithaca, NY: Cornell University Press.

Maisel, R., Epston, D., & Borden, A. (2004). *Biting the hand that starves you: Inspiring resistance to anorexia/bulimia.* New York: Norton.

May, T. (2005). *Gilles Deleuze: An introduction.* Cambridge, UK: Cambridge University Press. Retrieved August 4, 2009, from http://lib.myilibrary.com/Browse/open.asp?ID=43141&loc=vii

McGoldrick, M., & Gerson, R. (1985). *Genograms in family assessment.* New York: Norton.

Mederos, F. (1999). Batterer intervention programs: The past, and future prospects. In M. Shepard & E. Pence (Eds.), *Coordinating community responses to domestic violence* (pp. 127–150). Thousand Oaks, CA: Sage.

Milewski-Hertlein, K. A. (2001). The use of the socially constructed genogram in clinical practice. *American Journal of Family Therapy, 29,* 23–38.

Miller, J. K., & Slive, A. (2004). Breaking down the barriers to clinical service delivery: Walk-in therapy. *Journal of Marital and Family Therapy, 30*(1), 95–103.

Miller, S. D., Duncan, B. L., & Hubble, M. A. (1997). *Escape from Babel: Toward a unifying language for psychotherapy practice.* New York: Norton.

Morgan, W. D., & Morgan, S. T. (2005). Cultivating attention and empathy. In C. K. Germer, R. D. Siegel, & P. R. Fulton (Eds.), *Mindfulness and psychotherapy* (pp. 73–90). New York: Guilford Press.

Morson, G. S. (1994). *Narrative and freedom: The shadows of time.* New Haven, CT: Yale University Press.

Myerhoff, B. (1986). Life not death in Venice: Its second life. In V. Turner & E. Bruner (Eds.), *The anthropology of experience* (pp. 261–286). Chicago: University of Illinois Press.

Nylund, D. (2005). Deconstructing masculinity through popular culture texts. *Catching the Winds of Change conference proceedings* (pp. 104–114). Toronto, Ontario, Canada: Brief Therapy Network.

Nylund, D. (2007). *Beer, babes, and balls: Masculinity and sports talk radio.* Albany: State University of New York Press.

Paré, D., & Lysak, M. (2004). The willow and the oak: From monologue to dialogue in the scaffolding of therapeutic conversations. *Journal of Systemic Therapies, 23*(1), 6–20.

Parry, A., & Doan, R. (1994). *Story revisions: Narrative therapy in the postmodern world.* New York: Guilford Press.

Pence, E., & Paymar, M. (1993). *Education groups for men who batter: The Duluth model.* New York: Springer.

Pence, E., & Shepard, M. (Eds.). (1988). *Coordinating community responses to domestic violence.* Thousand Oaks, CA: Sage.

Pentecost, M., & Speedy, J. (2006, March 2). Poetic mindedness and poetic writing: A means of "doubly listening" towards, and capturing, the stories people tell us in therapeutic conversations. International Narrative Therapy Festive Conference, Adelaide, Australia.

Rajchman, J. (2000). *The Deleuze connections.* Cambridge, MA: MIT Press.

Ramey, H. (2007). *A sequential analysis of therapist scaffolding and child concept formation in narrative therapy.* Unpublished master's degree thesis for faculty of Child & Youth Studies, Brock University, St. Catharines, Ontario, Canada.

Ray, W., & Keeney, B. (1993). *Resource focused therapy.* London: Karnac Books.

Ramey, H., Young, K., & Tarulli, D. (In press.). *Scaffolding and concept formation in narrative therapy: A qualitative research report.* Manuscript submitted for publication.

Rennie, D. L. (1994). Storytelling in psychotherapy: The client's subjective experience. *Psychotherapy, 31,* 234–243.

Rosenbaum, R., Hoyt, M. F., & Talmon, M. (1990). The challenge of single-session therapies: Creating pivotal moments. In R. A. Wells & V. J. Giannetti (Eds.), *Handbook of the Brief Psychotherapies* (pp. 165–189). New York: Plenum Press.

Russell, S., & Carey, M. (2004). *Narrative therapy: Responding to your questions.* Adelaide, Australia: Dulwich Centre Publications.

Schön, D. A. (1983). *The reflective practitioner: How professionals think in action.* New York: Basic Books.

Shepard, M., & Pence, E. (Eds.). (1999). *Coordinating community responses to domestic violence: Lessons from Duluth and beyond.* Thousand Oaks, CA: Sage.

Slive, A., McElheran, N., & Lawson, A. (2008). How brief does it get?: Walk-in single session therapy. *Journal of Systemic Therapies*, 27(4), 5–22.

Speedy, J. (2005). Using poetic documents: An exploration of poststructuralist ideas and poetic practices in narrative therapy. *British Journal of Guidance & Counselling, 33*(3), 283–298.

St. James O'Connor, T., Meakes, E., Pickering, R., & Schuman, M. (1997). On the right track: Client experience of narrative therapy. *Contemporary Family Therapy, 19*(4), 479–495.

Stern, D. (2004). *The present moment in psychotherapy and everyday life.* New York: Norton.

Stourdeur, R., & Stille, R. (1989). *Ending men's violence against their partners.* Newbury Park, CA: Sage.

Tallman, K., & Bohart, A. C. (1999). The client as a common factor: Clients as self-healers. In M. A. Hubble, B. L. Duncan, & S. D. Miller (Eds.), *The heart & soul of change: What works in therapy* (pp. 91–131). Washington, DC: American Psychological Association.

Tinsley, R. & Lebak, K. (2009). Expanding the zone of reflective capacity: Taking separate journeys together. *Networks, 11*(2), 1–11.

Turner, V. (1977). *The ritual process: Structure and anti-structure.* Ithaca, NY: Cornell University Press. (Original work published 1969)

van Gennep, A. (1960.) *The rites of passage.* Chicago: University of Chicago Press. (Original work published 1909)

Vygotsky, L. S. (1978). *Mind and society: The development of higher psychological processes.* Cambridge, MA: Harvard University Press.

Vygotsky, L. S. (1986). *Thought and language.* Cambridge, MA: MIT Press.

Walter, J. L., & Peller, J. E. (1994). "On track" in solution-focused brief therapy. In M. F. Hoyt (Ed.), *Constructive therapies* (pp. 111–125). New York: Guilford Press.

White, M. (1984). Marital therapy: Practical approaches to long-standing problems. *Australian Journal of Family Therapy, 1,* 27–43.

White, M. (1986). Negative explanation, restraint & double description: A template for family therapy. *Family Process, 22,* 255–273.

White, M. (1994). *Recent developments in the narrative approach.* American Association of Marriage and Family Therapy (AAMFT): Learning Edge Series videotape of 50th anniversary conference in Miami Beach, Florida.

White, M. (1995a). *Re-authoring lives: Interviews & essays.* Adelaide, Australia: Dulwich Centre Publications.

White, M. (1995b, March 22 & 23). Therapeutic conversation as collaborative inquiry. Two-day training sponsored by Brief Therapy Training Centres International (a division of Hincks-Dellcrest Centre, Gail Appel Institute), Toronto, Ontario, Canada.

White, M. (1997). Narratives of therapists' lives. Adelaide, Australia: Dulwich Centre Publications.

White, M. (1999, April, 7, 8 & 9). *Migration of identity map in narrative therapy.* Three-day training sponsored by Brief Therapy Training Centres International (a division of the Hincks-Dellcrest Centre, Gail Appel Institute), Toronto, Ontario, Canada.

White, M. (2000). *Reflections on Narrative Practice: Essays and Interviews.* Adelaide, Australia: Dulwich Centre Publications.

White, M. (2003). Narrative practice and community assignments. *International Journal of Narrative Therapy and Community Work, 2,* 17–56.

White, M. (2004). "Working with people who are suffering the consequences of multiple trauma. *International Journal of Narrative Therapy and Community Work, 1,* 45–76.

White, M. (2005, April 11 & 12). *Mapping narrative conversations.* Two-day training, sponsored by Brief Therapy Training Centres International (a division of Hincks-Dellcrest Centre, Gail Appel Institute), Toronto, Ontario, Canada.

White, M. (2006a, February–September). *Seven-month narrative therapy training program.* Sponsored by The Dulwich Centre, Adelaide, Australia.

White, M. (2006b, February 20–24). *"One-week special intensive narrative therapy training training course."* Sponsored by the Dulwich Centre, Adelaide, Australia.

White, M. (2007a). *Maps of narrative practice.* New York: Norton.

White, M. (2007b, October 29 & 30). *Addressing the consequences of trauma: A narrative perspective.* Two-day training sponsored by Brief Therapy Training Centres International (a division of Hincks-Dellcrest Centre, Gail Appel Institute), Toronto, Ontario, Canada.

White, M. (2007c, December 10–15). *Level 2 narrative therapy training.* Sponsored by the Dulwich Centre, Adelaide, Australia.

White, M., & Epston, D. (1990). *Narratives means to therapeutic ends.* New York: Norton.

Winslade, J. (2009). Tracing lines of flight: Implications of the work of Gilles Deleuze for narrative practice. *Family Process, 48*(3), 332–347.

Wyschogrod, E. (1989). Derrida, Levinas, and violence. In H. J. Silverman (Ed.), *Continental philosophy II: Derrida and deconstruction* (pp. 182–200). New York: Routledge.

Yllö, K., & Bograd, M. (1988). *Feminist perspective on wife abuse.* Newbury Park, CA: Sage.

Young, K. (2008). Narrative practice at a walk-in therapy clinic: Developing children's worry wisdom. *Journal of Systemic Therapies, 27*(4). 54–74.

Young, K. (2006). *When all the time you have is now: Narrative practice at a wain therapy clinic.* Retrieved from www.brieftherapynetwork.com/papers.htm

Young, K., Dick, M., Herring, K., Lee, J. (2008) From waiting lists to walk-in: Stories from a walk-n therapy clinic. *Journal of Systemic Therapies*, *27*(4), 23–39.

Young, K. & Cooper, S. (2008). Toward co-composing an evidence base: The narrative therapy re-visiting project. *Journal of Systemic Therapies*, *27*(1), 67–83.

Index

absent but implicit, 98–99
abusive behaviors, men who have used
  cognitive-behavioral model, 208
  diagnostic labeling, 191
  dualisms in therapeutic intervention, 111–112
  feminist thought, 208–209
  shortcomings of standardized treatment, 210–211
  see also group narrative therapy with men who have used abuse
acknowledgment, 7
action, landscape of, 14–15, 32, 70, 101, 195
act one of three-act play
  conversational posture of, 44–45
  creating backstory in, 53–55
  developing storylines in, 47–52
  establishing therapeutic conversation in, 45–47
  genogram construction in, 55–59
  identifying point of story in, 52–53
  participation of significant others in, 59–61
  points of inquiry, 41
  reflecting summary, 64
  removing backstory constraints, 61–66
  separation goals, 41, 47
  therapist stance, 44
  transition to act two, 62–66
  trauma therapy case example, 169–175
  see also three-act play
act two of three-act play
  evaluating effects in, 74–82
  goals, 79
  as journey phase, 66–67
  pivotal events, 72–74
  points of inquiry, 42
  recognizing discrepancies in problem-saturated stories, 69–72
  reflective summary, 79–82
  therapeutic relationship in, 67–68
  trauma treatment case example, 175–184
  see also three-act play
act three of three-act play
  goals, 82–83
  points of inquiry, 42
  receiving context, 84–87
  temporal orientation, 83

act three of three-act play (*continued*)
  trauma treatment case example, 184–185
  see also three-act play
Adams, D., 208
addiction
  case example, 3, 188, 189, 192–193, 197–204, 231
  labeling and totalizing approaches to treatment, 188, 191, 194
  narrative therapy strategies, 188–189
  relapse conceptualization, 200, 202–203
  residential treatment, 199–200
  role of re-membering conversations, 197
agency, 138
Alcoholics Anonymous, 3, 191, 199, 200, 201, 202
ambiguity, 133
Anderson, H., 8–9, 55
assessment
  client's values and preferences, 195–196
  in walk-in clinics, 148–149
  written, 116–119
Augusta-Scott, T., 211

backstory
  clinical significance, 53–54
  constraints, 61–62
  eliciting, in therapy, 54–61
  trauma treatment case example, 173–175
Bakhtin, M., 69, 72–73, 136, 137
Bateson, G., 209
Berg, I., 24
Bird, J., 101
brief strategic therapy, 24
broader audience of therapeutic conversations, 16–18
Bruner, J., 32, 192, 195
Buttell, F., 210
Campbell, J., 27, 29, 31, 62–63
Carey, M., 51, 99
centering
  circulation of language in, 10
  goals, 9–10
  role of outsider witnesses, 17
  work with men who have used abuse, 218–219
Chambon, A., 114–115, 229
change
  construction of alternative storylines for, 11, 41
  in dialogical therapies, 10
  eliciting client's values and preferences for, 195–196
  imagining future preferred states, 59
  as migration of identity, 42–43
  pivotal moments in, 13–14, 122
  as receiving context, 84–87
  as series of events, 194
  story construction for, 35–36
  see also outcomes
chaos narrative, 113
circulation of language, 2
  conceptual basis, 102–103
  in recentering of therapy, 10
  therapeutic goals, 190
cognitive-behavioral model of abusive behaviors, 208
common factors research, 25
concept map
  conceptual development, 7–8
  context, 16–18
  development of alternative storylines for, 11–15
  examination of dialogical conversation, 8–10
  landscapes of identity and action in, 14–15
  overall design, 18, 19

pivotal moments in, 13
purpose, 18–20, 229–230
re-membering conversations in, 17–18
therapeutic documents in, 18
confidentiality, 120
congruence, 17
construction of meaning
circulation of language in, 10
contextual factors, 16–17
decentering of therapist in, 9
in dialogical therapies, 8, 9, 12
role of outsider witnesses, 17
story metaphor for, 38
truth and, 39, 194
conversational maps, 1
composition, 41
conceptual origin and development, 37, 38
points of inquiry, 41, 88–89
purpose, 43, 89–90
in three-act play, 41
for trauma treatment, 167–168, 186
critical pedagogy, 20
critical reflection, 2
conceptual and technical evolution, 4–6
definition, 4
implementation structure, 6
importance of, 20, 37
power relations as element of, 5–6
as practice, 6
for theory development, 5
critical social theory, 4, 6

D'Cruz, H., 4
deconstruction, 4, 5
deconstructive listening and questioning, 48–50, 68, 133
definitional ceremonies, 20
Deleuze, G., 91, 98–99, 103–104, 105, 108, 110–111, 112, 114, 116
Denborough, D., 211
depression, 54
Derrida, J., 51, 91, 98–99, 100–101, 103, 142
de Shazer, S., 24, 43
determinism, 138–139
dialogical conversation
as construction of meaning, 8
decentering of therapist for, 9–10
development of concept map, 8–10
goals of act one of three-act play, 44–45
in narrative development, 10
power relations in, 9
therapeutic goals, 10
therapy as, 8–9
see also conversational maps; therapeutic dialogue
documentation
ethical considerations, 120
of therapy in walk-in clinic, 156–157
in walk-in clinics, 149, 164–165
Dooley, M., 100
double listening, 50–51, 153, 154

empathy-building, 223
Epston, D., 23, 27, 88, 158, 192, 228
Ericsson, S., 211
ethical practice, 20, 28, 39, 119, 120
eventness, 72–74, 137, 176
evidence-based practice, 2, 20
externalizing conversations
clinical role, 10, 15, 163–164, 189–190, 203–204, 215–216
in group narrative therapy with men who have used abuse, 215–216

family structure and functioning
outsider witnessing process, 157–158
social and cultural concepts, 56
family therapy, 24

feminist thought
  in evolution of narrative therapy, 24
  family violence research, 207, 208–209
  narrative therapy and, 206, 210
Fisher, A., 111, 211, 223
Fook, J., 4, 5, 6, 76, 77
foreshadowing, 138–140
Foucault, M., 91, 114–115, 190, 194
Frank, A., 113, 115, 118–119, 132, 191–192
Freedman, J., 38, 44
Freire, P., 20

Geertz, C., 149, 192
genogram, socially constructed, 55–59
Gergen, K., 74, 192
Glancy, G., 209
Goffman, E., 192
Griffiths, M., 20
group therapy with men who have used abuse, 3, 231
  acceptance of responsibility, 217–218
  avoiding labeling and totalizing language, 217–218
  behavioral outcomes, 224
  centering client knowledge in, 218–219
  conceptual basis, 209–211
  current knowledge base, 206–207
  empathy-building in, 223
  externalizing conversations in, 215–216
  facilitators, 212–213
  future research, 225, 226
  identifying preferred ways of being, 221–223
  "internalized other" interviews in, 223
  limitations of research on, 224
  narrative therapy techniques in, 224–226
  partner contact procedures, 213
  recruitment, 211–212
  research design, 211–212
  research goals, 211, 224
  session recording and analysis, 214–215
  storyline development, 219–221
  structure, 212
  see also abusive behaviors, men who have used
Guilfoyle, M., 9

Healy, K., 4, 194
Hero with a Thousand Faces, The (Campbell), 29
Hoffman, E., 134
Holmgren, A., 99
hope, 15
horizontal scaffolding, 97–98
Hoyt, M., 128

identity
  addiction as, 191, 192
  backstory, 54–61
  community formation, 18
  constraints to, 61–62
  diagnostic labeling, 190–191, 201–202
  distinguishing person from problem, 158–162, 163, 189, 190–191
  internalized discourses, 189–190, 215–216
  landscape of, 14–15, 32, 70, 101, 195
  migration of identity map, 42–43
  poststructural approach to psychotherapy, 38–39
  reincorporation of, 82–87
  re-membering conversations and, 54–55, 196
  social construction of, 34–35
  socially constructed genogram, 55–57
  storyline construction, 31–32
  totalization of, 38, 47–48, 106–107, 194, 217
  trauma outcomes, 169, 179
  work with men who have used abuse, 216

interpretation, psychoanalytic, 116
intuition, 5

James, W., 129–130
Jenkins, A., 209–210

katharsis, 123, 143, 150, 151
  clinical significance, 130–131
  definition, 130
Katz, J., 211
Kline, M., 116
knowledge, as theme of critical reflection, 5, 6

landscapes of identity and action, 14–15, 32, 70, 101, 195
language
  of assessment, 116–119
  clinical significance, 91–93, 101, 119
  creative stammering, 110–116
  dualisms in, 108–109, 110–111
  feigned misunderstanding in therapy, 113–114
  flight and migration metaphors, 108–110
  introducing new words in therapy, 93–98
  limitations of, 100–102, 107–108, 119
  pathologizing, 105–107, 190–191, 201–202, 205, 217
  philosophical basis of narrative therapy, 98–99
  in postmodern era, 119
  rhizome analogy, 103–106, 180
  taken-for-granted usage, 114, 120
  therapist self-examination, 120–121
  therapy goals in walk-in clinic, 162–165
  see also circulation of language; dialogical conversation
Levin-Rozalis, M., 210–211
liberation theology, 20

Maisel, R., 204, 205
maps
  migration of identity, 42–43, 88, 200
  of problem effects, 77–78
  storyline, 32–33
  see also concept map; conversational maps
master narrative, 61–62
May, T., 108
migration of identity map, 42–43, 88, 200
Milewski-Hertlein, K. A., 56
mindfulness, tranquility and, 13
monomyth, 29
Morgan, W. D., 13
Morson, G., 69, 72–73, 123, 134–135, 136–137, 138–140, 141–142

narrative therapy
  concept of expertise in, 210
  conceptual and technical evolution, 1, 2, 229
  critically reflective research methodology, 6–7
  cultural context, 230
  eliciting client's values and preferences in, 195–196
  evidence-based practice and, 2
  introducing new words in, 93–98
  outsider witnessing in, 17
  risk of secondary trauma, 140–141
  word choices in, 91–93
  see also group therapy with men who have used abuse; story metaphor; walk-in clinic settings
not-knowing stance, 9
Nylund, D., 211

Oedipus, 139–140
outcomes
  anger and aggression treatment research, 209

outcomes (*continued*)
  client factors, 25
  common factors, 25
  extratherapeutic factors, 25–26
  group narrative therapy with men who have used abuse, 224–225
  role of client's life story in, 25–26
  significance of process versus, 20, 28, 30
  for therapist, 185–186
  see also change
outsider witnessing, 10, 17, 157–158, 162, 173
  trauma treatment case example, 176

Paré, D., 124
Parry, A., 39
Parton, N., 189–190
pivotal moments
  clinical significance, 2, 13, 122, 123–124, 129, 137–138, 143
  in concept map, 13
  concept of sideshadowing and, 140–141
  conceptual evolution, 124–128, 143
  conditions favoring emergence of, 127–128
  definition, 129, 143
  duration, 129
  experience of, 13–14
  katharsis in, 130–131, 143
  as ministories, 129–130
  temporal orientation, 122, 129, 134–143
  therapist role in eliciting, 131–134, 143
points of inquiry
  purpose, 41
  in three-act play, 41–42
position maps, 77–79
postmodernism, 4, 5, 119
poststructural theory, 38–39, 45, 153, 194
power relations
  in dialogical therapies, 9
  participants in therapy, 64–65, 204
  social justice elements of narrative therapy, 204–205
  as theme of critical reflection, 5–6
preferred ways of being, 221
present moments, 122, 123
pre-session questionnaires, 148–149, 156, 158
pulls, 10–11

quest metaphor, 33, 53

Rajchman, J., 111
re-authoring conversations
  addiction treatment case example, 193
  client understanding of concept of, 193
  in concept map development, 15
  definition, 192
  landscapes in, 14
  role of, 10
receiving context, 84–87, 133–134
recordings of therapeutic process, 121
  development of dialogic approach, 124–125
  ethical considerations, 120
  re-visiting project, 152
reflective practice
  in act two of therapy, 74, 75–77
  clinical significance, 77
  conceptual development, 5
  in dialogical therapies, 10–11
  levels of, 20
  for reinterpretation of experiences, 75–77
  session summary, 64–66, 79–82, 156, 171–172
  terminology, 4
  therapist self-assessment, 90
  see also critical reflection
reflexivity, 4, 5, 37
relativism, 39, 194
re-membering conversations, 10

in addiction treatment, 197–198
in backstory construction, 54–55
concept of identity and, 196
function, 17–18, 55, 196, 197
research
content analysis, 6–7
data collection, 6
demands of evidence-based practice, 2
evolution of narrative therapy, 2, 3–4
field research, 3–4, 7
group therapy with men who have used abuse, 207, 209–215
impact of researcher on subject of, 5
methodology for study of narrative therapy, 6–7
re-visiting project, 152
re-visiting practices, 151–152
rhizome analogy, 103–106, 180
rites of passage, 28–29, 30–31, 42, 88
Rites of Passage, The (van Gennep), 28
ritual and ceremony, 28–29
Ritual Process: Structure and Anti-structure (Turner), 29–30
Rosenblatt, P., 38
Russell, S., 210

scaffolding conversation, 10, 11–12, 65, 67–68, 97–98, 132, 133
Schmidt, C., 209
Schön, D. A., 5
self-disclosure, 11
sideshadowing, 140–141, 193
social and cultural contexts
backstory in, 53–55
of concept map, 16–18
concept of family, 56
concepts of time, 134, 136
diagnostic labeling, 190
of narrative therapy, 230
reflexive practice, 5
rites of passage, 28–29
storied therapy approach, 39
story construction, 34–35, 37
universal story form, 27–35
social constructionist theory, 38
socially constructed genogram, 55–59
solution-focused brief therapy, 24
stammering, 110–116
statement of position maps, 13
Stern, D., 122, 129
storyline structure
awareness of multiplicity, 73
client agency in construction of, 31–32
coconstruction, 11–12
concept map development, 7–8, 11–15
development in act one of three-act play, 47–55
development of alternative storylines, 11–15, 41, 68–69, 140–143, 153–155, 192, 219–220
dialogical conversation in development of, 2, 9, 35
empowerment in choice of, 205
map metaphor, 32–33
poststructural approach to psychotherapy, 38–39
recognizing discrepancies, 69–72
role of therapist in development of, 31–33, 35–36
social construction, 34–35
temporal aspects, 38, 39
universal story form, 27–31
work with men who have used abuse, 219–221
see also conversational maps
story metaphor
application to therapeutic process, 31, 38
conceptual evolution, 23–27
pivotal moments as ministories, 129–130
therapeutic goals, 41

story metaphor (*continued*)
universal story form and, 27–31, 35
see also storyline structure
stream of consciousness, 129–130

technique and process
assessments, 116–119
common outcome factors, 25
deconstructive listening and questioning, 48–50, 68, 133
development of alternative storylines, 11–15, 68–69
in dialogical therapies, 8–11
double listening, 50–51
eliciting pivotal moments, 131–134
feigned misunderstanding, 113–114
flight and migration metaphors, 108–110
innovative ideas in narrative therapy, 230
intuition and artistry in, 5
participation of significant others, 59–61
re-membering conversations, 10, 17–18, 54–55
session review, 15, 64–66, 79–82
storyline development, 31–33
story metaphor, 31, 38
temporal orientation, 122–123, 124, 132–133
theory development and, 5
therapist self-disclosure, 11
tolerance for ambiguity, 133
transparency in, 11
working with addictions, 188–189
see also circulation of language; group therapy with men who have used abuse; pivotal moments; three-act play; walk-in clinic settings
temporal orientation
act three of three-act play, 83
concept of eventness, 137
concept of open time, 140–142
creativity and, 138–139
cultural values and, 134, 136
diseases of the present, 123
imagining future preferred states, 59
of pivotal moments, 122, 129, 134–143
of storied therapy, 38, 39
of therapeutic process, 122–123, 124, 132–133
therapist self-examination, 144
theoretism, 136
theory development
bottom up approach, 5
critically reflective practice for, 5
origins and evolution of narrative practice, 1, 2
therapeutic dialogue
broader context, 16–17
flight and migration metaphors, 109–110
outsider witnessing, 157–158, 162
temporal orientation, 132–133
tentativeness in, 133
theoretical and technical development, 124–125
therapist curiosity in, 133
in zone of proximal development, 67
see also dialogical conversation; scaffolding conversation
therapeutic documents, 18
therapeutic relationship
in act one of three-act play, 44, 45
conversational posture, 45
decentering of therapist, 9–10
deconstructive listening and questioning, 48–50
politics of, 10
power relations in, 64–65, 204
therapist posture, 153
therapist responsibility for conversation, 13
in transition states, 67–68
welcoming attitude, 132

three-act play
conceptual origin and development, 37, 38, 88
conversational maps and, 41
goals, 42
purpose, 43, 88, 89–90
rite of passage analogy, 42, 88
stages of inquiry, 41
of storied therapy, 40–41
for trauma treatment, 167–168, 186
see also act one of three-act play; act two of three-act play; act three of three-act play
Tinsley, R., 67–68
tranquility, in therapeutic process, 13
transition states
from act one to act two, 62–66
characteristics, 30
social context, 28–29
social support in, 60
story form and, 30–31
therapeutic relationship in, 67–68
in three-act play, 42
see also act two of three-act play
transparency in therapy, 11
trauma and abuse experience, 3
act one case example, 169–175
act two case example, 175–184
act three case example, 184–185
case example, 168–169, 173–174, 230–231
self-perception outcomes, 169, 179
therapeutic strategies, 167–168, 186
truth, 11, 39, 43, 194
Turner, V., 27, 29–30, 31

universal story form, 27–35, 35

values and preferences, client's, 195–196
van Gennep, A., 27, 28–29, 30–31, 42
Vygotsky, L. S., 13, 67

walk-in clinic settings, 2–3, 230
advantages, 147
agenda-setting in, 155
development of subordinate storylines, 153–155
distinguishing person from problem, 158–162, 163
documentation of therapy in, 156–157, 164–165
goals of narrative therapy, 150–151, 162–165
historical development, 148
narrative therapy effectiveness, 165
narrative therapy rationale, 149–150
operations, 148–149
outsider witnessing in, 157–158, 162
pre-session questionnaires, 148–149, 156, 158
re-visiting practices in, 151–152
therapist posture, 153
White, M., 1, 11–12, 13, 20, 23, 24, 26–27, 32, 33, 39, 41, 42, 50, 51, 54, 56, 64, 67, 88, 92, 98–99, 103, 113–114, 120, 126, 128, 149–150, 168, 189, 190, 191, 192, 195, 209, 219, 228
Winslade, J., 99
witnessing, 7
Wyschogrod, E., 106, 107

zone of proximal development, 13, 67